BLACK MESA

THIRD MESA

SECOND MESA

FIRST MESA

Oraibi Wash

Polacca Wash

akavi

Kikeuchmovi
(New Oraibi)

Oraibi

Payupki

Tewa Village
(Hano)

Tsikuvi

Keuchaptevela

Shipaulovi

Shongopovi

Mishongnovi

Wepo

Kanelva

Kukeuchomo

Sikyatki

Terkinovi

Polacca

Walpi

Sichomovi

Keam's Canyon

ANTELOPE MESA

Meusiptanga

Chakpahu

Kawaika

TO GALLUP ▸

Awatovi

Huckyatwi
(Badger Butte)

POLACCA

WASH

Route 4

JEDITO

WASH

◂TO WINSLOW

Route 6

TO HOLBROOK▸

BUTTES

HOPI BUTTES

Indian Wells

Route 15

Big Falling Snow

Big Falling Snow

A Tewa-Hopi Indian's Life and Times
and the History and Traditions of His People

by Albert Yava

Edited and Annotated by Harold Courlander

CROWN PUBLISHERS, INC., NEW YORK

Inquiries should be addressed to
Crown Publishers, Inc., One Park Avenue, New York, N.Y. 10016
Printed in the United States of America
Published simultaneously in Canada by
General Publishing Company Limited

Library of Congress Cataloging in Publication Data

Yava, Albert, 1888-
  Big Falling Snow.

  Bibliography: p.
  1. Hopi Indians. 2. Tewa Indians. 3. Yava,
Albert, 1888- 4. Tewa Indians—Biography.
5. Hopi Indians—Biography. I. Courlander, Harold,
1908- II. Title.

E99.H7Y38 1978   970′.004′97 [B]   78-658
ISBN 0-517-53244-1

Book Design: Huguette Franco

Introduction

This book, *Big Falling Snow*, contains recollections and commentaries of Albert Yava, a Tewa-Hopi Indian, whose life spanned a critical period of adaptation by his people to what he calls a flood of white culture and authority across the mesas of Northern Arizona. He was born in 1888, when the weight of the white man's presence was beginning to be fully felt in the Hopi villages. It was then that the village children were being forced to attend day schools and boarding schools established by the Government. Many older people feared what this white man's schooling would do to their children and their traditional way of life, and there was stubborn resistance to the processes of "modernization" and "civilization." At this same time, the surrounding Navajos were beginning to recover from their "long walk" and their nearly fatal imprisonment at the Bosque Redondo, and in their quest for land and security they were occupying territory that the Hopis had long considered to be their own. The Hopi Way, as it has been called, was threatened by dynamics that the villagers could not control and which they did not fully understand.

As to the virtue, civic merit and propriety of turning the Hopis and Tewas into trails blazed by the white man, the Government and its agents had no doubts whatever. Forced schooling for the young, European-style haircuts, white man's clothing and food, reorganization of the traditional landholding system, and Christian names were considered to be the Indians' first steps to salvation. In 1888 the impact of the white man's religions had not yet been felt. The Catholic Church had penetrated the villages in the seventeenth century, but its gains were soon wiped out by the Pueblo-Hopi rebellion of 1680, and from the start of the eighteenth century until the latter days of the nineteenth, the Arizona villages did not have to cope with religious intervention. But by the 1890s, proselytizers of various sects were seeing the Hopis and Western Tewas as prime prospects for conversion. The Mormons already had a mission close to Moencopi, the westernmost Hopi village, and the Mennonite missionary H. R. Voth was established in the village of Oraibi—ominous threats, as seen by some Hopis, to ceremonialism and ancient traditions. For the moment, however, ceremonialism remained vigorous despite missionary efforts to weaken it. But intravillage strains over how to deal with the white man and his endless demands (as well as his gifts) were engendering frictions and struggles within the community that were to continue in various forms for almost a century. Such were the conditions of Hopi-Tewa life when Albert Yava was born.

Much has been written about these Indian inhabitants of Northern Arizona, but a few words about them here may help to place Yava's recollections and observations in their appropriate context. The Hopis now inhabit a number of villages along the southern fringe of Black Mesa close to, if not exactly, where the settlements were located before the arrival of the first whites. Anthropologists generally believe that ancestral Hopis settled this region some time around the twelfth century after migrating southward from the San Juan Valley because of drought, later to be joined by people coming from various directions. Hopi traditions say the immigrating groups came as clans over a period of time. Some of these clans, like the Snake and Horn, apparently speaking a dialect of Shoshonean, are said to have originated in California and to have come to Hopi country by way of Navajo Mountain in the north. Others, such as the Water and Tobacco clans, came from a place far to the south, their place of origin recollected only in legend. Still others, speaking Tewa, Keresan or Zunian, came from the Rio Grande Valley. At least a few Utes, Paiutes and Great Plains Indians may have been absorbed into the Hopi cultural complex, but whether Pimans or Yumans in significant numbers were among the immigrants is not specified in the traditions.

The founders of Tewa Village on First Mesa arrived from Rio Grande country about the beginning of the eighteenth century. Some of the settlements established by other incoming groups have disappeared, though some of their old ruins may still be seen. Today a dozen Hopi villages are strung in an east to west direction over a distance of some seventy-five miles. Tewa Village shares the top of First or East Mesa with Walpi and Sichomovi, and below the mesa is a growing village called Polacca. On Second Mesa to the west are Shongopovi, Mishongnovi and Shipaulovi. Old Oraibi is on Third Mesa a few miles further west, with New Oraibi, or Kikenchmovi, [1] below the cliffside, and sharing the mesa top are Hotevilla and Bakavi. Beyond, near Tuba City, is the village of Moencopi.

The First Mesa Tewas have retained what they regard as a distinct identity by preservation of their language and traditions, even while absorbing Hopi mainstream culture. Their situation as it relates to the Hopi mainstream is somewhat comparable to that of other ethnic minorities as they relate to American mainstream life. They speak Hopi as well as Tewa, intermingle and marry with Hopis, and share Hopi ceremonies and life in general, while as best they can they tenaciously hold on to their Tewa identity. Their retention of their particular traditions is paralleled by each Hopi clan's nurturing of its own history, legends, beliefs and accomplishments. Thus the Water Clan and its affiliated clans preserve the story of their origins in the south, along with the rituals and "medicine" commemorating those origins. And the Snake and Horn clans preserve and celebrate their memories of their beginnings in the north.

What are loosely referred to as "Hopi traditions," therefore, is a collection of traditions brought by numerous groups from a variety of places and now coexisting side by side. Certain clans assert special affiliations with particular deities that appear to predate their arrival in the Hopi villages. Huruing Wuhti (Hard Substances Old Woman) is claimed by some clans to be the creator deity who placed the sun in the sky. Other clans say it was Gogyeng Sowuhti (Spider Old Woman) who performed this deed. Such conflicts of beliefs, and there are many, point to separate traditions brought together on the Hopi mesas. But Hopis are tolerant of these contradictions and even consider them to be elements contributing to cultural enrichment.

There is already a substantial literature on Hopi life and it would be presumptuous to attempt to summarize in this brief introduction what is known to scholars about Hopi institutions and social organization. But to focus light on the basic Hopi view of land, work and property, I borrow here from a document appearing among the Appendixes of this book, a letter addressed to "The Washington Chiefs" by spokesmen of the villages:

"The family, the dwelling house and the field are inseparable, because the woman is the heart of these, and they rest with her. Among us, the family traces its kin from the mother, hence all its possessions are hers. The man builds the house but the woman is the owner, because she repairs and preserves it; the man cultivates the field, but he renders its harvest into the woman's keeping. . . .

"A man plants the fields of his wife, and the fields assigned to the children she bears, and informally he calls them his, although in fact they are not. . . .

"Our fields are numerous but small, and several belonging to the same family may be close together, or they may be miles apart, because arable localities are not continuous. . . .

"In the Spring and early Summer there usually comes from the Southwest a succession of gales, oftentimes strong enough to blow away the sandy soil from the face of some of our fields . . . ; as the sand is the only fertile land, when it moves, the planters must follow it, and other fields must be provided in place of those which have been devastated. Sometimes generations pass away and these barren spots remain. . . .

"The American is our elder brother, and in everything he can teach us, except in the method of growing corn in these waterless sand valleys, and in that we are sure we can teach him."

This was the world into which Albert Yava was born. Though his father was a Hopi, his mother was Tewa, and since descent was counted on the mother's side, he was Tewa. He grew up in Tewa Village (which the Hopis called Hano). The name given to him by his paternal aunts was Nuṿayoiyava, Big Falling Snow, alluding to his father's membership in the Water Clan, snow being an aspect of rain. But the name Nuvayoiyava did not survive his early school days because his teachers could not handle Indian names, and it became shortened to Yava. As was their custom, his teachers gave him a familiar personal name, and so he became Albert Yava. Later when he was initiated into the One Horn kiva fraternity he was renamed Eutawisa, meaning Close In the Antelopes, but to his friends he remained Yava, or more commonly, Albert.

It was not his father's membership in the Hopi tribe that made Yava a Hopi as well as a Tewa, but initiation into the One Horn Society. Even Hopi-born men were not considered to be complete, qualified Hopis unless they belonged to one of the major kiva fraternities. It was in those kiva groups that a person learned the traditions of the clans and the ceremonial cycles on which Hopi life was based. After initiation Yava was entitled to speak of himself as a Hopi, though in his own mind he identified himself first of all as a Tewa. By the time he was a village elder he was regarded as an authority on both Hopi and Tewa ways. An insider in the Hopi community, still he saw Hopi events and traditions with an "outside" perspective. The years he spent at the Chilocco Indian School in Oklahoma and working for the Indian Agency at Keam's Canyon increased the depth of the perspective. He could measure Tewa and Hopi life against the white man's view of the world and the white man's beliefs, achievements and vanities. But seeing Indian life more objectively never adulterated his sense of identity with his Tewa and Hopi brothers or with the religious traditions and cycles that regulated life in the villages. Although he never doubted that the villages had much to learn and gain from the outside world, he had deep regrets as he watched the erosion of traditions and the death of certain kiva societies and ceremonies.

True to the Hopi-Tewa sense of what is fitting, Yava does not tell everything he knows. As an elder of the Stick, or Spruce, Clan, affiliated with the Bear Clan group, he can speak with authority regarding the beliefs of those clans, and as a member of the One Horn Society he speaks with authority regarding its traditions. But of the traditions of other clans and kiva groups he speaks conditionally, noting that what he relates is what he himself has observed or what has come from the mouth of a qualified person. He is always careful not to tell what he is not authorized to tell, either because it is a ceremonial secret or because it should properly come from a qualified person of another clan or fraternity. In his final review of the manuscript of this book he deleted certain portions that he knew to be true but which he felt to be beyond the limits of what was permissible for him to say. He does not reveal what his kiva group has pledged him to keep secret. Among some Hopis it is believed that revealing kiva secrets could bring supernatural as well as social punishment. But I am certain that Yava's motivations stemmed primarily from pledges given and his sense of honor. On one occasion he said, "I can't give you the details of what went on in this ceremony, but that anthropologist Fewkes has written about it, and what he tells is absolutely true. You can find it all in that book of his."

I don't want to repeat in this brief introduction what Yava says well for himself in the pages that follow. But it should be observed that he would rather speak of his people, the clan and the village than of his personal life. In the Hopi-Tewa way he believes that the individual is less significant than the interaction of individuals and groups. Mostly he talks with the attitude of an observer of the scene and a teller of traditions. He is able to see his own culture in the large, and at times he assesses that culture and draws conclusions. For example, he notes that there run through Hopi history readily visible moral impulses and, at the same time, endless frictions and tendencies towards quarrelling. He notes that many villages were destroyed or abandoned in legendary and historical times as a result of dissension, inner conflicts or the desire to escape corruption, and that some of the old flaws continue to show themselves in modern Hopi-Tewa life.

Though much of Albert Yava's personality is revealed in his comments, these recollections are not a personality study. Unlike Don Talayesva's book *Sun Chief*—conceived and structured by its editor to reveal one man's behavior in response to the stresses of his culture—Yava's *Big Falling Snow* looks at Hopis and Tewas collectively. Yava can see a ceremony externally as well as through the eyes of a participant. The experience he communicates is substantially different from Talayesva's, which is largely internal, the experience of a participant cast by fate in a role. Talayesva describes supernatural events as aspects of everyday reality. Yava, though dedicated to the values of his group, finds it relatively easy to say "they believe" or "they" do this or do that. These two men, "old-timers" to the young, are close in age. They attended school together at Keam's Canyon, from where they went on to separate schools, Don to Riverside, California, and Albert to Chilocco, Oklahoma. Both absorbed much from their formal educations. Yet Don emerged as a person still enclosed by his culture, its pressures, its beliefs, its literal explanations, while Albert began to see himself from the outside. Don acted out tradition in his personal experiences, whereas Albert became narrator and chronicler.

In *Sun Chief*, Don Talayesva tells of a "dream" experience he had when he was ill at Sherman Indian School at Riverside. In this dream he goes to Maski, the Land of the Dead. What he witnesses and experiences on this journey is the substance of a traditional Oraibi story of a young man who journeys to Maski and afterward returns to the land of the living. (See pp. 99–104.) Whether Don actually dreamed that story or whether he consciously undertook to make himself the protagonist of the tale cannot be said with certainty. Albert has no impulse to be personally involved, and he tells the Maski story with full attribution to its source. Yet he is no less "Indian" for all his objectivity. In one section of this book he describes apparitions that appeared to him one night, and tells how he exorcised them through a ritual learned in his One Horn kiva. On concluding, he asks, "Well, now, what do you call that? Imagination?"—leaving it to the reader to characterize the experience for himself, but at the same time not rejecting the reality of those apparitions.

Big Falling Snow developed out of recording sessions with Albert Yava over a period of years while I was gathering traditions, tales and legends in the Hopi villages from a number of informants. Some of the materials collected appeared subsequently in *The Fourth World of the Hopis* (1971). In certain instances the narrations in that collection were composite versions, with details provided by two, three or more persons. The versions appearing here among Albert Yava's recollections, however, are told as he himself heard them from older people, and except for relatively minor editing they may be taken as near-literal texts.

H. C. Voth's *Traditions of the Hopi*, published in 1905, remains one of our most valuable sources of Hopi texts. Though he occasionally misunderstood or mistranslated, and though some knowledgeable Hopis today contend that his informants did not always tell him the truth but sometimes distorted or invented stories to please him or "get rid" of him, nevertheless Voth's *Traditions* is a treasury of myth-legends and historic legends as they were remembered in the villages three quarters of a century ago. Yava's narrations are of particular interest in that they reveal the extent to which certain of the traditions have survived through a period of acute cultural stresses.

He clearly perceives the distinction between history as it is understood in the outside world and the Hopi-Tewa legends, but he believes that many historical truths are contained in traditional tales. The story of the Tewas' migration to First Mesa from their Rio Grande village, Tsewageh, for example, he considers to be true in all those details that ha e survived. At the same time he acknowledges that parts of the story have been forgotten and become "lost history." As for the myth-legend of Tewa origins and migrations before reaching Tsewageh, Yava does not have the fundamentalist point of view that everything happened the way tradition describes it. He sees the myth-legend in part, at least, as symbolic, although he considers the place-names it mentions as elements of factual importance.

Tewas and Hopis alike tend to literalness in their telling of traditions for the reason that if one is not literal, if one is willing to omit or pass over a troublesome detail, if he changes something to make a story smooth, he may be losing a fragment of historical truth. For example, one of my informants once objected to the written version of his story indicating that a footrace was run to a certain piñon tree. He stated that it should have been a cottonwood, not a piñon, though the species of tree had no bearing whatever on the story, its outcome or its meaning. In the Hopi and Tewa view, literalness is a preserver of reality and authenticity. To let a cottonwood go as a piñon would be to lose one more bead from the long strand of beads reaching into the past. Yava frequently lamented that he was never able to acquire a tape recording made by his uncle, George Cochaase, telling of all the migration of the Tewas before they reached First Mesa, for in that recording were many details now lost to Tewa Village.

Well aware that traditions vary from place to place and person to person, he does not claim that his versions are more authentic than others, only that they are what were told to him by the old people. He does not pretend to tell the Tewa story as it is known to the Eastern Tewas, acknowledging that the Rio Grande people may remember details of the Tewa past that are now forgotten on First Mesa. But he does consider Tewa Village to have better knowledge than others of the migration to First Mesa and all that developed from it. He listens with attention, however, to whatever his Eastern Tewa cousins have to say about their past.

My first recording sessions with Yava were in 1969, and they continued thereafter from year to year whenever we could manage to get together at First Mesa. What he had to say went far beyond story narrations. He spoke of his experiences, of clan beliefs and conflicts, of ceremonial life, of Hopi-Tewa relations, of problems between the villages and the Navajos, and of difficulties with the Government. By 1975 it seemed to us that what he had voiced on tape might be sorted out and set down as a book of recollections. Members of his family urged him to do this, believing that such a book would pass on to younger generations the story of how life had been in the old days and preserve information and traditions that otherwise would fade away. Though modest about what his recollections might contribute, and shy about putting himself forward, he agreed.

There remained the process of transcribing many hours of recordings and notes and of bringing all the pieces together into their appropriate context. Once the transcribed material was structured, a continuing correspondence between Author and Editor helped fill gaps in the narration. In November 1975 Dewey Healing, Mr. Yava's son-in-law, went to the Colorado River Reservation, where Albert was then living, and spent several days with him recording further comments and explanations. Mr. Yava received the resulting draft of the manuscript in early 1977 for corrections, deletions, additions and whatever second thoughts he might have. In July 1977 he met with the Editor again on the Hopi Reservation, where he reviewed the manuscript page by page and recorded further comments. As nearly as possible, Mr. Yava's own words are retained throughout the final text, and even where editing was required, the substance remains faithful to his intentions and meanings. In those places where I have considered it useful to make comments or explanations, I have not intruded them into the text but placed them in back notes and appendixes. Likewise, I have tried not to tamper with Mr. Yava's language and style of narration any more than was required by the task of bringing into unity the substance of innumerable recording sessions.

I am sure that I speak for Albert Yava as well as for myself in thanking Dewey Healing, himself now one of First Mesa's respected elders, for his dedicated assistance in getting these recollections ready for publication. He sat with us for long hours in Tewa Village, in Polacca or on Second Mesa helping Albert sort out answers to my troublesome, sometimes naïve, questions. Other Hopis and Tewas also helped, in ways of which they may not have been aware, and to them also I express our appreciation. We are particularly grateful to the late Dr. H. C. (Dutch) Diehl, a longtime friend of Yava's who was learned in Hopi-Tewa ways, history and language. He reviewed many pages of the manuscript of this book, and made numerous suggestions that proved valuable. We are indebted to him for providing some of the Hopi documents that appear among the Appendixes. Thanks are due also to Phyllis M. Kaye, who helped to research the ethnogeography of the Tewas in New Mexico, and to Professor Alfonso Ortiz, who provided information about the location of Tsewageh, the village site from which a group of Tewas migrated to the Hopi mesas. My wife, Emma, accompanied me on an exploration of that site, and was present, and gave moral support, during most of my recording sessions with Yava. To her, also, my appreciation.

A number of the photographs in this book were obtained from the National Archives, the Division of Political History and the Anthropological Archives of the Smithsonian Institution, and the Museum of Northern Arizona. I want to express my thanks to those institutions, to the University of Oklahoma Press, and to the individuals who located the photo materials and made prints available—Katherine Bartlett, Edith Mayo, Byrtis Thomas and Richard C. Crawford. I am also grateful to Mrs. Henry S. Bothfeld for the portraits of Albert Yava and his father which were taken by Walter Collins O'Kane. Appropriate credits appear with the photos taken by persons other than the Editor.

Harold Courlander

This is a true story of events that happened in my lifetime, things I learned through living, and things that were taught to me by the old ones who were here before I arrived. If I have set down anything wrongly or incompletely, it is only because what a person recalls from the past is a combination of what he remembers and what he forgets. To the best of my recollection, this book tells things truly. As for those things I know but cannot speak about, I am sure I will be forgiven.

Albert Yava
Tewa Village, First Mesa
July 10, 1977

My people were Tewas from the Rio Grande Valley who came here to live with the Hopis on First Mesa some time around the year 1700. They settled near the Hopi village of Walpi, close to the southern edge of the mesa-top gap from which Walpi took its name. Hopis and whites often refer to our settlement as Hano. That is because we were thought to be Tanos, or T'hanos, but we were true Tewas and the proper name for our settlement is Tewa Village. In the old days, if a group came from a distant place and made a village, other people gave that village a name indicating what tribe or clan settled at that place. There were Kawaikas (now they are called Lagunas) who settled on Antelope Mesa, and their village was called Kawaika. Some people called Payupkis from the Rio Grande came and made a settlement on Second Mesa, and their place was known as Payupki. After a while they went back, according to what we were told, to the Rio Grande to live in the Pueblo of Sandia. Quite a few other eastern Pueblo groups came here at different times. Some of them merged with the Hopis, but most of them only stayed for a few years and then left. We First Mesa Tewas are the only ones who came and remained without losing our own culture and our own traditions. We still speak the Tewa language, and we speak it in a more pure form than the Rio Grande Tewas do. Over there in New Mexico the Tewa language has been corrupted by the other Pueblo languages and Spanish. We also speak Hopi fluently, though there are very few Hopis who can converse in Tewa.

My father was actually a Hopi, but we count descent on the mother's side, and as my mother was a Tewa, I am a Tewa. My mother, Iechawe, which means Blue Smoke in Tewa, belonged to the Pehtowa, or Wood [Stick], Clan, so that is my clan also. Hopis call it the Spruce Clan. Though

I am a full-fledged Tewa, I am also a Hopi—not because of my father being a Hopi, but because I was initiated into the Kwakwanteu, or One Horn kiva society. It is one of the four major kiva fraternities among the Hopis. A member of any one of those fraternities is considered to be a Hopi. On First Mesa, the One Horn fraternity is regarded as the most important of the four. They tell us that you can be born in a Hopi village of Hopi parents and speak the Hopi language, but still you aren't a complete Hopi unless you go through the initiations and become a member of one of the four kiva groups. That's because it's only within these societies that you can get all the important teachings that have been handed down mouth to ear from one generation to another. Only by having a place in the kiva can you possibly understand all the ceremonial relationships within the village—who the important figures within the clans are, how the clans relate to one another, which of them has ultimate authority in particular matters, who has the right to be the kikmongwi, or village chief, what the different kiva groups stand for, where the responsibility lies for things that have to be done, what the traditions of the different clans are and how they are shared, and the special rights claimed by this clan or that clan.

Our traditional Hopi society is a complex tangle of relationships. When two people meet for the first time they try to figure out what their relationship is, because it's important to the way they act toward each other. As a Tewa, I have ceremonial ties with many Hopis through my kiva society. As a member of the Spruce, or Wood, Clan, I have a tie with anyone from that clan, whether he's a Tewa, a Hopi, a Zuni, a Supai, a Navajo or a Paiute. Certain clans are linked together. My clan is affiliated with the Bear, Strap, Grease Cavity, Bluebird, Spider and Gopher clans, so people of those clans are, you might say, my relatives. But certain particular clans are especially close. The Spruce and Spider clans go together. The Bear and Strap clans go together. And the Gopher, Grease Cavity and Bluebird are close together. People of those closely related clans can't intermarry. At least it was that way in former times, but I think that young people are ignoring clan relationships these days, not bothering to follow the old restrictions.

Whenever we men sit together in the kiva to smoke, one person passes the pipe to another saying "my uncle," "my father," "my younger brother" or "my older brother" to indicate a relationship. "Brother" isn't literal. It means a person with whom you are in harmony, and whom you respect. If he is older than you, you say "navaypaday" or "navaypipi," meaning "ahead of me" in age. Everybody in the kiva has a particular relationship with the others. You have to know a man's clan or you won't know your appropriate relationship with him or how to behave toward him. If someone offers tobacco to you you may not feel like smoking, but if that man is a member of the Tobacco Clan you never refuse, because tobacco is sacred and it is a special kind of gift coming from a Tobacco Clan member. We are never allowed to forget how our society fits together, and only if you are exposed to the teachings of the kiva societies can you fully understand these things.

The name that was given to me when I was born was Nuvayoiyava, meaning Big Falling Snow. You can also translate that as Big Falling Snowflake. I received this name because my father belonged to the Rain-Cloud, or Water, Clan. It was traditional for aunts on the father's side to name a child, and they usually selected a name that revealed the father's clan affiliations. Snow is an aspect of rain, so Nuvayoiyava indicated my father's clan. If you meet a man named Hontoechi, meaning Bear Moccasins, you know that his father was a Bear Clan person. If a man's name is Chucka, meaning mud, you know that his father was Sand Clan, because earth and sand together cover the breast of Mother Earth. If a name has tawa in it, meaning sun, that means the father belonged to the Sun Clan, which claims a special affiliation with the sun. However, a person's name doesn't reveal his own clan, which is the same as his mother's. Nuvayoiyava was the only name I had till I went to school. Because my teachers couldn't pronounce it very well they shortened it to Yava. But that wasn't enough for them. They didn't like it that the children had no family names. So they sort of turned our individual names into family names and then gave us personal names like John, Mary, Henry, Peter and so on. One teacher wanted to call me Oliver, but another one who took a personal interest in me said, "No, I like the name Albert, and that's what we're going to call him." This explains how I came to be Albert Yava. Later on in life when I was initiated into the One Horn Society they gave me a ceremonial name, Eutawisa, meaning Close In the Antelopes. It was supposed to drown out my original name, but people still call me Yava.

What we people are like has been studied by lots of anthropologists, but they were able to find out only so much about us and quite a bit of their infomation has been wrong. A lot of it has been right, of course, we don't deny it, and some anthropologists in particular have had a great gift of learning about our ways, even learning some things that should have been private to our kivas. But I am one of the old men here now, and if I tell something about my life and what I recall of our traditions, maybe a little bit will be added to what is publicly known, and maybe certain errors will be corrected. Maybe, also, our own people will want to know these things.

I was born in 1888 and I probably remember some events and traditions that will be forgotten soon if they are not set down. Quite a few of our traditions have already slipped out of memory because so many knowledgeable old people have been called by the Great Spirit. The children spend days and years away at school, and I think most of them speak better English than Hopi or Tewa. Also, there isn't much mouth-to-ear teaching in the kivas any more. So I am going to recall some of the things I know, the way I saw them or heard them, or the way they were taught to me. Maybe our young people will get an inkling of what life was like on this mesa when I was a boy, or how it was in the time of our fathers and grandfathers. If I seem to say a lot about myself, it is really my times that I am thinking about. I am merely the person who happened to be there at a particular time. It is hard to put down something with myself as a center of interest— that is, to say I did this or that. It makes me out as important, which isn't the way I see it. We Tewas and Hopis don't think of ourselves that way. In our histories and traditions we don't have individual heroes with names to remember. It is the village, the group, the clan that did this or that, not a man or woman. If an individual happens to stand out, we probably don't remember his real name, and if a name is required we probably have to make it up. Anyway, I am going to tell about some of the things that I know or remember, and you will understand that I am really talking about my people, the Tewas and the Hopis, and their experiences and recollections.

These villages up here on First Mesa looked quite different when I was just a boy and growing up. If you ever happen to see any old pictures of Walpi and Tewa Village at that time, you'll notice that quite a few of the houses had second stories up above. They were terraced buildings. I myself was born in an upper level house. But all those upper stories decayed and were never replaced. Some of the lower stories have also disappeared, and here and there you can see walls still falling apart. Probably some walls were already coming apart back in the 1880s and 1890s when I was growing up. But the fields that the people kept in those days were in good shape. We used to get more rain than now. There was a lot of grass and all kinds of growing things that you don't see any more. Some of those growing things were higher than your head. Sunflowers were everywhere. When the plants were in bloom there were hummingbirds all around. Nowadays you don't often see them. If we were out in the fields when it rained, the washes would quickly fill with water and we couldn't cross, so it was hard to get home.

Even though there was more rain in those times, life was a struggle for everybody. I don't think the Hopi people ever had an easy time of it from the beginning. It seems that they were living up to a prophecy that was made when the people first came out of the underworld. That is the basic

Hopi creation story, that humans emerged into this land from a world beneath the earth. When the people came out, the mockingbird arranged them according to tribes, the tribes they were going to be. He said to one group, "Sit over there. You will be Comanches." To another, "Sit over there. You will be Hopis." Another, "Sit over there. You will be Bahanas, or white people." After that, the mockingbird set out the corn. He put out different kinds of ears, all the varieties of corn that we know. He told all these tribes to take whichever ears they wanted, and he told them what each ear meant. He said, "Now, this yellow corn will bring prosperity and enjoyment, but life will be short for whoever chooses it." And when he came to the short blue ear he said, "This one, the blue corn, means a life of hardship and hard work, but the people who choose it will have peaceful times and live to a ripe old age." He described all the different ears, and the leaders of the tribes sat looking at the corn trying to make up their minds.

Then one big tall fellow, a Navajo, said, "All right. You people can't decide." So he reached out and grabbed the long yellow corn that meant a short life but much enjoyment. The others said, "Ayih! He's always grabbing!" Then everybody began to grab. The Supais took the yellow speckled corn. The Comanches took the red corn. The Utes took the flint corn. Every tribe got its corn, but the leader of the Hopis sat there without taking anything until only one ear was left, the short blue corn. He picked up the short blue ear and said, "Well, this ear is mine. It means we will have to work hard to live, but we will have long, full lives." And all through their migrations after that there were prophecies that the Hopis would make their final home at an austere place where life would be difficult, but their guiding spirit promised to watch over them if they led decent lives. The Hopis were not supposed to accumulate wealth, but to be generous with everything. And when they settled here in this country they said, "Life will be hard in this place, but no one will envy us. No one will try to take our land away. This is the place where we will stay."

Whenever life was difficult in the Hopi villages, the old people would explain that the Hopis were destined for this kind of living. In the time of my boyhood the thing that people had to strive for was to raise enough food to tide them over the year. They'd go out early in the day to cultivate their fields of corn, beans and melons. They were always trying to produce better crops. In the summertime, the men were always in the fields. You'd hardly ever see them in the villages until evening. At other times of the year, of course, they did things like weaving blankets, kilts and sashes. They didn't know how to waste time. The women worked just as hard. Even getting water wasn't easy. There were several springs down at the foot of the mesa, but the water didn't flow very fast. The early risers were the ones who got their water right away. Women who came later had to wait for the springs to fill up again. If a woman came late and couldn't fill her water jar, she set it by the spring to stake out her turn. The next woman would set her jar behind, indicating that her turn would follow. Sometimes they had to make several trips a day to get as much water as they needed. Nowadays the young people don't have any inkling of this. Since those old days the Government has drilled wells for us, improved the springs and even piped water to the top of the mesa. Now there is a tank with a standpipe on the mesa, waiting for the people to come and get their water.

We young boys were expected to get up early and help with the fields or other chores. We generally did what we were expected to do. But if a boy became careless about getting up on time and doing his work, his mother called on her side of the family—her clan relatives—to do something about it. They'd take you from one house to another where your relatives lived, and they'd pour cold water on you. When a boy went through this experience he was embarrassed and ashamed, and after that he did what he was supposed to do.

One of our responsibilities was to keep the field rats from eating the corn seeds. If we found a little mound where a rat had made a fresh hole, we would dig down till we found the rat, and we'd kill it if we could. But sometimes that rathole had a second entrance and the rat would run out there, maybe right behind you. So one boy would dig and another would be watching for the rat to come out somewhere else. To keep us alert to the right way to dig for rats, some of the older people told us, "Watch what you're doing. If the rat escapes behind your back while you are digging you will get a hunchback." In order not to get a hunchback you kept your eyes open.

There were lots of crows to contend with too. We young ones were sent out to keep the crows away from the corn and melons. Everybody would have a particular place where he was supposed to stay to either shoot the crows with bows and arrows or scare them away. (We used the bows and arrows given to us on ceremonial occasions, such as the Home Dance. They weren't very good and we never hit any crows with them.) The job they gave me was to roll up a sheep pelt and hit it with a stick. It made a sound like a gunshot, and when the crows heard that they just took off. We had one boy, his name was Cheeda, he'd stick something up his nose to make it bleed. Then he'd smear a little of the blood on a cornhusk and put it somewhere to attract the crows so he could shoot at them. Sometimes when we were in the fields we'd pretend to be warriors fighting each other—Hopis against Comanches or Utes or some other tribe—throwing corncobs. After the game was over we'd go back to guarding the corn and melons from the crows.

Another thing we did when we had time was to go after prairie dogs. They were good to eat. We would strip down and crawl along the ground as quietly as possible. Whenever a prairie dog came out of its hole and barked, we would try to shoot him. If we were lucky enough to get one we would clean it out, burn off the hair, put salt on it, wrap it in corn leaves and roast it in hot ashes. That was always a great treat for us young ones.

Another responsibility we had was to watch over those long-legged goats and sheep that some families owned. If a family had only one or two ewes they'd bunch them up with other people's animals, and we boys would stay with them and keep them together. If we were a good distance away from the village we might have to stay out all night, and we younger ones would be scared but we tried not to let on to the others. We also had the responsibility of taking care of the melons in the fields. We had to build windbreaks to protect the plants from wind and drifting sand. If a windstorm came up at night we would have to go out in the morning and uncover the plants. I learned about all these things from my stepfather. He would take me out to the fields with him and show me just the right way to do things. If a melon vine was covered with dust, he would show me how to gently clear it off, how to tap the soil firmly around the stem where it came out of the ground. We'd take snake brush, the root part, and set it in front of the plants for wind protection. We would build up brush for shade to keep the ground cool. If the young watermelon plants weren't kept cool their roots would rot away.

I also learned a lot about corn from my stepfather. Our Hopi corn has to be planted deep, maybe six or eight inches, so that it gets some moisture. You can't plant Iowa corn that deep because it won't grow. Of course we couldn't fertilize our corn like the white man did, and like some eastern Indians are supposed to have done. Our best rains would come in June or July, and we would expect the floodwaters to flow over the fields and bring something along to fertilize them. The water must have washed down minerals of some kind. And of course we left the cornstalks in the fields where the blowing sand would cover them up, and this helped fertilize the ground.

My stepfather was very patient about teaching me all these things. His name was Peki, meaning Turned Over, and he belonged to the Corn Clan. He took care of me just as if I were his own son. He tried hard to keep me well clothed. He really cared for me and was always wondering what I might need. One time he even bought me a saddle, and I know he had to give up something else for that. He was respected by everybody in the village, both for his character and the way he conducted himself. He knew what was right or wrong, but generally he was gentle and softspoken. Nobody ever knew him to avoid work. If he wasn't working in the fields he'd be out trading with the Navajos for sheep. Then of course he had to give a lot of time to kiva affairs. In important ceremonies he was the one that laid out the sacred path with cornmeal. I was the only boy in the family for a while, and so I was the only one to work with my stepfather. Later on I had two half brothers and a half sister. But I always had a special role in working with my stepfather, and even after I was older and went away to school, whenever I came home I'd help him in the fields, or take his turn when he was supposed to be out herding the sheep.

When I was very young I never saw very much of my real father, Sitaiema. He belonged to the Water Clan and to the Kwakwanteu, or One Horn kiva fraternity. He left me and my mother, as they say, while I was still in the cradle. However, in later years, after I was initiated into the Kwakwanteu, I saw a lot more of him and he told me many things about Water Clan traditions that I would never have heard anywhere else. The One Horn rituals were brought here by the Water Clan (we Tewas call it the Cloud, or Mist, Clan) and its related clans when they came from a place in the south called Palatkwa. The real meaning of the clan name in Hopi is Dwelling On Water, or Houseboat, alluding to the tradition that they once crossed a great body of water in their migrations. My father was the headman of the One Horn fraternity and he wanted me to be in it. Eventually when I was old enough I was made a member. So as it turned out, I learned about rituals, ceremonies and traditions from my father, and from my stepfather I learned how to make the land fruitful. Today the young people aren't getting any of this. Initiations into the main kiva societies seem to have come to an end on First Mesa, and you hardly ever see young children working in the fields the way we did. There is a big break between the old ways and the new ways.

Of course, it wasn't all work and no fun for the children in the old days. We had lots of games. Some of them were pretty simple, but they were great sport for us and I guess you could say they kept us out of mischief. One game was pretty much like shinny. The ball was made out of buckskin stuffed with deer hair, and the players all had specially shaped sticks to knock it around with. Hopis call that game nahoydadatsia, Tewas call it huntamaylay. There was a sloping piece of clear ground, and we used to play over there. This game is the one the two warrior gods, Pokanghoya and Palengahoya, are supposed to be playing all the time. You hear about it in the old stories.

We also had a dart-throwing game. We made the darts out of corncobs, with feathers at one end and a sharp greasewood point at the other. We had teams. We would throw at a target made out of corn leaves, or something like that, or throw at hoops. Another game we had that was great fun for the boys was a sort of throwing race with corncobs. You'd have a corncob, or a ball as a substitute, tied to a string, and the other end of the string was tied to a little crosspiece made of wood. A boy would put the crosspiece between his toes, lie down on his back, and flip the corncob with his foot as far as he could over his head. Then another boy would flip it. The last boy down the line would start the corncob going back the other way. Whichever side got its corncob back to the starting place was the winner. We also had another corncob game, but we played it a little differently. The objective was to throw the corncob down into the kiva.

Most of us young children in the village didn't have decent clothes to wear. Up to a certain age we ran around naked, but at some point we wanted to have something on us. There weren't many nearby trading posts where clothes could be bought even if people had the money, which a great many of them didn't. A few kids had overalls, which gave them distinction. I had an uncle that used to go out trading to different places, and sometimes he would bring back a twenty-pound sack of flour for my mother. She used to mix the white flour with our own blue corn flour to make it last longer. When the white flour was gone my mother converted the sack into a kind of tunic for me by ripping out the bottom. One time my uncle brought some white muslin, and my mother made it into something like pajama pants. It was the first pants I ever wore.

Another thing about those days, the children weren't allowed to wander around like they do now from one end of the village to the other. Unless they were down in the fields with their parents they were expected to stick pretty close to their homes. They were warned to stay away from the kivas, couldn't go near them. People used to tell them that if they got too near to a kiva one of those man-eating monster kachinas would come out and get them. Kids were really scared of those monster kachinas, who used to go around the village on certain occasions to see if the youngsters were behaving themselves.

I was five or six when I first went to the day school below the mesa at Polacca. It was a small stone building that belonged to an uncle of mine, of the Tobacco Clan, and it was used as a temporary school until they finished building the new day school. The old building is still there, and now it has gone back to the Tobacco Clan. On our first day at school they gave us all new clothes, white man's style. We didn't like those clothes very much because they made us feel ridiculous. Altogether, we felt pretty strange, getting educated in a language we didn't understand. When the teacher sent us outside for recess we took off the clothes and hid them under some bushes, then we ran naked back to the village up on the mesa. We tried to be invisible up there because the truant officer, a Hopi uncle of mine, Chakwaiena, was coming after us. He had to chase us all through the village and over the roofs to catch us. When he did, he took us down to the school and we had to put those clothes on again and listen to the teacher, a tall white man named Mr. Spink, trying to teach us things in English. We ran away several times before we gave up.

One of the things Mr. Spink taught us was how to count, "One, two, three, four, five," but we couldn't get it because we didn't know what he was talking about, and we just sat there dumb. Chakwaiena, the truant officer, was sitting in the room, and one time he jumped up and said, in Hopi of course, "What's the matter with you kids? Don't you understand anything? Just say like I do, 'One and two and hai hai hai!'" It sure made us laugh. Even later, remembering it made us laugh. We'd say to each other, "What's the matter with you? One and two and hai hai hai." When the new day school opened we were transferred over there. We had a teacher named Miss Cunningham. It was still hard for us to understand English and to pronounce English words. Our mothers told us, "Watch your teacher's tongue, then you'll know how to say the words." I had a girl cousin in that class, and she went home and told her mother, "Oh, that teacher's tongue is so loose! She says, 'A-atah, o-cha-tah!'" My cousin must have thought that was English.

You have to remember that this school business was new not only to the children but also to most of the people in the villages. There had been a big commotion when the Government gave the order that all the children would have to attend school. There was a lot of resistance. Over on the other mesas—in Oraibi, Shongopovi and Mishongnovi—the reaction was even stronger than on First Mesa. The conservatives—you can call them that or Hostiles—felt very strongly that the white man was cramming his ways down our throats. Many people felt that the Government was trying to obliterate our culture by making the children attend school. And if you want to be honest about it, the schooling the children have been getting over the past seventy-five or eighty years has educated them to the white man's ways but made them less knowledgeable about the traditional ways of their own people. A lot of what they have been taught is good. It makes them able to understand the way the white man thinks, and to compete in the outside world. But at the same time, they aren't getting as much of their own traditions as they should. Something important is being gained, but something important is being lost.

In the years just before I appeared on the scene, the villages were split down the middle over whether to allow the children to be sent to the day schools or the boarding schools. The struggle was mostly between the village leaders, the men who were spokesmen for the rest of us—the village chief and his advisers, the clan leaders and the leaders of the kiva societies. For example, in Walpi—including Sichomovi, which was a Water Clan offshoot of Walpi—the resisters included the kikmongwi (his name was Simo) and the heads of the four main kiva fraternities. Naturally, the leaders of the kiva societies were worried that our traditional ways of doing things were going to be undermined. Up to then, it was in the kiva organizations that young people were educated to Hopi history and beliefs. Nobody really knew what the Government schools were going to do to the children.

But the other groups, the progressives, or Friendlies (called that because they were in favor of cooperating with the whites), saw that if the next generation was going to survive, the children would have to learn a lot about white ways. We Tewas were mostly on the progressive side. One of our prominent Tewas, Tom Polaccaca (the Hopis called him Polacca), was very determined that the children should have a modern education. Polacca village at the foot of the mesa is named after him. Another Tewa who came out strongly on the progressive side was a man named Kalakwai. Among the Hopis a man named Haneh, of the Tobacco Clan, also urged the people to send their children to school. But with all the pushing and pulling, it took quite a while for the struggle to be resolved. More than once the Government had to send troops into some of the villages to round up the children and cart them off to school. When the split came in Oraibi in 1906, the conservative bunch, led by the Fire Clan and the Water Coyotes, established the village of Hotevilla, and once they arrived there they refused to let their children go to school, so in 1911, as I recall, the Government sent in troops to round up the Hotevilla children and take them to boarding school by force. By that time I was working for the Bureau of Indian Affairs in Keam's Canyon, and I was sent with a team and wagon to Hotevilla to pick up a load of children. We brought them to the Oraibi day school and kept them there overnight, and the next day we took them to Keam's Canyon and settled them at the boarding school.

So you can see that when I was starting school at the age of five or six, around 1893-94, the problem had not yet been settled. Some of the First Mesa families were still resisting and weren't happy about the Government forcing them to let the kids have an education. But the progressives won out, and the Tewas were mostly on that side of the argument. Tom Polaccaca exerted a lot of influence on the side of education. The conservative Hopis were always complaining about him. In later years, after that school business was all settled, he continued to receive a lot of criticism from them, and whenever something went wrong they would say, "Well, you can thank Tom Polacca for that."

In 1896, when I was eight years old, I was transferred from the Polacca day school to the boarding school in Keam's Canyon, about ten miles from First Mesa and quite a bit further from the other mesas. The boarding school was in what they later called "the old plant," because a new building was finished in 1903, and that one was called "the new plant." When we kids arrived on the first day of school, the first thing they did was to give us baths and cut our Hopi-style hair and make it white man's style. Our families didn't like our hair being cut. Our traditional hairstyle was meaningful. The long hair we boys wore on the sides symbolized rain, you might say fertility, and it seemed to our parents that the whites were pretty high-handed and insensitive, as well as being ignorant of our ways. Still, quite a few of the teachers were pretty nice people. All the teachers were whites, but there were Indians performing other jobs. Tom Polaccaca was there. He was what you might call a law officer, and we had another law officer named Charlie Avayung. They kept things under control around the school. If some kid ran away from school to go back to his village, which happened once in a while, one of the teachers named Frank Ewing got on his roan horse and went after him. Mr. James, a half-Cherokee, was the school carpenter. His wife, also part Cherokee, was the cook.

The new school building that was opened in 1903 was pretty modern for those times. It had an electric power plant, electric lights, and steam heat from coal-fueled boilers. To hear what some of the kids had to say, they would rather have been anywhere but in that school, at least in the beginning. Still, a lot of us liked it and were glad to have a chance to learn the white man's ways so that we'd know how to cope in later years. That was one thing that was always on my mind. I was glad to learn or experience something new. We had a gardener at the school, a man named Bennet Hill who was a Civil War veteran. Eating the vegetables he raised was my first experience eating white man's crops.

Of course, a good many things were sort of primitive in those days. When our parents came to visit us they rode burros or walked from the villages. Burros are pretty slow. You can walk as fast as they can. At the school they had a couple of horses and a buckboard for the teachers or other Indian Agency people if they had to go to Holbrook to catch a train or meet someone. They would stop overnight at Indian Wells, where there was a trading post. That trading post is still there. The next day they would go on from there to Holbrook.

When I was at Keam's Canyon we had Navajos to deliver mail to Holbrook by horseback. A Navajo mail-rider carried a locked leather mail sack behind his saddle. Those Navajos were hard riders. They aimed to get to Holbrook in one day, and that's more than seventy miles. The next day they would bring mail back from Holbrook. Before the Agency had Navajo mail-riders, Hopi runners used to carry the mail on foot.

The Hopis had a great reputation as runners. You hear about that in the old stories. One story that everyone knows is that men and boys from Oraibi used to run all the way to Moencopi to tend their fields there, and when they were finished they would run all the way back. There's no doubt that they did it, but I think the story tended to become a little bit exaggerated the way some people told it. They said the men and boys ran to Moencopi in the morning, tended their fields and came back the same day. Oraibi and Moencopi are about fifty miles apart, so that seems like a little too much running for one day. Just the same, it is true that Hopis have always been known as great runners.

I knew some of those Hopis who carried mail from Keam's Canyon to Fort Defiance—Lowiwaya (Getting Out of the Rain), Le'etayo (Fox or Swift Fox), and a younger man named Tilchi (Roasted Corn). One of the runners who later became a relation of mine was a man named Yoyiwina (Rain Standing). He was said to have carried the mail to Holbrook in one day, returning the next day to Keam's Canyon. I guess you could say that it was special delivery.

When the smallpox epidemic hit the villages in 1898, I was ten years old and at the old plant school at Keam's Canyon. It was a very bad experience for the Hopis. It seems that a group of Hopis and Tewas went to Zuni to put on a dance over there. My mother and stepfather were in the group. None of them knew that there was smallpox at Zuni. After the group returned, people on First Mesa and Second Mesa began to fall sick. One thing that was done right away was to isolate the schoolchildren to keep them from having contact with the villages. Oraibi wasn't affected much, but on First Mesa and Second Mesa quite a few persons died. In the Second Mesa villages so many people were sick that there were not enough well persons to bury the dead properly, and they disposed of the bodies by putting them in rock crevices. On First Mesa the dead were buried. We children at the Keam's Canyon school were not allowed to come home during the summer, not until the following spring. When we did come home, a lot of people we knew on First Mesa and Second Mesa were missing. Almost every family had lost somebody. I was very lucky because my family weathered it.

After the epidemic was over, things were pretty hard in our village. It was a struggle to get enough to eat. My mother and stepfather and a woman who had lost her husband from smallpox wanted to go down to St. Jo (that's what they called it then—now it's called Joseph City) to do some gleaning. The people around there were Mormons. After they'd cut their wheat they would let Indians come in and glean the fields. So a party of us set out from First Mesa on burrows. It was a long trip. When we got to St. Jo we looked around and found where the wheat fields had been cut. Then we went to the man in charge of the fields and asked if we could go in and glean. I was the main one to do the talking because I knew a little English. He said okay, so we went through the fields picking up every head of grain that we could find and putting it in a cloth. At night, we would beat the cloth to thrash out the wheat heads.

We also did a little trading. Those Mormons were almost as poor as we were, and if we had something they needed they were glad to swap food for it, mostly wheat and molasses. When the Keam's Canyon school closed down for the summer they gave us kids a few clothes, and I received a pair of knee pants and a striped shirt. My mother had brought those things along to St. Jo, and she was able to trade them to the Mormons for some kind of food, I don't remember exactly what. I guess I didn't mind too much, particularly about the shirt because I didn't care about wearing it in the village anyway. We didn't get much wheat from the gleaning, since the Mormons didn't leave much behind in the fields. But it was an interesting experience for me because I learned something about the white people's way of living. I saw the way they made their houses, with big windows and porches. I thought that some day I might be able to live in a house like the ones I saw.

When I was in the eighth grade I began to wonder what I was going to do with myself when I was through at the Keam's Canyon school. At that time the children were detailed to work half a day and attend classes half a day. Once when I was working in the kitchen with Mrs. James she said to me, "Albert, wouldn't you like to go away to school after you are finished here?"

I said, "Where to?"

She said, "Mr. James and I have been transferred back to Oklahoma. There's a big Government school there at Chilocco. The students are from different tribes."

I said, "Well, I'm interested in doing something. There isn't really anything for me on the reservation. We don't own much livestock to take care of. I'd like to go further in school and learn something useful. How should I go about it?"

She said, "Talk to the superintendent. Maybe he can get you enrolled."

The superintendent was an elderly man with a long beard. His name was Lemon. I went to his office and knocked at the door. He asked me to come in. He looked at me over his glasses and said, "What do you need, my boy?"

I said, "I'd like to go away to school."

He jerked his head up. "Are you sure about that? You really want to go?"

I said, "Yes. I heard that Mr. and Mrs. James are going to Oklahoma, and I would like to go to the school at Chilocco that Mrs. James mentioned."

We talked some more. He said, "Well, I'll write to the people in charge over there and see if they can pay for your transportation. I will make out the papers, but somebody has to sign for you. If your father and mother are alive, they have to approve."

I went back to the kitchen and told my friend Claude who was working there. He said, "I believe I'll go and talk to Mr. Lemon too." After Claude talked to Mr. Lemon, we were both pretty sure we were going to Chilocco. Mr. Lemon let us go home to talk to our people about it. As soon as we got to First Mesa I went right to my mother's house to tell her.

My stepfather didn't say anything, but my mother said, "No, I want you to stay here."

I argued with her. I said, "Mother, I don't have anything waiting for me here. No livestock to take care of, nothing. I want to learn a little more than I already know. I want to improve my English."

My mother was not persuaded. She just kept saying she didn't want me to go away. Somehow my father heard about what was going on and he came to the house. He said, "I hear you want to leave."

I said, "Yes, I want to go to school at Chilocco."

He said, "No, you can't go. I'll fight the superintendent on it."

I said, "Father, the superintendent hasn't anything to do with it. I'm the one that wants to go to that school."

All my father would say was "no," but I was getting more and more determined. I know that my father and mother didn't mean me any harm by opposing the idea. I'm sure they believed I'd be better off staying in the village. Most people were not very comfortable about letting their children go away to school. Still, there were a number of young people who were going to Phoenix or Haskell and other places like that for schooling, and some were going to the Indian School at Riverside, California.

I went and found my friend Claude. We sat at the edge of the mesa, looking down. I asked, "How did you make out?"

He said, "My father and mother won't let me go."

I said, "The same thing with me."

But just the same, we had made up our minds. So we left the village and went back to school. We talked all the way back to Keam's Canyon about how we were going to manage it. We agreed that when it came time for Mr. and Mrs. James to leave, we would just get in the wagon with them. But we kept that plan to ourselves, didn't tell anyone.

As it happened, one of my uncles, Irving Pawbinele, was employed at the school as a watchman. He heard about my problem, and he was in favor of my going to Chilocco because he'd been at the Phoenix Indian School and knew what schooling could do to help a person. He encouraged me to keep trying and said he would help if he could. By this time, quite a few boys were interested in going to Chilocco. Among them were James Palengahoya, Willie Hantiwa, Jackson Lomakema, Nelson Polaccaca and my cousin Hugh who, in the Hopi way, I called brother. Mostly all of them got permission from their families to go, but I still didn't have an okay. So I went to Mr. Lemon and told him, "My father and mother don't want me to leave. But there's a policeman here in Keam's, Nelson Oyaping. He is my uncle. In the Hopi-Tewa way, he is responsible for my welfare. He will sign for me." I wasn't sure Mr. Lemon would accept that, but he did. He said, "Good boy!" So I took the papers to Nelson Oyaping and he signed them. My friend Claude was getting ready, too. His parents still opposed his going, but he got someone else to sign for him.

Finally the day came for us to take off. We packed up our clothes, and with us Indians whenever we were going on a long trip we always took food along, so I asked Mrs. James if I could take some dried prunes. She laughed and gave them to me. My Uncle Irving gave me a little canvas satchel, and I put some of the prunes in there, and I also put some in my shirt. My uncle also gave me two dollars. I remembered that there was a light fall of snow that day. The team and wagon drove up to the dining room, and all of us who were going to Chilocco piled in. We were all boys except for one Navajo girl.

We got as far as Indian Wells the first day, and stayed overnight at the trading post. The next day we arrived at Holbrook after sunset. Most of us didn't like the idea of staying in Holbrook overnight. Claude and I didn't want to hang around there because we thought some of our people might be following us to take us home, since our parents had not given their approval. Mr. and Mrs. James thought it would be good to try a night train, so after dinner they took us to the railroad station. Mr. James asked me about the little canvas satchel I was carrying, said, "What's in it?" I told him it was prunes. He said, "Oh, you didn't have to bring that. We'll get our food along the way." It embarrassed me because it showed I didn't know anything about travelling the white man's way. So I just shoved the satchel under a bench and left it there when we got on our train. We rode all night to Albuquerque, and we had to change there for a different train. We had breakfast at the station and got on another train going east.

About ten o'clock or so, a man came through the cars with a tray of fruits. He was saying, "California fruits, California fruits." Well, among us Indians whenever we had visitors we offered them something to eat as hospitality, and it seemed to me it must be the same way here. So I grabbed a little basket of plums and started eating them instead of the prunes I'd left behind in Holbrook. The man stood there quite a while looking at me. My brother Hugh nudged me and asked, "Did you pay?" I said I thought it was just hospitality. He said no, I had to give the man money. So I had to take out one of those dollars my uncle had given me and I paid the man. He gave me change, of course. I thought how different the white man's ways were from ours.

Well, about noon the man came through the cars again, and this time he had something I hadn't ever seen before—bananas. My brother bought two and gave me one. I took it for granted that you were supposed to eat bananas like pears or peaches, and I went ahead. My banana was sweet inside, but the rind was pretty tough. When I was about half through eating it my brother asked me what I'd done with the peeling. I said, "What peeling?" He looked at what I had been doing. He thought it was real funny. He showed me how to take the outside off. That was something else I learned when I went out in the world, how to eat a banana.

Somewhere in Kansas we had to change trains again, and we went into the station restaurant to eat. I sat on a stool but I kept falling off because I felt like I was still riding and swaying. Everybody thought it was a great joke, how I couldn't stay put on the stool, but I think some of the other kids felt that way too. We had to wait quite a while for our next train, so I wandered around the shop in the station looking at all the things they were selling.

There were lots of odds and ends and curios, but two things in particular caught my attention—some dark specs and a big box of pencils. I was always curious about specs, and wondered what you could see through them. If my teacher was wearing specs I would sort of get around in back of him and try to get a glimpse through them, but I was never successful at that. Also, I was always impressed that the teachers carried big bunches of pencils in their pockets, and it seemed to me that the pencils had a lot to do with being educated. I still had a dollar and some change left, so I bought a pair of the dark specs and a handful of pencils. I stuffed the pencils into my inside jacket pocket, but they were sticking out and everybody could see them. They asked me why I had all those pencils. I said I'd got them for school, because all the teachers wore pencils like that. They poked fun at me, but I didn't mind. When I put the specs on, though, I was disappointed. I couldn't see anything but the same things I'd seen before, it was just that they were darker.

When we eventually got to Chilocco, they took us to the school in surreys. It was about a mile from the railroad. They took us right to our dormitory buildings, one for girls, the other for boys. There was a Sioux

Indian, Asa Little Crow, who took us boys in charge. He turned on the light in the sleeping quarters—it was late at night—and I got a big surprise. Most of the boys who were there were real light skinned. I said to Hugh, "Hey, this is a white school." Here and there you could see a boy dark skinned like us, but most of them even had light hair. I found out later that they were Indians, all right, but they were Cherokees and other tribes. It was the first time I ever knew that Indians came in different colors.

The next morning we were awakened by a bugle call, and somebody shouted, "Roll out! Roll out!" The boys made their beds first, then went downstairs to wash up. The adjutant, as they called him—his name was Amos Dugan—marched us around like soldiers. Everywhere we went, we marched, until we were dismissed. This place was run like the army, like a military training school. Everything was done according to military discipline. The other boys kept looking at us new arrivals. Only one Hopi had been at that school before us, and we were a curiosity. It was a big institution, and we First Mesa boys were impressed with everything. Like some of the other kids, I felt pretty homesick for a while. I thought I had done myself wrong by coming to Chilocco. But some of the older boys talked to me and encouraged me, and after that I began to feel okay. Whatever the other fellows were doing, I did it too.

One thing, though, for some reason I never understood, they put me back in the fourth grade. I had completed the eighth grade at Keam's Canyon, and here I was, suddenly, back in the fourth. They were teaching stuff in my class that I had had long ago. The books they were using were the same fourth grade books I'd had back at Keam's. I was bored and discouraged by this, and I just sat and drew pictures on paper most of the time. I guess my teacher, named Mrs. Richards, figured out what the matter was, and at the end of the year she had me skip two grades, and so I was back nearer to where I should have been, but not all the way. Now I started to really study. I didn't fool away my time. I got into athletics too—running, junior football, baseball and things like that.

Chilocco had a trade school program for the boys. We would work at a trade half a day and go to our classes the other half. They were trying to teach us something practical, like carpentry, blacksmithing, making harnesses and shoes, and so on. I was always interested in leather, so I asked to get in the shoe- and harness-making program. In the end, I got a harness maker's certificate. While we were still learning we made shoes for our track team and harnesses for other reservations.

During the summer vacations about three hundred of us went over to Colorado to thin beets. We worked in several different groups. The foreman of our bunch was a Sioux named Alex Whirlwind. I also did other things during our summer vacations. I worked with a pipe-laying gang, and once I worked on the Otoe Reservation baling hay.

Claude and I had signed up for three years, but at the end of that time we were not prepared to go home because we didn't know what we could do for a living on the Reservation, so we stayed on. I finally graduated in 1910. My half sister, Pinini (her married name is Chloris Anah), still has my diploma hanging in her house in Tewa Village. I can't say I was well educated, but I did learn some things that have been useful to me all my life, and I am grateful that the Government made it possible. But looking back from where I am now, I think my life really began when I returned to the Hopi Reservation. That was when I had to meet my problems face to face.

I went back to helping my stepfather with his work. I cultivated fields for him and herded sheep. Sometimes he and I worked together at herding. That was a pretty difficult thing, getting the sheep to grass or something edible and to water. We had to move around a lot, and we were always thinking about the water problem. Sometimes over on the east side of the mesa my stepfather would motion toward a certain sand hill and say, "I've heard from the old people that there's a spring over there somewhere." I'd say, "Where?" and he'd say, "I don't know. Nobody living has ever seen it. There's a ruined village up above. Those people must have had a spring somewhere close by." He mentioned this often and urged me to see if I could find the water.

Quite a few times later on when my half brother Taft and I were herding in that vicinity we would circle around that sand hill looking for some signs of a spring. Once when I was out there alone I noticed that a couple of cottonwood trees were growing at the bottom of the hill, and I said to myself, "Those cottonwoods must have water. Maybe they know what they are doing." So I started digging here and there. Every time I went out with the sheep I took a shovel with me. I shovelled a lot of sand near the cottonwoods without discovering anything. Then one day I noticed some rocks on the side of the hill. They had been uncovered by the wind. I could see three rocks, two side by side, the third on top of them. So I started shovelling again and found that the rocks were the top stones of a wall. I worked a long time digging down to expose the whole wall. It was pretty evident that the old-timers living up above had built it to keep the sand from drifting into their spring, but there wasn't any water visible.

Sometimes my half brother and I would go out there without the sheep just to dig. And one day we got down to where the sand was damp, and a little further down water started to flow in. I have to say it was a wonderful find. It was a gift from those old-timers who had lived in the village up above before it became a ruin. It was also a gift from my stepfather Peki who had remembered something handed down from the past and urged me to dig. Now we had water for our sheep, only a few miles from the village.

Some years later while I was working for the Indian Agency at Keam's Canyon, in my spare time I built a stone house and a storage building near the spring, and that was my sheep camp, my half brother's and mine. We got some help from the Government to protect the spring. They built a cement cover over it to keep the sand out. I planted some peach trees there too. When I eventually left the Hopi Reservation and went to live on the Colorado River Reservation, my half brother worked the sheep camp by himself.

Going back to the time when I returned from Chilocco, I think I was pretty discouraged by what I found on the Reservation. There didn't seem to be any opportunities to earn money. We didn't have much livestock to count on, and I didn't see any way of using that learning I had gotten at school. I got little jobs here and there, and I did the best I could. I was doing work of one kind or another at the Indian Agency in Keam's Canyon when someone told me that my stepfather was very sick. I left right away, but when I got to Tewa Village he was already dead. It was a very sad thing for me. I will never forget that kind man and what he did for me when I was growing up.

One of the jobs I had was in Winslow. A group of us young men went down there to see if we could get work. Some of us were lucky and some weren't. I got a job in the railroad roundhouse. The main thing I had to do was to haul ashes and dump them in boxcars. Sometimes I filled in for one of the men who fired the boilers. There wasn't any place for us to stay in town, and we had to camp out among the rocks. We built shanties and did our cooking over open fires. The nights were pretty cold. It was a rough life, but we stuck to it because we needed the money. Then some people from First Mesa who had come to Winslow after some freight found me at the roundhouse and told me that my mother was pretty sick. I hated to give up that job, but I knew I had to go home and do what I could for my mother.

I started out the next day on foot. I had a woolen blanket, and I bought some bread and potted ham at the store. I found an old whiskey bottle, cleaned it out, filled it with water and put it in my belt. Then I started walking. At Bruckman's Crossing I met some Hopis going to Oraibi. I followed them for a while, then left them and went cross-country, north toward First Mesa. I crossed a river and reached Yellow Bird Spring—the same place where the Water Clan people stopped when they were on their journey from the south. When I got to the top of the plateau I could see First Mesa and the Gap in a faint silhouette, and I headed for that.

The land was all hills and sand dunes, and it was hard walking. Eventually my water was gone and I started looking for some place to get a drink. Eventually I saw some late-flow water in a wash. It was frozen over, but there was a spot where the cattle had walked and broken the ice, and I was able to get some water there. It didn't taste good, but it quenched my thirst. My route took me across the old Flagstaff Road, and about sundown I reached Bull Springs. With darkness coming on I began to look around for a place to stop. I was pretty sure there were some Hopis around there somewhere with their stock, and pretty soon I hit a sheep trail. I could smell the sheep camp all right, but for a while I couldn't locate it. Finally I heard a lamb calling over by a little stone hill. I went in that direction, and sure enough there was a small house built up against the rocks.

I knocked at the door and the man who opened it turned out to be a clan relative of mine. He said, "What you doing way down here?" I told him I was coming from Winslow because my mother was sick. He said, "You'd better stay here for the night. You can't travel in the dark. Tomorrow you can take one of my burros and ride it home." He gave me some stew, and after I had eaten he said, "Lie down over there and get some sleep." He gave me a sheep pelt to cover myself with.

The next morning I got up early, and my relative told me again to take a burro. So I caught a burro and started riding. But that burro walked so slowly that I got off and let him loose, then I was on foot again. I went past what they call Little Giant's Chair near the old Flagstaff road. When I finally reached First Mesa I'd walked about sixty-five miles from Winslow. I immediately went to my mother's house in Tewa Village. She was pretty sick, all right, but she was glad to see me. I urged her to go to the hospital at Keam's Canyon, but she didn't want any of that. My two half brothers and my half sister were pretty young, still going to school. So I stayed on in the village, doing whatever I could to keep things going.

I made several trips to the Indian Agency office in Keam's Canyon trying to get some work. There weren't any jobs available for some time, but eventually they gave me a job taking care of the horses. I'd learned a lot about horses and mules when I was at Chilocco. I also drove a coal wagon and shovelled coal for the powerhouse. I earned fifteen dollars a month for this kind of work, and in those days it seemed like a lot of money. The Agency had some Hopi interpreters, and some time later when those men left, the job was given to me. I did other work as well, but whenever they needed me to interpret they called me. As interpreter I earned twenty dollars a month, which made me feel rich.

One of the things I had to do every so often was to go over to Hubbell's Trading Post in Keam's Canyon and get the mail for the Agency. There was a Tewa girl working at the trading post by the name of Ida Haupove. I used to see her whenever I went for mail. I was interested in her, and she liked me. I guess we used to meet pretty often. But her family didn't seem to care much for me. I was up on First Mesa one time going to Albert Naheu's store when Ida's mother stopped me. She said, "Come here."

So I went over to her house and stood outside the window. She was talking to me from inside. She said, "I heard that you're going around with my daughter."

I said yes, that I'd been seeing her.

She said, "Well, I want you to stop it. I don't want you to see her any more. We don't want you. We don't accept you."

I said, "All right, if that's the way it is. But you'd better tell her, because I have to go to the trading post to get mail. That's how I met her."

From then on I didn't visit with Ida very much, but one day she was purposely sitting outside the trading post waiting for me to come. She said, "What's wrong?"

I said, "Like I told you, your mother doesn't want me to see you any more. That's why I haven't been coming around."

Ida put her head down. She said, "Well, I don't care what my mother says, I want to marry you. If we can't get married the Indian way we can get married white man's style. We can go to the Agency office for a license."

That was what we finally did. We got our license from the Agency and went to the Keam's Canyon Baptist Church to be married. It was a sad business, because all of Ida's folks were down on us, at least all of her mother's clan. Only one of her relatives was at the wedding, her grandmother on her father's side. And only one of my relatives came, my uncle, Irving Pawbinele. But later my own people arranged an Indian wedding for us. That made everything better. It was sort of a hard beginning, and I always felt bad that Ida's folks didn't want me.

Ida and I really cared for each other. We had three children, all girls, Juanita, Sarah and Patricia. I hate to talk about the way the marriage ended. Ida and two of the children were in a car on the cliffside mesa road when the brakes failed and the car went over. The children came out okay, but my wife was killed. Even now, after all this time, I find it hard to talk about.

I was about twenty-four years old at the time, and for quite a while I felt lost and restless, but I kept working at the Keam's Canyon Indian Agency. Some time later I married a Hopi woman. Her name was Taiyomana. (It really isn't proper, in our Tewa way, to be giving the names of my wives, as I have been doing. We don't speak of them by name, but only as "my wife." It's the same with your mother's name. You never mention it, you only say, "my mother." It's an attitude of respect. But I can see that you have to use names when you are putting down your recollections, particularly if you've had more than one wife.) My marriage to Taiyomana came about because I felt sort of lonesome in Keam's Canyon and decided to go home to First Mesa to see the Niman Ceremony, the Home Dance. That is the last time the kachinas make an appearance before they supposedly return to the San Francisco Mountains. There was a fellow at Keam's Canyon named Fini, and he was sick in bed. I mention that because in a way he was responsible for things that followed. Anyway, when I got to First Mesa I went to see a friend named Cheupa. His English name was Edgar.

Just before I arrived at Cheupa's house somebody called to me, "Yava!" It was Cheupa's sister and her aunt, Taiyomana. They said, "Edgar isn't home. He's gone to Piñon to work on the windmills."

I said, "Oh, I thought he was here."

They said, "No, he's gone."

So I said, "Well, no use for me to stay around, then. I guess I'll go back."

They asked where I was going and I said Keam's Canyon. They said, "You just arrived."

I said, "I know it. But I've been restless since I lost my wife. I guess I just came to spend a little time with Cheupa."

They said, "We heard Fini is sick. Can we go back to Keam's Canyon with you to see him?"

I said sure. So I took a bunch of people to Keam's to see Fini, and then I brought them all back again.

Taiyomana had three children, but she wasn't living with her husband. They hadn't been together for some time. Still, she was worried that her husband would hear that she'd gone to Keam's Canyon with me. That's one reason I brought the whole party right back after seeing Fini. Then I parked my car down below and went up to see the Niman Dance. I was standing there watching when Taiyomana's husband (or her former husband, depending on how you figure it) came up to me. His name was Preston Masa, and he was a distant nephew of my father's.

He said, "Did you come?" (That's a Hopi way of greeting, but it sounds peculiar in translation.)

I said, "Yes."

He said, "Let's go over to my house."

I wanted to watch the dance, but I went with him, and in the Indian way he fed me. When I was finished eating he said, "Let's go over to see my children's mother."

I wanted to see the dancing, but I said "Okay" and went with him. We went to where his wife and her three kids were living. Taiyomana was there but the kids were out watching the kachinas. I sat down and Preston sat down. Then he started, "Say, I understand you two are going around together."

She was surprised. "Yava and I?"

"Yes. He took you to Keam's Canyon."

She said, "Yes, he did, along with my sister Rita and a car full of people. We went there to see Fini. He's sick."

Preston said, "Evidently you two are going to get married."

I said, "No, nothing like that."

Well, then the old man went out and got the police, two Navajos and my Uncle Irving. He brought them into the house. He told them I was going to live with his wife. He said, "I want to know what you are going to do about it."

My uncle just sat there with his head down. The two Navajos looked at Preston but couldn't say anything. Preston kept talking, and finally one of the Navajo policemen said, "What do you want us to do? Marry them? We don't have anything to do with this kind of business. Ask the lady, she's the one to say, not us."

Taiyomana didn't say anything for a while. She was just sitting there laughing because Preston was so ridiculous, and also, I suppose, because she was ashamed to be put in such a position. Then she said to Preston, "What's wrong with you? I hardly know Yava. You know him better than I do. You used to come with him when he visited his aunt. I don't know that man. So why are you doing this?"

One of the Navajos said, "It's up to you people. It's up to the lady. If she wants him, that's up to her."

After that the three policemen walked out. But Preston wouldn't give up. He said to me, "All right, I'll give my wife to you."

I said, "No, I don't even know her."

That was the end of it for the moment.

One day I was visiting my daughter Sarah at my father's house, and when I came out I saw Cyrus Tangovia standing there at the edge of the mesa. Cyrus was Taiyomana's brother. He worked in Winslow at the ice plant, but he'd come to the village to see his wife. He called me. He was laughing. He said, "Say, did old Masa get to talk to you?"

I said, "Yeah, he sure did. During the Niman. I wanted to see the dancing, but first Taiyomana got me to take a bunch of people to Keam's Canyon and back, and then Preston took me to see your sister. He offered to give her to me. I guess he was jealous."

Cyrus said, "That old man is no account. He's no good. He never took care of my sister or her kids. He never lived with her. I have to support her." He was thinking, and then he said, "How about it? Would you be willing to marry her?"

I said, "Cyrus, that's ridiculous. I don't even know her."

But there was something going on in his head, and he took me over to

Taiyomana's house and started talking. He said, "Why don't you two get married just to spite the old man? That'll give him something to think about."

Well, we kept talking about it and I kept saying no, but Cyrus had it on his mind and wouldn't let go. And after a while Taiyomana and I began to know each other. Eventually we agreed to get married. That's the way it happened.

She had those three children, so I acquired a ready-made family. It was a peculiar situation, with Preston lurking in the background, and I wanted everything to be clear and legal. I said we'd have to have everything done properly, so we went to Keam's Canyon and were married by a missionary over there. The house Taiyomana was living in in Walpi had belonged to my father's mother before she moved to the Middle Village, Sichomovi. After we were married, my wife had an addition built onto it. It was her house, and she had the responsibility for doing this. I provided her with a lot of buckskin things that she used to pay for the construction.

We were together about eight years, but I never had any children from her. There were those three children that she and Preston had together, and later, when her sister died, she took in her sister's children. After a while her own three children decided that they wanted to go and live with their father. They were talking about it a lot, and trying to get Taiyomana to go back too. It looked to me as if that was what she wanted to do. The way it was going, I had to leave. I told her brother Cyrus, "In the Hopi way, Preston is her true husband, even in the land of the hereafter." [2] I said to Taiyomana, "Okay, then, go back to your old man." So I left her. We'd been legally married in the white man's way, so we had to go to the Tribal Court to make our divorce final.

My third wife was Virginia Scott, a Navajo woman from Leupp. She and her husband used to herd sheep for me. Her husband left her, Navajo style, decided he didn't want to be with her any more. I said to him, "Are you leaving Virginia?" He said, "Yes, if you want to live with her, okay." She and I had a legal marriage. I didn't want to live with someone I couldn't call my wife. We had five children together—Albert, Estelle, Eddie, Aaron and Leonarda. My oldest son, Albert, was killed by a train near Kingman. The other four are all living and doing well. Eddie was in the army and served in Korea, Vietnam and Germany. Leonarda is married to a doctor in Gallup. Like her Navajo husband left her, Virginia left me and the children after we moved down to the Colorado River Reservation, so I had to raise the children by myself.

I think I've said more than enough about my personal life. I keep wondering who in the world could be interested in these details, but

Juanita, my son-in-law Dewey Healing and Estelle have kept after me to
put all this down on paper so there will be some kind of a record apart from
hearsay. I have to admit that scattered recollections have their limitations.
And I regret that my stepfather Peki or my father Sitaiema or some of our
other old-timers weren't able to put their experiences and recollections
down in writing. If they had, we'd know a lot more about the past than we
do.

Anyway, I believe it's time to say something about how we Tewas came
to be living here on First Mesa along with the Hopis.

A little over two hundred and seventy-five years ago, the Hopis living on
this mesa were suffering a great deal from attacks by raiding tribes—the
Utes, Paiutes, Comanches and Apaches. In those days the Navajos hadn't
yet become a problem, though I think they were already out there to the
north of Hopi country somewhere. The Hopis distinguished between these
tribes but regarded them as sort of related. The Comanches, Paiutes and
Utes all spoke Shoshonean. The Navajos and Apaches spoke dialects of
Athabascan. The Hopis' word for Utes was Utam. They called the Apaches
Uche'em, and the Navajos were called Tasavem or Tsavem. Those people
moved around a lot, and they frequently raided other groups if they needed
supplies. They raided the Hopi fields for corn, and sometimes they fought
their way into the villages and took food, women and children. Many Hopi
men were killed defending the villages. Walpi was really suffering from
these attacks, and sometimes other Hopi villages attacked them too. The
people of the Hopi villages didn't think of themselves as belonging to the
same tribe. They considered themselves to be Walpis, Mishongnovis,
Shongopovis, Oraibis and so on. The village was their nationality, you might
say. There are a number of stories on First Mesa of Oraibi attacks against
Walpi.[3] But it was the outsiders—the Utes, Apaches and Comanches,
mostly—who were giving the Walpis serious trouble.

How many people were living in the village at the time, I can't really say,
but according to what we Tewas heard, the population was down to seven
families, and they were feeling pretty desperate. The Bear Clan and the
Snake Clan were the leaders. Their chiefs decided that they would have to
get help from somewhere if they were going to keep the village alive. But
where could that help come from? The Tewas over in the Rio Grande
Valley had a reputation as fighters, and so they sent a delegation over there
to see if they could get some Tewas to come and settle somewhere near
Walpi. The distance from Walpi to the Rio Grande Tewa villages must be

about three hundred miles, so you can guess how long it took the delegation to get there on foot, which was the only way there was to travel in those times. When they reached the area where the Tewas were living, they went from one settlement to another trying to find a group that would be willing to come to Hopi country. It seems that they heard more and more about a certain Tewa village called Tsewageh or Chekwadeh. It had that name because in the cliffs behind the village there was a long horizontal white stripe of limestone or some similar kind of rock. The name means broad white line or wide white gap. The site was two or three miles east of where Española, New Mexico, is today, on a hill south of what is now called Santa Cruz Creek. The people had good running water at Tsewageh and they were flourishing.[4]

When the delegation from the Walpi Bear and Snake clans arrived at Tsewageh, they met with the chief and other important leaders. They told about Walpi's difficulties. They said, "Our brothers, we need help. We want you to come and make your home in our country. Living close together, we will all be secure." The Tsewageh leaders did not refuse, but they said they would have to have time to reflect on the matter. So the Hopis returned to Walpi and reported on their conversations with the Tsewageh Tewas. Walpi waited a long time for a message from Tsewageh, but they didn't hear anything.

After a while they sent their delegation again. When the Bear and Snake clan representatives arrived at Tsewageh they said that things were getting worse at Walpi and requested an answer. The Tsewageh chief said that he and his advisers had not yet finished considering things. He said for them to go home and he would let them know the outcome. So the delegation returned home. Again the Walpi leaders waited for a message, but nothing happened. After a while they sent the delegation the third time. It went, it returned, but still no word came.

At last the Walpi leaders said, "We'll try once more. If the Tsewagehs don't come, that's the end of it." So the delegation went to Tsewageh for the fourth time. They brought a bundle of prayer feathers, pahos, for the Tsewageh leaders. There were three feather sticks—we call them uudopehs in Tewa—and they represented three things. One was a male paho and one was a female paho. The feathers are the same, but the sticks are painted differently. The male and female pahos together meant people, you might say population. The third paho was plain, not painted, and it represented land. These pahos were a pledge to the Tewas. They meant that if the Tewas would come to help Walpi they would be given land and they'd be allowed to take Walpi's sons and daughters as husbands and wives. Land and people, that was the pledge. This time the Tsewagehs accepted. They received the pahos as a sacred promise. They said, "Go home, tell your people we are coming." The delegation returned to Walpi, and the Snake and Bear clan chiefs waited for the Tewas to appear.

The compact that the Hopis and Tewas made at Tsewageh is still memorialized in Tewa village. When we carry out certain rituals one of our masked figures carries a tall stick with cotton strings and feathers attached, representing land and people. They recall the sacred promise made by the Hopis to the Tewas.

Well, the Tsewagehs prepared for their journey. The chief called them all together and announced to them what had been promised to the Walpis. He said, "Whoever wants to cross the river and make a new settlement with the Walpis, get yourselves ready. We will help them survive. Whoever wants to stay behind, let him stay." But all the people wanted to go. The chief didn't want his village to disappear, so when half the people said they were ready to go, he said that the other half would have to stay behind. The group that left was led by a man named Agaiotsay, meaning Yellow Star.[5] On that long march they made four stops that we know about. The first was at a place near what is now called Canoncito, a little bit north of Laguna Pueblo. They rested a while there and then went on. Their next stopover was at Awpimpaw, Duck Spring, near present-day Grants. They rested there for a while and then went on. Next stop was at Bopaw, Reed Spring, over near Ganado. They planted some sacred things there, and after resting some time they continued their way. Their fourth stop was at Kwalalata (Pawsaiyeh in Tewa), Place of Bubbling Water, in Keam's Canyon, and they planted sacred things there also. How long the Tewas remained at these places I can't say, but it seems that they stayed long enough to build temporary houses. From Kwalalata they continued on toward Walpi, but when they arrived there they weren't welcomed immediately. The Walpis let them settle a little below the mesa on that low ridge on the east side, but wouldn't let them come any closer. The Tewas must have remained there for a while, because they had to build temporary houses again. You can still see broken pottery and the ruined walls of those houses on the ridge.[6]

I can't say why the Walpis didn't allow the Tewas to come any closer at that time. Maybe it was because there were so many Tewas in the group that they made the Walpis uneasy. It was quite a large party. According to what we were told, there may have been as many as two hundred men, women and children in the group. Maybe the Walpis began to wonder whether they should have invited the Tewas to come. In any case, they weren't as hospitable as they should have been.

Then the Walpis did something that's hard to explain. They contacted the Utes and challenged them to make an attack on Walpi. They said,

"We've got some real fighters here now. Why don't you come and try to drive them off?" If this story is true, then it must be that the Hopis had a change of heart and really wanted to get the Tewas out before they had a chance to settle, or maybe they just wanted to test them. Anyway, the Utes accepted the challenge. And four days later a messenger from Walpi came down to the Tewa camp and said that the Utes were coming. Now, how in the world did the Walpi people know that the Utes were coming? It's something our people often thought about.

The Tewas said, "Well, even if we're not ready we'll have to show ourselves and meet the enemy." They began to fix up their bows and arrows and other weapons. That night they sent scouts out to see if the enemy war party was really on the way. The third night out, the scouts saw many campfires at Black Mountain, and they reported this news back to their war captain. "There's somebody coming," they said. "We think they are Utes travelling at night on horseback." The Tewas didn't have any horses. They had to fight on foot.

The next day the scouts reported again. They said, "We spotted many men riding this way. We're sure they are Utes because they're wearing mirrors that reflect the light." Agaiotsay was the leader in everything. He was village chief, spokesman and war chief. He said, "Well, now those Utes are going to find out what kind of fighters we are. We'll use our tried and tested tactics. We'll split our force into two parts. One will hit them in front and the other behind." They put on their battle clothes and their war paint. Some of the women were fighters too, but all of the women were told to stay where they were camping, and some of the older men were also told to stay to help defend the place if necessary.

At this point, a group of Hopi officials came down from Walpi and said, "What we told you is true. You can see that they are coming." The Tewas went up to the top where the gap is. At that time there were sand dunes there, north of the gap, but since then they've all blown away. From that spot they could see the Utes coming dressed in bright colors with their little mirrors reflecting the sunlight. The Utes were down in Wepo Wash, where they thought they wouldn't be seen. They dismounted and led their horses into a smaller wash, not knowing that the Tewas were watching. There they planned their attack.

The Tewas prepared to go down from the gap. Their leader, Agaiotsay, said, "Now our party will break into two parts. My group will meet the Utes in front, and while we are engaging them the other party will go around behind. Get the Ute leaders first. After that, watch to see who takes command, then get him. Aim for the heart. If you can't get the man, get his horse." The Hopi leaders said, "We'll wait for you here till you return."

The Tewas went down from the high ground, one group going to the left, the other to the right. The party that was going to engage the Utes from the front hid among some large rocks. The other party went around on the west side through a dry wash. The first group moved forward, trying to stay concealed among the rocks, and they came to a certain place where they waited. The other group kept moving, crawling through the wash to get behind the Utes. About this time, the Utes remounted their horses and rode out into the open. Now they were wearing their war bonnets. They rode fast, not knowing that the Tewas were waiting for them. They gave their war cry.

Out in front of the other Tewas there were two brothers. One of them shot an arrow at the Ute war captain and killed him. The other brother killed the man who took his place. Arrows were flying from both sides. The Utes made a rush, using their lances. Agaiotsay said, "If you can't hit a man or a horse with an arrow, use your war club." The Tewas ran among the Utes and knocked some of them off their horses. The Utes backed off, then made another rush. By that time the other Tewa party was behind them. The Utes were in the middle, pinned on both sides, and they began to draw away toward safer ground. But the Tewas kept pressing them on two sides. The Utes reached the place where they'd left their bags of pounded meat. There was nothing else to protect them, so they got down behind their meat bags and shot arrows from there. Before the battle, that spot didn't have a name, but afterwards it came to be known as Tukyu'u, Meat Point.

For a while the Utes were able to hold their ground there. But the Tewas again came at them from two directions, and the Utes had to fall back. From there on they didn't have any place to dig in. Now and then they'd stop and try to make a stand in the open, then they'd fall back again. The Tewas tried to encircle them, but the Utes kept moving till they came to some rocks, and they fought from behind the rocks and tried to hold their position. That place didn't have any name then, but now it's called Kokwadeh, Stone Wall.

By this time dead and wounded men and horses were lying scattered all through the valley. Only three able-bodied Utes were left behind the rocks. One of them threw his bow out and waved something white. The Tewa leader said, "Hold your arrows. There are only three of them left. Let us see what they want." He put his weapons down and approached the Utes.

He said in sign language, "What is it? What do you have to tell me?"

The Ute who had given the signal said, "What people are you? We see you are not Hopis."

He said, "We are Tewatowa."

The Ute answered, "My cousin, we didn't know it was you."

The Tewa leader said, "Yes, it is us. We came from Tsewageh."

The Ute said, "I'm sorry, my brothers, that we fought against you."

"Yes," the Tewa leader said, "now you are sorry. But why do you make war on these peaceful people at Walpi? They don't threaten you."

The Ute answered, "We just came to get some corn and things like that."

The Tewa leader said, "You made a mistake. We Tewas are going to stay here now. Remember it, then you won't be coming back any more."

The Ute said, "No, my brother, we'll never come back to fight. Take my bow as a token. It's not made of wood but of elkhorn. Elkhorn will never rot. Only when this bow rots will we ever meet you again in battle. So you see we will have peace forever."

The Tewa leader said, "That is good. You three men who have survived, we will not kill you. Return to your people and tell them that if they ever return we'll be waiting to meet them."

The Utes went away. The Tewas started back to their camp, gathering the bows and other weapons that were scattered across the battlefield. They also took some scalps.[7] They selected the bodies of four of the bravest Ute warriors, split their breasts open and took out their hearts. When they reached the spot where they first met the Utes, the Tewa war captain said, "Now we'll bury these courageous hearts here in the earth. Let us see what grows out of their grave. Whatever it is, we'll protect it and keep it growing." They dug a hole an arm length deep, buried the hearts, and made a ring of stones around the place. Today we call that spot the Place of Hearts—Pingto'i in Tewa, Eunaktana in Hopi. A juniper tree is growing there now inside the ring of stones.[8]

When the Tewa warriors returned to the mesa gap, the Hopi dignitaries were still waiting. The chief of the Bear Clan was there, also the chief of the Snake Clan. The Tewas put some of their battlefield booty in the hands of the Hopis, along with some scalps. They said, "Take these trophies. Now we have shown you that we are worth something. We Tewas have lost some of our men in this fight, but the Great Spirit was with us and the rest of us survived."

The Hopi leaders handed the scalps back, saying, "No, the scalps are yours. Keep them to recall what you accomplished in this battle." Now, even today when we have our midwinter ceremonies in Tewa village, those scalps are brought out and displayed to commemorate the victory over the Utes.

So the Tewas and the Hopi leaders stood there at the gap of the mesa, and when they were through discussing the battle, the Hopi chief said, "Well, now, my children, you may leave your camp and come to the top of the mesa. Make your village over there on the north side of the gap."

The Tewa leader said, "My friend, your village is at the point south of the gap. If we build where you say, the gap will separate us. How can I protect you if I am over here and you are over there? How would I even know if the enemy attacked you? No, I want to be a watchdog sitting in front of your door."

The Hopi chief said, "Well, then, come and make your village just on the south side of the gap."

So they went together to look at the spot the Hopi chief had in mind. The Tewa chief said, "My friend, how do you expect us to live on this little piece of land? Do you think we're not going to increase? We Tewas are going to grow. We need more room."

Then they all walked south from there to the place where there is now a shrine with a large piece of petrified wood sitting at the boundary between Tewa Village and Sichomovi.[9] At that time, however, Sichomovi did not yet exist, and there was a wide open space there. The Hopi chief said, "Well, then, let your village extend up to here. Now you have ample room."

Agaiotsay said, "Yes, all right, now we have room to build our village. But we also spoke of land. Where are we going to have our fields?"

The Hopi chief said, "Over there in the east, where the mesa juts out, that is Eagle Point. And to this side, to the west, you see Big Water Point. These points mark the extent of your land." The land designated for the Tewas included what is now called Keam's Canyon, but today there are no Tewas cultivating over there.

After they were finished speaking about the land, the Hopi chief said, "When we sent for you we promised that you could take some of our women for wives. That was our promise, and we will be true to it."

But Agaiotsay said, "Wait, let us not go too fast. It is too soon to speak of that. We are not ready for it. First we have to see how well our villages live together. Suppose we took Hopi wives now, and then after a while you people become angry with us for some reason and we have to break apart. It would be too hard for us to have to go away from here and leave our children and grandchildren behind.[10] No, we couldn't go through all that. It would break our hearts. Later on, when we're sure that things are going well, then we can talk about taking Hopi wives. Not now. We'll let the matter rest for a while."

After that the Tewa leader said, "Another thing, my brother, we want you to know that we are going to remain Tewas forever. No matter what you do, we will follow our own ways." He took a small ear of corn and handed it to the Hopi chief. He said, "Chew it up but do not swallow it." The Hopi chief chewed the corn. The Tewa chief said, "Now give me what you have chewed." The Hopi chief spat the chewed corn into his hand. The

Tewa chief took the chewed corn, put it in his mouth and swallowed it.

The Hopi chief asked, "What is the meaning of this?"

The Tewa chief answered, "It means that we will take from your mouth the language you speak. We will speak Hopi."

The Hopi chief said, "It is good that you will speak Hopi. Now you chew up some corn and give it to me." The Tewa chief chewed some corn, and the Hopi chief put out his hand to receive it. But the Tewa chief did not give it to him. He had his people dig a deep hole in the ground, and he spat his corn into the hole. They filled the hole with earth and covered it with heavy rocks.

The Hopi chief asked, "What is the meaning of this?"

And the Tewa answered, "It means that you will never have our language in your mouths. We will speak Hopi and Tewa, but your people will never speak the Tewa language. If you were to speak Tewa you would be able to infiltrate into our rituals and ceremonies. You would interfere with our way of doing things."

They placed a piece of petrified wood there to mark the boundary of Tewa Village. Today Sichomovi, which we sometimes call Middle Village, is on the Hopi side of the boundary, but in those days it didn't yet exist.

The Tewas built Tewa Village right where it stands today. It has never moved. People built their houses according to the clans they belonged to. The Bear Clan and its affiliated clans built their houses on the four sides of the central court, with a shrine in the middle. Those were the leading families. The other clans built around the Bear Clan houses according to how they ranked. The Sun Clan and the Cloud Clan built at the end. The Corn Clan built on the east side to guard the entrance there. Then came the Tobacco Clan, the Green Corn Clan, the Parrot Clan, the Cottonwood Clan and the Shell Clan. There also were others. My clan—Wood, or Spruce—was affiliated with the Bear Clan, so we were with them in the center. A number of these clans have become extinct in Tewa Village, but my clan and the Bear Clan have increased. When the Tewas took over the land that Walpi assigned to them, they gave a portion to each of their clans.

That is the story of how we Tewas came to be here on First Mesa. I guess the outcome hung on that battle with the Utes. If the Utes had won, the Tewas might never have settled in this place. Someone inscribed the record of the fight with the Utes on the cliff wall down below. When you come up the road from the main highway you can see the markings. There's a Tewa shield and a long row of marks indicating the number of Utes that were killed. Underneath that pictograph is another one referring to a battle the Tewas and Hopis had later on against the Apaches. In the fight against the Utes, however, no Hopis took part, only Tewas.

It was Agaiotsay and his group from Tsewageh who established Tewa

Village.[11] Other Tewas came from time to time, but they are kind of vague in our minds. One Tewa Side Corn Clan group came later and made a settlement down in Wepo Valley, due west of the spring. When that settlement broke up, some of the people came up to First Mesa and lived in Tewa Village. According to what we were told, another group of Tewas settled for a while on the south side of the mesa near what is now called Five Houses. We also know that a large party of Tewas left their Rio Grande home, went south to Zuni for a while, then came to Hopi country following the Zuni Trail. One bunch of Tewas is said to have arrived here in a heavy mist, and because of the mist people didn't know the direction this group came from.

Now, our traditions say that the Tsewageh people came here in response to the invitation of the Walpis,[12] but those other groups that followed from time to time came because they wanted to get away from the Spanish who were giving them a hard time in New Mexico. The Rio Grande Tewas had played an important part in the insurrections against the Spanish. The leader of the main revolt was a Tewa named Popay. So when the Spanish returned after having been driven out in 1680, the Tewas and some of the other Pueblos decided to come over here to Hopi country to get away from them.

The Tewa party that came on the Zuni Trail is supposed to have brought important ritual paraphernalia and masks with them. We still have those masks that these Tewas are supposed to have brought. In former times, Tewa Village had a ceremony every ten years and brought out the masks, four of them, to commemorate how we emerged into this world at Sibopay and began our long journey that eventually led us to Hopi country. One mask represents the Stick, or Spruce, Clan. It leads the other three masks, because the Spruce Clan, affiliated with the Bear, lead the other clans. It's called Simpeng'i, Black Man. The mask has diamond-shaped eyes, a wide mouth with zigzag teeth, long hair with big eagle feathers on top, and two horns coming out from the sides. The man wearing the mask is dressed in a bearskin robe, and underneath the robe he's wearing a kilt and scarfs and shell beads. This masked personage leads the other masks around the village four times. Then he's taken to a place where he has to sit on his haunches all day without any water until the ceremony is finished.

Those masks, as I said, were supposed to have been brought by the Tewas. But I believe they were made right here on First Mesa, because in the old days before they came here the Tewas didn't use masks. It was only after living with the Hopis that they began to use masks and prayer feathers. If you examine those old Tewa masks carefully you can see that they were copied from certain Hopi masks. For example, the one I described, representing the Spruce, or Stick, Clan, was copied very closely from an old Hopi Bear Clan mask. The Bear and Stick clans being affiliated, whoever made the Simpeng'i mask considered it to be appropriate. I believe all these old Tewa masks were made on First Mesa to help the Tewas remember their old traditions and not get swallowed up by the Hopis. Before the Tewas came here, the main ritual thing they had was cornmeal, which represented our living bodies and all life.

Anyway, you can see that we Tewas aren't exactly newcomers in Hopi country. We arrived shortly after the Walpis had moved to the top of the mesa from their old village, Kenchaptevela, which was on the shelf down below. That big Laguna Village on Antelope Mesa, Awatovi, had died just before we got here. It was destroyed in 1700, and we arrived, according to our tradition, about 1702.[13] You might say that the ashes of Awatovi were hardly cold. I'll tell you about that event later. I've already mentioned that our Middle Village, Sichomovi, didn't yet exist, and the village of Moencopi hadn't yet been established. The Payupkis still had a village over on Second Mesa during the 1700s, and we were here about forty years before they picked up and went back to the Rio Grande and settled, we think, at Sandia Pueblo. Tsikuvi, about a mile north of Payupki, also was still a living village. We were here two hundred years before the breakup of Oraibi. We were here when the first Anglos arrived from the East.

So you have to agree that we aren't newcomers. Everything before 1700 sort of tapers off into distant legends. Not that legends aren't part of the history of the Hopis and Tewas. Our historic legends recall a lot of real events of the past. Every one of the Hopi villages has its own traditions. Every clan has its own traditions. The clan traditions don't always agree, and sometimes they contradict one another. Even in a single clan there can be arguments about such things. For example, what the Reed Clan says about its past in one village can be contradicted by the Reed Clan in another village, because different parts of clans had different experiences in their travels.

We Tewas have had our ups and downs with our Hopi brothers, and every now and then there has been contention between us. Some of it still goes on today. But that isn't much different from the experience various Hopi clans have had with one another. Some clans have found it almost impossible to live together without friction, and some have had to move away. Yet we Tewas are still here. In the past hundred years Hopis and Tewas have intermarried quite a bit. Many Hopi men have Tewa children, and many Tewa men have Hopi children. We participate in each other's festivals and kachina dances. We share the same weather and rain. We are clan relatives. We respect each other's rituals. And we have shared the same experience in our relations with the whites—the Blue Eyes, as the Tewas called them.

As to where all these Hopi clans came from, every clan is the custodian of its own story. But adding it all up you can say that they came from just about every direction. Some of those who came from the north, from the neighborhood of Tokonave (which the white people renamed Navajo Mountain)—they include the Snake and Horn clans—originally were from farther west, probably in California. Other clans came from a place far to the south called Palatkwa. No one knows for sure where Palatkwa was. A number of clans travelled up and down the Colorado River and the Little Colorado for a good many years, maybe centuries, before they arrived here. Some, like the Coyote Clan (not the same as the Water Coyote Clan) came from Eastern Pueblo country.

Looking at all these facts, it's clear that the modern Hopis are descendants of numerous different groups, including Plains Indians, that merged after gravitating to this place. Those people who say we are all descendants of those Basketmakers who lived up in the San Juan Valley make it sound too simple. We Hopis (you have to remember that I am a full-fledged Hopi as well as being a Tewa) can't be explained so easily. Those migrating groups that came here spoke several different languages. For example, the Water Coyote group that came here from the north spoke Paiute or Chemehuevi or some other Shoshonean dialect. We had clans, even whole villages, coming here from the Eastern Pueblos, where various languages are spoken. We had Pimas coming in from the south. And there's an Apache strain too. Those clans that came here from Palatkwa, such as the Water Clan, the Sand Clan and the Tobacco Clan, brought Pimas and Apaches with them. My father's group, the Water Clan, claims to be Uche—that is, Apache—in origin. It could be that the first people to settle these mesas were Shoshonean-speakers from the San Juan Valley, but other people joined them and it was this mixture that came to make up what we now call Hopitu, the Hopi People.

Anthropologists believe that the earliest Hopi villages were established around the twelfth or thirteenth century when a big drought came to the San Juan Valley and drove the people south. Shongopovi is supposed to have been our first village—the old Shongopovi, that is, built down below the mesa at the place called Masipa. It was settled by the Bear Clan. But from the evidence, you'd have to say that those Bear Clan people weren't actually the first to settle in this region. For one thing, according to their own tradition, the first morning after they arrived they saw smoke rising from Antelope Mesa. They investigated and found that a village was already established up there. That village was Awatovi.

All through this country around here are hundreds and hundreds of old ruins. Anthropologists haven't paid much attention to them, only to the larger, more spectacular ruins. Some of those people living in the smaller villages of only a few houses may have been here long before the Bear Clan, the Snake Clan and other clans built the main Hopi settlements. In fact, some other clans claim to have arrived here before the Bear Clan. There could have been settlements scattered all through this mesa country long before Betatakin and Mesa Verde were abandoned.

One thing we can be sure of is that people weren't just moving down from the north. They were travelling in all directions. It isn't clear to us as to what they were looking for. Maybe it was water and good fields. Maybe they were told in their old prophecies to behave in such and such a way, or to find such and such a place. According to the main Hopi creation story— there are a number of different creation stories, but this is the one most Hopis accept—the beginning of our earthly experience was when the people emerged from the underworld. Where they emerged from, that was already their Third World, and up here it was the Fourth World. At that time they were advised to look for a place called Sichdukwi, Flower Mound. The clans separated and went in different directions, but eventually they converged here in the belief that Sichdukwi was at First Mesa. At least, that is the traditions that some clans have. The ones that gravitated to the other mesas had another thing that they were looking for. Some clans say they went in that direction looking for Masauwu, the Death Spirit who owned all the land around here.

But there's another reason for all the migrations and the abandonment of one village and another. Time after time, contention within a village, or between villages, or between clans caused the people to leave, and in the journeys that followed, they were looking for a place of harmony where they could follow good teachings and a good way of life. That didn't mean having bounteous crops, but living together as people who were civilized and worthy of being in the Fourth World. Time after time, in our traditional stories, the people had to leave a certain place because they'd fallen into evil ways. Sometimes their villages were destroyed because of the corruption that had come into their lives. Sometimes one village had to pack up and leave because of dissension with another village. Palatkwa, that southern village of the Water Clan, was destroyed and the people had to leave because they'd forgotten about spiritual values.

The people of Sikyatki had to go away because of evil things that had occurred, and because of enmity with Keuchaptevela, the old Walpi. The chief of Awatovi asked that his village be destroyed by the other villages because his people had lost respect for their spiritual traditions and had become undisciplined and ungovernable. The Snake Clan had to leave Tokonave because of friction with other people in the village. The chief of Pivanhonkapi had his village destroyed because, as in the case of Awatovi, the people had turned away from decent living. The Payupkis abandoned their village because of quarrels with nearby Tsikuvi. Oraibi was broken in two by dissension, so the Fire Clan and the Water Coyotes had to go away and build new villages.

Sometimes, traditions say, sorcerers were responsible for these events. That is a way of saying that evil forces came into play. Always, time after time, there is that theme of flight from evil and the search for virtue and balance. The theme goes back to the first recollection of all, the emergence of the people from the underworld. That's where it begins. The story is usually told to boys after they have been initiated into the Kachina Society. It's quite long, with elaborate details, but I will make it brief, telling enough, though, to explain about that long flight from sorcerers, dissension and evil.

Way back in the distant past, the ancestors of humans were living down below in a world under the earth. They weren't humans yet, merely creatures of some kind. They lived in darkness, behaving like bugs. Now, there was a Great Spirit watching over everything, and some people say he was Tawa, the sun. He saw how things were down under the earth. He didn't care for the way the creatures were living. He sent his messenger, you might say his representative, Gogyeng Sowuhti—that is, Spider Old Woman—to talk to them. She said, "You creatures, the Sun Spirit who is above doesn't want you living like this. He is going to transform you into something better, and I will lead you to another world."

So Tawa made them into a better form of creatures, and Gogyeng Sowuhti led them to another world above the place where they were living. This was the Second World, still below the ground. The creatures lived here for some time, but they were still animals in form, not humans. There were some with tails, some without. The ones that were eventually to become human did not have tails.

But life in the Second World wasn't good. The creatures didn't behave well. They didn't get along. They ate one another. There was chaos and dissension. So the Great Spirit sent Gogyeng Sowuhti down again after he transformed those beings without tails into a humanlike form. But they weren't yet true humans, because they were undisciplined—wild and uncivilized. Gogyeng Sowuhti led them to another world up above, the Third World. Things were better at first, but after a while there was more chaos and dissension. Evil individuals caused all kinds of difficulties. There were sorcerers who made people fall sick or quarrel with one another. The evil ones made life hard for everyone.

When at last things became too difficult to bear, the ones who wanted to live orderly and good lives said, "This must come to an end. When the Great Spirit brought us up here he wanted us to be better than we were before. How can we get away and leave the evil ones behind?"

Gogyeng Sowuhti told them, "Above us is a Fourth World. Up there life will be better for you. But to get there we have to go through the sky of the Third World. And there are other problems. The Fourth World is owned by Masauwu, the Spirit of Death. You will have to have his permission to go there."

The way this story is told by our old ones, there were four layers of worlds. You might say that this idea describes a way of existing, the transformations that had to be gone through for the people to become truly human. In the Fourth World they were supposed to acquire good values and become civilized.

The people who wanted to escape from the Third World decided to send a scout up to see what it was like up there and make contact with Masauwu. They chose a swift bird, the swallow.[14] The swallow was swift, all right, but he tired before he reached the sky and had to come back. After that they sent a dove, then a hawk. The hawk found a small opening and went through, but he came back without seeing Masauwu. Finally they sent a catbird. He was the one that found Masauwu.

Masauwu asked him, "Why are you here?"

The catbird said, "The world down below is infested with evil. The people want to come up here to live. They want to build their houses here, and plant their corn."

Masauwu said, "Well, you see how it is in this world. There isn't any light, just greyness. I have to use fire to warm my crops and make them grow. However, I have relatives down in the Third World. I gave them the secret of fire. Let them lead the people up here, and I will give them land and a place to settle. Let them come."

After the catbird returned to the Third World and reported that Masauwu would receive them, the people asked, "Now, how will we ever get up there?" So Spider Old Woman called on the chipmunk to plant a sunflower seed. It began to grow. It went up and almost reached the sky, but the weight of the blossom made the stem bend over. Spider Old Woman then asked the chipmunk to plant a spruce tree, but when the spruce finished growing it wasn't tall enough. The chipmunk planted a pine, but the pine also was too short. The fourth thing the chipmunk planted was a bamboo. It grew up and up. It pierced the sky. Spider Old Woman said, "My children, now we have a road to the upper world. When we reach there your lives will be different. Up there you will be able to distinguish evil from good. Anything that is bad must be left behind down here. All evil medicine must be thrown away before you go up. Sorcerers cannot come with us, or they will contaminate the Fourth World. So be careful. If you see an evil person going up, turn him back."

The people began climbing up inside the bamboo stalk. How they got through the bamboo joints I don't know, because the story doesn't explain about that. The mockingbird guarded them on the way up. He was like a scout. He went ahead, calling, "Pashumayani! Pashumayani! Pash! Pash! Pash!—Be careful! Be careful!" The people came up in groups, until everyone reached the top. The opening in the place where they came out was called the sipapuni. The people camped near where they emerged. The light was grey and they didn't know where they would be going.

Spider Old Woman—that is, Gogyeng Sowuhti—said, "Well, we are all here. Did you leave the evil ones down below?"

They said, "Yes, we didn't see any evil ones coming up."

Spider Old Woman said, "Good. Now plug the bamboo up with this cotton."

All this time, the mockingbird was telling the people how to arrange themselves, some over here, some over there, group by group, and he gave each group the name of a tribe. So there were Utes, Hopis, Navajos and so on, and one of the groups was called Bahanas, or white people.

After the bamboo was plugged with cotton, it turned out that an evil one had come up without being detected. When they discovered him he laughed.

They said, "We don't want you here. It was because of people like you that we left the Third World."

He said, "You couldn't get along without an evil one. I have a part to play in this world."

So according to this version of the story, the evil one taught them how to make the sun, moon and stars and to loft them into the sky to make the world light.

There are other explanations of who put the sun, moon and stars in the sky. Some say that Spider Old Woman told the people how to do it. There is also a story that Coyote scattered the stars in the sky. Over in Oraibi some of the traditions say that the spirit Huruing Wuhti, Hard Substances Old Woman, put the sun up there. But the way it was told to me, it was the evil one who came through the sipapuni with the people who showed them how to get the sky work done.[15] Sometimes you hear that the evil one was a powaka, a witch or sorcerer. Because he came into the upper world instead of staying below, sorcery and evil have plagued the people ever since. In my version of the story, sorcery and knowledge were sort of linked together. A sorcerer was supposed to know how to do things that ordinary people couldn't do. I suppose that in the old days they would have said that he was a man with powerful medicine. That's how the evil one knew what to do about making the sun and moon.

When the Hopis left the sipapuni to begin their migrations, they told the sorcerer that he couldn't come with them, because the whole purpose of the emergence was to get away from evil. So he went with the Bahanas, or white people, instead, and the Hopi leaders said that everyone must be wary of Bahanas if they met them anywhere, because their possession of the sorcerer would give them more knowledge than the Hopis could cope with. But time and again in later days other sorcerers found the Hopis and caused dissension and corruption in the villages.

You can see that the theme of dissension and evil, and of the search for a place of harmony, starts with the emergence story. I've told only a little of that story, because it's very long. Different villages and clans have their own special details, and different explanations. A clan in Shongopovi or Oraibi has different explanations than the same clan in Walpi has. The reason is that clan groups kept branching off during the migrations. The Bear Clan was going in a certain direction, then part of the clan left the group and went another way. They all expected to meet again somewhere, maybe at the place foretold in their prophecy. When the Water Clan was coming north from Palatkwa, it was the same thing with them. So you had different branches of clans scattered all across the country, and then they started coming together again at the Hopi mesas. By that time the fragments of the clan had accumulated different experiences. Up to the point when they'd separated, they all had the same traditions, but after that each branch acquired experiences of its own. When they came together again they couldn't tell the same story any more.

Nevertheless, the tradition that the people emerged from the underworld with the guidance of Gogyeng Sowuhti is accepted by most Hopis. The emergence through the sipapuni is commemorated in a great many ceremonies. Sometimes it is discussed and debated in the kiva. Like one night we were talking about it and someone said, "Now how in the world could all those people come through a bamboo? How could they get in? How could it hold their weight? How could they get through the joints?"

Those clowns that come out when a big dance is going on, they are there to entertain the people, of course, but they have a special meaning in some of the things they do. For older people like myself, they're a part of the serious ritual, though most spectators aren't aware of it. There used to be a Clown Fraternity in the old days. If you were initiated into that group you were a clown as long as you lived. That Clown Fraternity doesn't exist here any more. Nowadays when they need clowns they invite certain members of the community to be performers. I can't say for sure about the Hopi clowns, but our Tewa clowns have to go through preparations just as the dancers do. They abstain from various things to purify themselves and make themselves ready. They stay away from their women, don't have any intercourse with them. Sometimes they sleep in the kiva. They deny themselves salt or meat. It is a tribute to you if you are asked to be a clown. If you accept the invitation, your aunts on your father's side will furnish you with food.

I was telling you about the emergence from the underworld. Now, that tradition is involved in the clown rituals. Before they go to perform, the clowns have their own ceremony in the kiva. Just as in other ceremonies, the central theme of their ritual is rain. They sit in a circle, go through prescribed routines and sing. When they are finished with the song they all holler, "Yah hay!" Then they reenact the coming from the underworld. The leader climbs the ladder to the top. He sticks his head out, says, "Yah hay!" and ducks his head down again. He does that four times. Says, "Ne talat aou yama, I came out into the light!" After that, the next fellow does the same thing. It's a reenactment of the emergence into the upper world.

When they are all outside the kiva, they go to different places in the village. First they go to the home of the eldest woman of the Corn Clan or of the Tobacco Clan. This woman offers them piki, and they take small pieces four times. They thank her. They have in mind that corn is life, that it is the substance of our bodies. They have in mind that all things come from the Great Spirit. The piki that they receive from the woman is symbolic. It gives them the strength to perform. These things take place the day before the dance. They go to where the dancers and kiva leaders are having their rehearsal, and they rehearse with them, planning what they are going to do to entertain the spectators. They stay there all night, and early in the morning they return to their own kiva for a while before they make their appearance at the ceremony.

Many of the things they do in their performance are mischievous or, you might say, naughty. This behavior is really telling people how *not* to behave. Sometimes the things they do refer to certain individuals in the community. If someone has been acting in an improper manner, the clowns' actions or dialogue allude to this. They can be criticizing even an important person. While it may seem funny to many of the spectators, some of them understand that it is serious criticism. Those clowns are freed from the usual restraints, and it gives them an opportunity to say things that ordinarily wouldn't be said. But a lot of things they do are just nonsense, as if they didn't understand any proprieties. You see, they sort of represent people as they were when they came from the underworld. They are funny looking and they don't understand good manners. They are, you could say, uncivilized, as people were when they first emerged. By their actions they remind everyone how important it is to be decent and respectful and harmonious in their way of living.

To be absolutely truthful, I have to say that these clown ceremonies are dying out, slowly but surely. If some of us old-timers were involved in these things, we'd do it the way I've described it. But the younger generation doesn't have a grasp of it any more. They don't take it as seriously as we do. I'm afraid that most of the ritual aspects of clowning are gone.

Now that I have mentioned the Hopi tradition of emergence from the underworld, I ought to say something about Tewa origins and how we came to be in all those villages over there on the Rio Grande—Santa Clara, San Ildefonso, San Juan and so on. Of course, those names were given by the Spanish. The Tewas had their own names for their villages. San Ildefonso was Pokwode, Santa Clara was Kap'o. Pojoaque, that's a Spanish corruption of Posunwage.

Anyway, the story told to us by our elders is that the Tewas originated at a place called Sibopay. In some respects the story is similar to that of the Hopis. It says that the people came from down below. There weren't humans down there, only creatures of different kinds, and they emerged by climbing a tall spruce or pine. When they came out on the surface of the earth, that's when they became humans. The people who came out were Tewas, not mixed tribes as in the Hopi tradition. The sacred place where this happened is regarded as the navel of the earth. There's a lake over in Colorado, a briny lake, that's called Sibopay. I've never seen it, but they say it's located in the sand dunes somewhere north of Alamosa. I've heard that the Eastern Tewas accept it as the place where we emerged. I myself can't really say anything one way or another about the lake.[16] But over here we have another way of interpreting that emergence story. In our songs we say that we came from Sibopay, the mother that bore us. We emerged, somewhere, from the first woman. Our life cord was attached to her.

After the Tewas emerged they went on their journey. Of course, everything goes by fours, because it is a sacred number. So there were four places on this journey that are remembered. Sibopay, where we began, is the first. From Sibopay the people went out and arrived at Oga'akeneh, a big body of water. At that place they branched off from one another, but the main group made a long water crossing and arrived at Shonkyugeh, meaning Slippery Point. They settled there for a while and then they decided to move on. But they branched off again. It was all that splitting off that was responsible for there being numerous Tewa villages in the Rio Grande Valley. One group—you have to take it that they were my ancestors—went out from Shonkyugeh and settled at Tsewageh. That was the fourth place, counting Sibopay as the first.

The whole story is in the chant we sing in our Midwinter Ceremony in Tewa Village. The first part says:

> Somewhere, somewhere,
> Far away,
> What were you at Sibopay when you were born?
> That is what I am asking,
> What am I myself going to be?

When they finish with that part they get to a section about Oga'akeneh, that body of water, and then they come to Shonkyugeh, Slippery Point:

> I'm asking,
> What am I?
> Where am I going?
> Where do I come from?

From Shonkyugeh the song takes you on to Tsewageh, It says:

> Why did I come to Tsewageh?
> This is what our fath ?rs told us,
> Instructing us,
> Telling us how to conduct ourselves.[17]

It's a long chant. It repeats how life starts, how you are born, how you grow into childhood and get to be mature, and how you are supposed to conduct yourself until the Great Spirit calls you.

Someone is up at the kiva opening, watching the stars. There are three stars in a row, we call the Kweedeeing, meaning Strung Together. The white people call them Orion's Belt. When the man at the kiva opening says "The Kweedeeing's at the right place," then they stop the singing. They get into a circle in the kiva and purify themselves. They sing a purifying song. Anybody who has a guilty conscience or some bad thoughts that are bothering him, he is supposed to put it out of his mind, wipe it out of his heart, because they're going to repeat the Sibopay song again. After they have gone through the Sibopay song, they go into another one. They chant it the same way, and it sounds like a continuation, but the words are different. It is about things that happened after we Tewas left Tsewageh. The words tell about how we carry out the ceremonies, and the power we have to bring rain and produce good crops. They tell about the different waters and the four directions with their different colored clouds.

Instead of mentioning those sacred names of the first song—Sibopay, Oga'akeneh, Shonkyugeh, Tsewageh—they substitute place names in this region to commemorate what the Tewas saw when they came here. There's Muchoveh, the first point of the mesa that you see when you're coming this way from Keam's Canyon. There's Kanyegehping, meaning Moist Ground, a kind of mound off to the north of Tewa Village. Then Kwaaping, Oak Mountain, west of Piñon. And Saalaping, a large yellow stone standing just the other side of Wepo. All these places are landmarks that are commemorated in the chant. The song takes all night. About daybreak someone says, "Well, I think that one more time around with the song will be enough." Everyone is a little tired by this time and they begin to sing a little faster to get it over with. After that they purify themselves again. A person with a purifying feather—a buzzard feather, because the buzzard is a great purifier among the birds, he cleans up everything—comes forward. He's a member of the Bear Clan. He puts ashes on the feather and holds it out, and when the singers come to the last word of the song—a purifying song—everybody blows the ashes away. That completes the purification.

As to the Tewa origin story, it is all in the chant, as I said. But some years ago my uncle, George Cochaase, recorded that whole story on tape, from Sibopay to Tsewageh, and from Tsewageh to First Mesa, not singing it but narrating it in prose. I always wanted to borrow that tape so I could write the story down just as he told it in Tewa, and then make an English translation. It's something that the Tewa people ought to have because it is a very important document. They would have something authentic to refer to. What I've told you about our migrations is authentic too, but I'm sure I have forgotten some of the things my Uncle George remembered. It's always that way. Unless you have it written down, a little more gets lost with every generation. George Cochaase isn't living any more. But the tape is somewhere. I'm told that one of his people has it. I've asked about it a number of times, whether I could borrow it and transcribe everything that's on it so the Tewa people here on First Mesa could have a record. But George's people don't want to let it out of their hands. I think that's too bad. Tape recordings don't last forever.

In our First Mesa traditions there's a reference to a flood that occurred sometime in the ancient past. It's not very clear. There's no story about it, to my knowledge, and I don't know where the recollection comes from. The Hopis call their village chief a kikmongwi. We Tewas don't actually have a village chief, but we have a word for him, poa'atoyong, meaning leader-after-the-flood. Somewhere, sometime, there was a great flood that destroyed everything, and when the surviving people came together again, the person who took the leadership was called leader-after-the-flood. We still call chiefs by that title. It is predicted that another great destruction is coming, this one by fire. According to this prediction, the patterns of civilized living will deteriorate and people will cease to have respect for one another. Son will fight father, mother will fight daughter. Good living will come to an end, and after that the fire will consume everything.

I can't really say whether that prophecy comes from the Tewa side or the Hopi side.[18] But some people here on this mesa believe we are moving toward the destruction by fire because so many young people are turning away from the old religious beliefs, and because so few are being initiated into the kiva societies where discipline is learned. We can't control the young people any more. According to some, the destruction by fire can't be far off. They say that only two persons will be left, a male and a female, to repeople the earth.

When you start telling how the Hopis got to these mesas, you are in for some long stories. Every clan is the keeper of its own traditions, and sometimes you could call those traditions real history modified by legends. What the clan traditions contain has been very important through the centuries, because they give a clan its place in the scheme of things. I've already mentioned that the Fire Clan—sometimes they call it the Firewood Clan, or the Masauwu Clan—claims to be a relative of that spirit being, Masauwu, who owned all this upper world when the people emerged from below. Because of that, they have always put themselves forward as a leader clan, you might say as a royal clan. But the Bear Clan claims to have led the other clans in their search for the place where the people were supposed to settle, and to have arrived here first and established Shongopovi on Second Mesa. So they claim the leadership of quite a few of the villages. They are a traditionally paramount clan. Other clans claim importance because they own certain protective good spirits. For example, the Reed Clan and its affiliated clans—Eagle, Hawk and Wind—claim Pokanghoya and Palengahoya, the Warrior Brothers.

Those two fellows sometimes are referred to as twins, but they really aren't twins because one is older and one younger. They are spiritual beings that white people would call gods or deities. They were already up here in the Fourth World at the time of emergence from below. They're supposed to be grandchildren of Gogyeng Sowuhti, Spider Old Woman. In many of the stories you hear, Pokanghoya and Palengahoya appear as a couple of ornery kids who are always up to some kind of mischief. Palengahoya means "echo," because he does everything that his brother does. They play jokes on people—often on their grandmother—and spend a lot of time playing shinny.

But these boys have another aspect. They are creators and warriors, and they use thunder and lightning as weapons. When the people first emerged, a lot of this country in the Fourth World was nothing but mud and marsh. Well, the two brothers went from place to place turning the mud into stone and making mountains and buttes. Also, at that time there were monsters and giants roaming around, harassing and killing humans. The two Pokangs, as they're sometimes called for short, attacked the giants and monsters and drove them out or killed them off.

The Warrior Brothers figure in most of the Hopi Reed Clan ceremonies. That clan is responsible for the Hopi Somaikoli Ceremony, which features rituals for the Pokangs. It is also in charge of the Kaletaka warrior fraternity and its Momchitu Ceremony. (Among the Tewas, Somaikoli is under the direction of the Cloud, or Mist, Clan.)

My father, who was head of the One Horn Fraternity, and Nitioma, my sponsor, told me that the Reed Clan came from some warm place down south called Bakatnam. In their migrations they met the Eagle Clan, and the two of them travelled together. When they arrived, some of them moved in here with the Walpis and some settled over at Second Mesa and at Oraibi. I have heard it said that the Walpi Reed Clan people claim to have been actually created by the Pokangs at Lamehva, that spring below Second Mesa on the east side of Shipaulovi.[19] Their claim doesn't jibe with Reed Clan traditions in other villages. If the Walpi Reed Clan people stick to that contention, then of course their ancestors couldn't have emerged from the Third World with the other Hopis.

One other thing about the Reed Clan gave them a special place in the community. They don't have it any more, but they used to have a Yaya Society that was particularly noted for its special powers in sorcery or witchcraft. Before we Indians ever learned those English words we would have called it "medicine." The Yaya Society was closely affiliated with the Somaikoli activities, you might say sort of intertwined, because they were under the direction of the same clan group. But the Yayas had rituals that were distinctly their own. They wore eagle feathers and cornhusks in their hair, and they used to perform some mysterious and bloodcurdling acts. One thing they'd do was to take some of their members and throw them down into the kiva. Ordinarily, a person thrown down into a kiva that way would get badly hurt, break some bones or be killed. But after a Yaya was thrown down, he'd come up in a minute or two as if nothing had happened.

Another thing I remember about the Yayas is that one of them would put a long stick down his throat, like a circus sword swallower. Then, they had a big act with a skull. They'd chant and call the skull to come to them in the dance court. It would come out of some passageway and roll across the plaza to the men who were calling it. One thing I heard about them is that they once called a scarecrow to come up from the fields below the mesa on the west side, and the scarecrow came up the trail to where the ceremony was taking place. How they performed some of these tricks I can't say. But there are many such stories about the Yayas. One of them is that a Yaya priest pointed toward a certain butte and made white marks there, like writing. The Yayas always acted kind of wild, and they scared people. Sometimes they'd go up on the roofs and knock the chimney pots down. If there was ever a separate village of Yayas out there somewhere, as some Oraibi stories say, I don't know. I never heard about it myself. I know about the Yayas only as a Reed Clan fraternity.[20]

Well, the Reed Clan people have the Pokangs as protective personages. Then the Rain-Cloud group—all those clans affiliated with the Water Clan—claim Paleuleukang, the one-horned water snake of Palatkwa, as their good spirit. Some people say that Huruing Wuhti—Hard Substances Old Woman—is claimed by the Water Coyotes who came from the north, but to the best of my knowledge she's accepted by all Hopis. She is supposed to be the owner of all coral, turquoise and things like that. Usually when a person makes or strings beads he sings a song to Huruing Wuhti. The Sun Clan claims a special relationship with Tawa, the Sun Spirit, and other celestial things such as the moon and the stars. Alosoka belongs to the Two Horn Fraternity, composed of clans with the names of two-horned animals such as deer and antelope. Gogyeng Sowuhti, or Spider Grandmother—she represents the earth, which gives us everything we need to live—is claimed by the Bear, Spider and Spruce clans and all their affiliated clans. The Bear Clan says that in the form of a small spider, Gogyeng Sowuhti sits on the bear's ear, tells it what to do and guides it through all difficulties. Muyingwa, a germination spirit, belongs to the Water Clan.

You have to remember that a good many of those clan groups that arrived here weren't Hopis as we know them today. They came in with different customs, different traditions, even different languages. They brought ceremonies that the Hopis didn't know about, and they brought whatever guiding spirits, or deities, they happened to have. Before you can even begin to understand the inner relationships among the Hopis, you have to know a lot about the beliefs that the clans hold to. If clans are having a dispute of some kind, they might argue their cases by recalling something that happened back at the sipapuni or during the migrations. For example, the Fire Clan in Oraibi never stopped claiming its right to lead the village because it was their relative, Masauwu, who allowed people to settle in this world. This was one of the situations that led to the breakup of Oraibi in 1906.

If you don't have a comprehension of the clans and their claims on the community you will have a hard time understanding what is going on around you. This applies to Hopis as well as to outsiders. Before I was initiated into the One Horn Society I didn't have a very good picture of how the Hopi village functioned. Afterwards I began to understand who was who in the clans and the villages, and what the main forces of village life were. So I am going to tell briefly about some of the clan traditions that I am familiar with. With certain clans, their stories begin at the place of emergence. Quite a few things happened while they were camped at that place. For one thing, Spider Grandmother called a council of the leaders of the different groups—the Hopis, the Comanches, the Cohoninos, the Utes, the Tucom (the Sioux and all the other tribes that wore war bonnets, such as the Blackfeet, the Mandans and the Nez Percés), and the whites. She gave each one of these groups a direction for its journey. The tribes began to depart.

But the Hopis were arguing about who was going to lead them on their migration. Now, the Fire—or Firewood—Clan was the first to emerge from below, and because of that it was assumed that those people would take responsibility for leading the Hopis to their final destination, the place where Masauwu was living. So the Hopis were waiting for the leader of the Fire People to tell them what to do. That is the responsibility of any chief. But he sat there and didn't take any initiative.

Someone said, "You Fire People say that Masauwu is your relative because he gave you the knowledge of fire. Good. Then take the lead and we will follow."

But the chief of the Fire People said, "No, I don't want to lead."

They said to him, "What is the matter? When we were down below, you claimed that it was your right to lead."

He answered, "No, I don't want the responsibility. This is a new place to us and we don't know what might happen. If I take the lead and something goes wrong, I'll be blamed for it. I don't want to be accused of taking the people on a false trail."

They went on arguing. Finally, a heavy, stocky man jumped up.[21] He said, "All right, the Fire People don't want to lead, so I will take the responsibility. My group will go first and the others can follow."

Of course there weren't any clans yet, but this group that accepted the
lead eventually became the Bear Clan. The Fire People eventually became
the Fire Clan. Even though they refused the responsibility of leading, they
insisted that they would always be the paramount clan because of their
relationship with Masauwu.

So at last all those Hopis prepared for their migration, that is, their long
journey to where Masauwu was going to give them a place to live. When
they were ready, one of the good guiding spirits—maybe Tawa, the Sun
Spirit, or Spider Grandmother, the Earth Spirit—gave them some teachings
to carry with them. The Good Spirit said that even though they had
received the short blue ear of corn and would have to struggle hard, they
would have worthwhile lives if they remembered these teachings and were
peaceful except in defense of their villages. "Now that you have been
brought to the upper world, remember that I guided you here. I'll be with
you all the time. Listen to me. Listen to your conscience, that is my voice.
I'll be inside you. I'll be everywhere. If you want to do something and you
hear that voice inside you saying, 'Don't,' then turn away from that thing.
Your corn will help to guide you to a place of beautiful flowers, where you
will finally stay. Your journey will be a long one. I will guide you with signs.
If you reach a place where your corn doesn't mature, then you'll know
you've gone too far north and you'll have to turn back."

The journeys began. At first they all travelled together with the Bear
Clan in the lead. Then the groups started to branch off, some going one
way, some another, according to signs that were given to them. They took
clan names as they went. One group became the Sand Clan, and they
claimed a special relationship with Spider Grandmother, because sand is an
aspect of earth. The Fire People now became the Fire Clan, and they were
guided by sparks or flares of fire in the night. This is how the clans scattered
in the upper world, each going its own way in search of the place where they
were supposed to settle down and rest.

The group that became the Bear Clan went too far north in its journey,
into Colorado. It made some villages there and stayed for a while, but their
corn didn't mature and eventually they came south again. Those Mesa
Verde ruins in Colorado are supposed to be places that they built and
abandoned. How that group took the name of Bear Clan is this. During
their journey they came to a place where the carcass of a bear was lying. The
leader of the group looked at the dead bear awhile and said, "I think we'll
call ourselves the Honau (Bear) Clan from now on to distinguish us from
other clans." So his group took that name.

Other groups were following his trail, and when they came to the place of the dead bear and heard that the Bear Clan had named itself there, they also took clan names. One group cut straps from the bear's hide to make carrying straps, and they took the name Pikoysa (Strap) Clan. Another group saw fat in the dead bear's eye sockets, and they gave themselves the name Grease Cavity Clan. Another group found a bluebird pecking at the carcass, and they called themselves the Bluebird Clan. Another saw a gopher digging a hole underneath the carcass, and they became the Gopher Clan. Another saw a spider spinning a web across the bones and gave themselves the name Spider Clan. The last group to come that way saw a spruce tree growing through the skeleton and took the name Spruce Clan. This is the tradition of all those clans, and they tell this story to show how they became related, that is, affiliated.

The way they tell it, the Bear Clan stopped in various places and made villages when they had to grow their corn, then they went on. One of the places they stopped at was Wupatki, where those ruins are, north of the San Francisco Peaks. The Hopis call those mountains Nuvatikyao, Snow Peaks. After a while the wise old men told the Bear Clan people, "This is not the place we are supposed to go to. The land is too rich here. We will become obsessed with easy living. We are supposed to settle at a place where life will be austere. Let us move on. Our guiding spirit will take care of us." So they moved from there and eventually arrived at Hopi country.

Masauwu, the Death Spirit, was living over on Third Mesa near where Oraibi is today, according to the Oraibi Bear Clan story, and he saw them coming. (The Walpi people say Masauwu was living over here.) He went out to meet them, and asked who they were.

They said, "We are the Bear Clan."

He said, "I have been expecting my children, the ones called the Fire Clan. They are the ones I was going to give this land to."

They answered, "Well, the Fire Clan was the first to come through the sipapuni, we acknowledge that. But then they pulled back and refused to take the responsibility of leading the people. So we accepted the responsibility. This is the place we were told about, so we came here. We are the first of the clans to arrive."

Masauwu said, "Yes, since you are the first to come, I will give you a place to build your village."

The place he gave them was where the ruins of Old Shongopovi are, down below the mesa on the east side, and he assigned land for them to cultivate. They called that place Masipa.[22] I think I already mentioned that the morning after their arrival they saw smoke rising from Antelope Mesa in the east, and when they investigated they found that another village was already there. (That would be Awatovi, of course.) But that fact never interfered with their claim that they were the first to arrive in Hopi country. After a while some of their affiliated clans and other clans arrived and joined them.

Oraibi, over on Third Mesa, was an offshoot of Old Shongopovi, that is to say Masipa. According to tradition, Oraibi was started by a man named Masito, of the Bear Clan. According to what some people say, Masito was an honest fellow who didn't agree with everything other people believed about their traditions. He was a kind of dissenter, and he got to be troublesome to his clan. The chief in Masipa told him, "You are my brother, but if you don't want to follow me as a brother, then you'd better leave here, because you are making a lot of difficulties." Masito was independent minded. He took his family and left, going over to Third Mesa and building his house there, starting a new village. The location where he built was not on top of the mesa where Oraibi is now, but down on the southwest side. There are still ruins there.

The people of Masipa didn't know where he'd gone. But one day some men were out hunting rabbits and they found his place. They asked him if he was going to return to Masipa, but he said, "No, my brother didn't want me, and the people over there didn't want me, so I am going to stay here." When the people of Masipa found out where he was, quite a few families followed him, and people came in from outlying settlements to join him. His settlement grew so fast that in Masipa it was rumored that Masito was a wizard who was making all these people. This is one of the stories about Masito and the beginnings of Oraibi. But some people in the Bear Clan say he was sent there to maintain contact with Masauwu. There is a mound just a little southwest of Oraibi where Masauwu was supposed to be living. They called it Ojaivi (now corrupted to Oraibi), meaning On Top of the Rock, or Above the Rock. The village took its name from that spot.

Well, after a while the Fire Clan arrived. They found Masauwu and announced that they had come to receive the land he had promised them. He told them, "You Fire Clan people, you were the ones I selected to favor. But the Bear Clan came first. You were my chosen people, so why didn't you take the lead?"

The Fire Clan chief said, "Because we wanted to be respected. When we arrived up here in this world we didn't know any more about it than the others did. Everything was strange to us. We didn't want to be accused of leading the people in the wrong direction. If something bad happened, we didn't want the others to say we were guilty of bringing them into a hard life."

Masauwu answered, "Well, you let the Bear Clan get here first, and now they are the paramount clan. Still, you are my clan. You are the Fire Clan, the Masauwu Clan, and I will watch over you. But I don't want to stay where all these people are living. I'm going to disappear from this place. You won't see me any more, but I'll work with you in spirit. I'll guide you. I'll show you the right way by giving signs such as sparks or flares in the night." After that, Masauwu went away from there and didn't show himself to the people any more. He became invisible unless he wanted to show himself as an apparition.

The Fire Clan stayed on in Oraibi until 1906, when they were forced to leave. They founded a new village, Hotevilla. Still today, the Fire Clan has credentials going back, so they say, to the emergence from the Third World. They own a piece of a broken stone tablet that, according to their tradition, they have possessed ever since leaving the sipapuni. They say that the other portion of the tablet was given to good Bahanas right after the emergence. The reason for that was that there was already a prophecy saying that one day far in the future a good Bahana was going to come from the East bringing harmony and good fortune to the Hopis. But the Hopis had already been warned that there were bad Bahanas as well as good ones. So when the right Bahana came he was supposed to carry the portion of the broken tablet. If the two pieces fit together properly, then the Hopis would know that it was the good Bahana that arrived, not some impostor.

The broken tablet of the Fire Clan really exists, at least their part of it. They have it over in Hotevilla. A number of us have seen it. Yukioma, the last Fire Clan chief in Oraibi, went to Washington with a BIA official in 1911 or 1912, and he took that broken tablet with him just in case he might run into the white man who was supposed to have the other part. When he returned, some of the people asked him, "Did you find the real White Father who has the other part?" He said, "No, they took me to the Commissioner. That's as far as I got. I didn't get to see the Big White Father."

As I mentioned before, over here on First Mesa, people have a tradition that Masauwu lived up top where Walpi is today. That's where he was said to be living at the time the Snake Clan arrived from Navajo Mountain, and they had to get his approval before they were allowed to come into Keuchaptevela, the original village down below on the mesa shelf.

One thing has always troubled me about saying that the Bear Clan or some other clan arrived first at a certain place. It must have been a mixed group with other clans represented in it, because people of the same clan can't intermarry. A Bear Clan man has to have a wife from another clan, and a Bear Clan woman has to have a husband from another clan. So it seems to me that when the Bear Clan arrived here in Hopi country, they had to have other clans with them.

Anyway, after the Bear Clan made its settlement over on Second Mesa, other villages began to make their appearance, such as Shipaulovi, Mishongnovi, Tsikuvi and others. Some of those villages, like Tsikuvi, have disappeared—everything except their ruined walls. The Bear Clan was the founder of the original Walpi, old Keuchaptevela. You can see that ruins looking down from Walpi on the west side. There are also a number of old Bear Clan ruins scattered around on the mesa. Most of the old Hopi villages were dominated by the Bear Clan. Hotevilla and Bakavi on Third Mesa were started in 1906, when the Fire and Water Coyote clans broke away from Oraibi, and so they don't have Bear Clan leadership. Moencopi, near Tuba City, has Green Corn Clan leadership. And the Bear Clan is extinct in Walpi now.

One thing that is perplexing to a lot of people is that the Navajos have some of the same clans that the Hopis and Eastern Pueblos do. If a Hopi and a Navajo meet somewhere, the Navajo might ask, "Say, what clan are you?"

Hopi might say, "I'm Bear Clan."

Navajo might say, "I'm Bear Clan too, so you are my clan brother."

Hopi would say, "How in the world can that be? We Hopis took our clan names during our migrations, and there weren't any Navajos among us."

The Navajo would say something like "Just the same, I'm Bear Clan. Way back somewhere our people and your people got mixed together. Some Hopi woman joined the Navajos, or maybe she was captured by us. She was Bear Clan, and her children were Bear Clan. I'm descended from them so I'm Bear Clan also."

That is how we believe the Navajos came to have some of the same clans we do. They probably captured women from the wandering small groups, or maybe they all mixed peacefully, and the Hopis or Eastern Pueblos who were absorbed by the Navajos kept their clans going. Of course, the Navajos have some clans that we don't have. For example, they have what they call Black People's Clan. There is a story that a group of Navajos picked up a black man for a servant or slave somewhere. They adopted him into their group, and some time later they took the name Black People's Clan.

I am sure a lot of things having to do with clans seem strange to most white people. But clan traditions have always been extremely important to us, not only because they contain some of our history but also because they regulate our lives in many ways. Clan traditions are, you might say, the common law that governs many of our activities. They determine where a person can grow his corn, and whether he has prestige in the council. If it is a ceremonial question that has to be answered, only members of certain clans have the knowledge and authority to speak. Clans have a kind of rating, in some cases because of their being first arrivals, in other cases because of where they came from, or what other clan they are affiliated with, or because of some particular protective spirit that they claim as a relation. It is not possible to tell about the origins and experiences of all the clans. You can live your life among them without knowing all their claims and secrets. But if you are going to half understand the Hopis you have to know at least something about the more important clans. And so I am going to say a little now about two other groups that have been very influential up here on First Mesa—the Snake Clan and the Water Clan.

Up at Tokonave, Black Mountain, which the white people decided to call Navajo Mountain, there was a village known as Wuhkokiekeu, and there were people who spoke some dialect of Paiute. As yet, those people hadn't selected a clan emblem for themselves. After a while another group from out in California somewhere, a place they called Taotoykya, arrived at Wuhkokiekeu and were accepted into that village. They also spoke some dialect of Paiute. The first bunch were the ones that came to be known later as the Snake Clan. The second group came to be known as the Horn Clan. According to their traditions, the Snake Clan got its name through the experiences of one of their young men who made an expedition down the Colorado River.

They say that this young man used to sit at the edge of the river—probably the Colorado or one of its tributaries—watching the water flow and wondering where it was going. After thinking about it a long time, he decided to make a trip down the river. So he got a big cottonwood log and hollowed it out—made it into a hollow drum large enough for him to crawl inside. He made a tight lid that would keep the water out. Then he informed his parents that he was going to make this voyage to see where the water was flowing. He asked his mother to prepare some tusi (cornmeal made out of baked corn) for him, and also some piki.

His mother asked, "Why are you going?"

He said, "Day after day I see this water flowing. I want to know where it goes. So I've hollowed out a tree, and I will get inside and flow with the current."

His father said, "No, don't do it. It would be foolish. Some of our old people went down the river a long time ago. It was a very long journey. It took them years. They went through cactus country. They came to Patowahkacheh, the ocean. When they returned they brought back stories of many dangers."

He tried to dissuade his son, but the young man said, "No, I don't want to be dissuaded. I want to find out for myself."

So the father made prayer feathers, like the Hopis do today, and he gave them to his son. "Place these prayer feathers at the edge of the great water when you arrive there. Pray that your guiding spirit will protect you from the great difficulties you will meet." At last the young man was ready, and he went to the river and got into his hollow log. (They called it a poshikpi.) He fastened the lid down. He had made a very small hole in the top, and now he put a reed through it. He breathed through the reed. His parents pushed the hollow log into the river. The river carried him away.

After many days he felt his hollow log grate on sand. He wasn't moving any more, so he pounded the lid off and got out. All around him on both sides of the river were great stretches of cactus. He entered the log again, pushed it out into the current and replaced the lid. After floating for many days, the log grounded again. When the young man got out this time he saw that he had arrived at Patowahkacheh. There was water as far as he could see. He rolled his hollow log up on the bank. He placed his prayer feathers and prayed that his protective spirit would guide him safely. Then he took his food from inside his craft and began to walk.

He travelled a great distance, then he met some people. They spoke a language that was foreign to him, but they were able to communicate with the help of signs. They took the young man to a house. They set food in front of him. They asked him where he came from, and with the help of hand signs he explained that he came from a village in the north called Wuhkokiekeu, where the river began.

When they had talked for a while, the people said, "We are going to have a ceremony here. Do you want to participate?"

He said, "Yes, I would like to be part of it."

So they began teaching him all the chants. Then they took him out to gather snakes. They went east, west, north and south, all the four directions. They gathered the snakes gently. They called them snake brothers. They brought the snakes to their kiva. They spread sand on the floor and let the snakes wriggle around on it. At night they put the snakes away in bags. The next day they went out again. They took four days collecting the snakes. The next four days they spent fixing up their ceremonial paraphernalia and making moccasins. They gave him a ceremonial kilt that had seashells like a fringe along the edge. They showed him how to make himself up for the dance, painting his face and letting his hair hang down long. Everything that you see in the Snake Dance among the Hopis today, it was the young man who was instructed by these people how to do it. They held their ceremony, and after that the clouds gathered and the rain fell.

The young man stayed for some time. When he was ready to leave and go home, the people told him to select a young woman for his wife. He selected a young woman whom he liked, and the two of them carried the ceremony to the young man's village, where they arrived after many months had passed. When you see a young woman in the Hopi Snake Dance, throwing meal at the dancers, she represents the girl that the young man brought back with him.

You hear this story told in different ways.[23] One version says that the people the young man met were really snake people. They crawled around on the ground like snakes, but when they went down into the kiva they took off their snakeskins and became humans. In this version, after they were finished with their rain ceremony, all the young women turned themselves into snakes and the young man had to choose one of those snakes for a bride. A good spirit, probably Spider Grandmother, told him which one to pick, and when the snakes turned themselves back into humans he discovered he had chosen a very beautiful and intelligent girl.

Whatever story you hear, what happened after the young man and his wife came back to the village is pretty much the same. The whole village wanted to know about where he had been and all the things he had experienced. He told them everything and said they could have the Snake Ceremony for rain if they wanted it, because he and the young woman had brought all the knowledge with them. The chief and the other elders considered it, and they agreed to have one Snake Ceremony each year in the middle of the summer to bring rain. After that things went well in the village, until the young man and his wife began to have children. Then there was trouble. The children of this family began to bite other children, who died just as if they had been struck by poisonous snakes. When the villagers complained about it, the young woman said, "I'm sorry, but we and our children are snake people. We can't help it." The villagers were angry, however, and told the snake-people family that they would have to go away. So the snake family departed, and from that time they were known as the Snake Clan. From Tokonave, Black Mountain, according to their traditions, they travelled south and east.

Their journey covered a long expanse of time. They made many stops, at each of which they settled for a time, and then went on. It seems that they wandered back and forth a good deal. They got to Monument Valley, lived there for a while and left. Some of the ruins in Monument Valley are of villages built by the Snake Clan. The people went on till they reached Kalewistema, where those cliff ruins are in Tsegi Canyon, west of Kayenta.[24] It's an important place in Hopi tradition. A number of Hopi clans lived there at one time or another, including the Water Coyotes. While the Snake Clan was living at Kalewistema they heard that there were Bear Clan villages down here on the Hopi mesas, so they moved in this direction. Part of the clan broke off and went west to Oraibi, but the main body came to First Mesa.

Now, at this time the First Mesa village was still below on the mesa shelf and was called Keuchaptevela, and Masauwu, the original owner of the land, was said to be still living up on top of the mesa where Walpi is now. From the top Masauwu saw the Snake Clan approaching through Wepo Valley. He went down to the village and told the Bear Clan chief, "People are coming out there. Are you going to accept them?"

The chief said, "Well, I don't know. You are the one who owns all the land. You are the one who has to decide."

Masauwu said, "Those people, I don't know who they are. Someone ought to go and find out what they want."

The Bear Clan chief answered, "Well, I'm a recent arrival here. You are the one to go down and talk to them."

So Masauwu went down in the valley to meet the Snake Clan. In his usual form Masauwu was pretty frightening to look at, but he transformed himself to look like an ordinary human being before he arrived where the Snake Clan was resting. He talked to the leader of the group for a while and told him it was all right for the people to camp down there, but he didn't invite them to the village. Then he went back to the top of the mesa. The Snake Clan went on through the valley till they came to that big wash that runs down from Second Mesa, the Payupki Wash or Big Wash. The Snake Clan settled there for a while.

Masauwu decided after some time that he didn't want them living around there, so he came down with the intention of scaring them away. This time he appeared in his usual terrifying form. He was wearing a torn and bloody rabbitskin blanket. He didn't have any hair, and his head was shiny and black with encrusted blood. His eyes and mouth were horrible to look at, he had no ears, and his skin was marked with ugly fire scars. He came running at the Snake Clan people giving wild wolf cries. Most of the people were so terrified that they ran away or fell down in a faint. But the chief—of course he wasn't the same chief that the people had started out with from Tokonave, because many years had passed since then—didn't flinch. He just stood there with courage, facing up to Masauwu.

When Masauwu saw that the Snake Clan chief wasn't going to back off, he tapped him on the back with the long stick he carried in his hand. He said, "Well, I see you are a brave man. I came to test you and you stood up to it." Then he went behind a large rock and transformed himself to look human. He came back and said, "You people want to stay here, is that it? Before I allow you to stay you will have to show me what kind of powers you have."

So the Snake Clan people put on their ritual dress, the same as the Snake Dancers wear today. They began to sing their ceremonial song. They danced in a line, just as they do today. Snakes came crawling from the four directions and wriggled between their feet. The dancers stroked the snakes with feathers, picked them up and held them. Clouds gathered. It began to rain. Then, suddenly, the dancers rushed at Masauwu in a frightening manner. Masauwu pulled back. He said, "Enough. I don't want to see anything more. You people have great powers. You can come and live in Keuchaptevela."

That's how the Snake Clan arrived and settled here at First Mesa, according to the way the story is told in Walpi. You might hear a lot of embellishments, but that is the main line of the story. Over on Second and Third mesas the Snake Clan tradition is a little different, because that branch of the clan had different experiences as it came to Hopi country.

Quite some time after the Snake Clan left Tokonave, the people still living there began to have difficulties. For one thing, the rain stopped falling and the crops didn't grow. The people began to regret that they had sent the Snake Clan away, because the Snake Ceremony had brought them rain when they needed it. So they abandoned their village at Tokonave and set out to find another place to live. By this time there were several clans in this group, the Horn Clan, the Divided Spring Clan and some others. The Horn Clan [25] went eastward, but the other clans branched off and went in directions of their own choosing. Every now and then the Horn Clan discovered pottery or signs engraved on the rocks showing that the Snake Clan had passed this way ahead of them. In time they reached Kalewistema, that canyon of cave villages near Kayenta, and learned that the Snake Clan had been there a long time before.

How long the Horn Corn stayed at Kalewistema isn't known, but after living there for a while they went on to a place called Lenyanovi, where the Flute Clan had a village. The Horn Clan remained there for some time. When they moved on, the Flute Clan travelled with them. They went then to a place called Kwastapa, just above Wepo. There's a cave at Kwastapa with dripping water. They camped at that place and sent out scouts to search for the Snake Clan. When the scouts returned, they reported that the Snake Clan was living at Keuchaptevela, though some Snake Clan people had gone to Oraibi to live.

So the Horn and Flute clans went on. They passed Wepo Spring. They passed Kanelva, Sheep Spring. They came to Gogyengva, Spider Spring, at the base of the mesa where Keuchaptevela was located. They rested there a while, then the leading men of the clan went up to the village, where they were met by the kikmongwi and the chief personages of the Bear Clan and the Snake Clan at the village entrance. One of the Snake Clan priests made a line of meal across the trail, and that was as far as the Horn and Flute men could go.

The kikmongwi asked, "Who are you people?"

The Horn chief said, "Don't you Snake Clan people recognize us? We have come all the way from Tokonave searching for our cousins."

The Snake Clan chief said, "So! Is it really you?"

The Horn leader said, "Yes, we have come. How can you doubt us? Don't you recognize our language?"

The Snake Clan leader listened to the story told by the Horn spokesman. Finally he said, "Yes, we recognize you. You are the ones we left behind."

The Bear Clan and Snake Clan leaders conferred, and they agreed that the Horn and Flute people could enter the village. The line of sacred meal was rubbed away, and the Horn and Flute people entered. Since that day they have been an important part of the ritual life of Keuchaptevela and, later, Walpi.

Every second year they put on their Horn-Flute Ceremony. The ceremony comes in even years, and in odd years the Snake Ceremony takes place. The Horn-Flute rituals come in August, and commemorate the clans' arrival at First Mesa. The participants go out to Wepo Wash, and when they return they are in white clothes and have sunflowers all over them. The meaning is, "We are good people, we can bring flowers and joy to Walpi." It represents the time they were stopped at the entrance to the village by the chiefs of the Bear Clan and the Snake Clan until they could prove that they were worthy of entering.

Connected with the Flute Ceremony, there's an early morning race that begins out at Wepo Spring. The men and boys who enter the race stand off at a little distance till a gourd of sacred water is placed on a certain rock. When the signal is given, they race to the rock, and the first one there takes the gourd and starts for Walpi. If one of the other runners catches him, he takes the gourd and goes ahead with it. Anyone who catches the leader takes the gourd away, and the winner is the one who carries it into the village. This race is said to bring a blessing on the people. It calls upon the Great Spirit to "rain on his children." They have the same kind of race for the Snake Ceremony the following year.

Back in the earliest days of the First Mesa village, the Bear Clan was supreme. After the arrival of the Snake Clan, the Bear Clan was still on top, but the Snake Clan was strong and influential. Then the Horn and Flute clans came, and other clans. They all brought something to strengthen the village's religious life. Then the Bear Clan died out. The leader now is a Horn man, Ned Nayatewa. He's sort of acting for the Bear and Snake clans.

There's no Bear Clan in Sichomovi, either, since old Kootka died. I think you can sort of see, from what I have told, how the priority of certain clans and their relationship with one another affect the social structure, the rituals, and the everyday lives of the people.

The Water Clan, sometimes called the Rain Clan (Tewas call it the Cloud or Mist Clan), also brought important traditions to the Hopi villages. It was perhaps the fifth or sixth major clan group to arrive at First Mesa, following the Bear, the Snake , the Horn and Flute, and some people would add the Squash and Fire clans. Still, as I said before, different clans claim different things, and there's no fixed order of arrival that everyone will accept.[26] The Water Clan was the leader of a group of clans—the Sand and Lizard, the Tobacco and Rabbit (really Rabbit Brush), the Hawk and Eagle, the Sun and several others. Their story starts at that ancient village of Palatkwa in the south, whose exact location we don't know. The spirit-protector of the Water Clan was a great horned water snake called Paleuleukang. That group brought the Kwakwan, or One Horn, kiva society with them, or perhaps they started this society after they arrived here. The One Horn rituals all derive from the tradition of the horned water snake.

As I mentioned before, my father belonged to the Water Clan, and after I was grown and had been initiated into the One Horn Society he told me a good many things about Water Clan beliefs and traditions. I used to sit with him in the kiva and talk while he was making prayer feathers or something like that. Every once in a while he'd say, "Son, put on your ritual robe and deliver these pahos for me," and he'd tell me what shrine to take them to. There were shrines all around the village, up above on the mesa and also down below, and I'd take the pahos, sometimes a bowl of sacred meal, to the one my father had designated. We had lots of time to talk about ceremonial things while we were sitting in the kiva. One thing he passed on to me was the Palatkwa story as it was known to his clan. The other clans that had come from Palatkwa had somewhat different things to tell, some embellishments that I didn't hear about from my father. That is because each clan had a somewhat different experience, and also because each clan had its own storytellers. The story I'm giving here is just the way my father told it. And you will see that same old theme coming up— corruption and evil driving the people to leave their village and set out on a journey.

In Hopi the Water Clan is called Patkiwoema. That can be translated as Dwelling on Water, or Houseboat, Clan, as I mentioned before, and this refers to their tradition that sometime after they left the place of emergence

they made a long journey across a large expanse of water in boats with
dwellings constructed on them. The body of water is believed to be the
ocean, but just what part of the ocean it was we do not know. It seems that
the Water Clan had a big village somewhere before Palatkwa, but
corruption and evil set in and they had to leave. That is when they made
the ocean voyage. Palatkwa was their next big village. One thing you hear
from the Patki people is that in ancient times they were white, not Indian
color. They say, "My ancestors had white skins, but because of evil things
that happened, we lost all that." They also say, "The Patki people are the
ones who are supposed to teach the Hopis good moral values, how to lead
good lives."

After the Water Clan established their settlement at Palatkwa, meaning
Red Place, everything went well for a while, then evil and corruption crept
in again. People didn't behave well toward one another. They became
careless about their lives and didn't follow the rules of decency. Young
people ridiculed what old people tried to teach them, and had no respect
for their elders. Sometimes some young ones would see an old man
squatting down to relieve himself and they'd push him down in his excreta.
The same thing if it was an old woman. They thought it was great sport.
Things got worse, and the ones who were misbehaving would not listen to
the chief when he tried to correct them. Things came to a head when the
chief discovered that his wife was having sexual relations with another man.
The chief said, "Now we have come to the end of the trail." He believed
that what his wife had done could not be repaired, for the chief's wife is
supposed to be respected as the mother of the village. He decided that the
village would have to be destroyed and that the people would have to go on
a long journey, leaving their wickedness behind, and build their lives all over
again.

He went into his kiva and sent for a young man who was his nephew. He
said to him, "My nephew, I have a task for you. You see that mountain out
there in the distance? Tomorrow morning get up early, run toward the
mountain until the sun rises. I want you to develop yourself until you
become swift, until you can reach that mountain, circle it, and return home
by the time the sun rises."

The young man did not question anything, because when an uncle tells
his nephew to perform a task, it is done without asking for explanations. He
arose early in the morning and went running toward the mountain. When
he had gone only partway the sun was coming up and he did not have the
strength to go further so he returned home. The next day he went further
before the sun rose, and the next day further still. Each day when he
returned he reported to his uncle, the kikmongwi.

On the fourth day he reported, "This morning I just reached the mountain before the sun rose."

The chief said, "That is good. Go on with the running for four more days."

And the fourth morning after that, the young man went to the mountain and returned home just as the sun was rising. The kikmongwi said to him, "It is good. You have become strong. Now, tomorrow you will rest, but the day after that I will have another task for you."

And so, two days later the young man came again to the kiva. His uncle, the chief, laid out four bundles of prayer feathers. He said to his nephew, "Select one paho from each bundle." The young man did that. The chief said, "Today you will go to the west where you see those peaks. You will find deer there. Select a buck that is in its prime. Get the spike horns from its antlers. In exchange, give him these prayer feathers."

So the young man went running west. He came to the place of the deer. He selected a buck that was in its prime and pursued it. The deer ran swiftly, but the young man was also very swift. He caught the buck and threw him down.

The deer spoke. He said, "Is my father going to be hard on me?"

The young man answered, "I have to do it, but I am sorry. Here are four prayer feathers to take with you to the spirit world. There you will live on in a spiritual form."

He killed the deer and took its horns, which he wrapped up in his kilt. Then he returned running to his village. He gave the horns to his uncle. His uncle said, "That is good. Now listen closely to what I am going to tell you about your next task."

The kikmongwi said, "I have prepared four masks and other medicine for you. Tomorrow go to the mountain out there. Put this medicine in your mouth." It was fire, so that when the young man breathed, flames would come out. Then the chief said, "Put on this mask." It was a Kiwan Kachina mask. "Now, on top of that one, place this mask." It was the mask of the Auheulani Kachina who appears in Soyalana, the winter solstice ceremony. "On top of that one, put on this mask." It was a Talavai Kachina, the one who comes to distribute beans at dawn on the last day of the Powamu festival. "On top of all of these masks," the kikmongwi said, "put this one on." It was a Masauwu mask, with red hair and a spotted face. The kikmongwi said, "When darkness falls, come running into the village and circle it four times. Then go to the highest roof, sing the song I am going to give you, and grind the corn-grinding stones together as if you were making meal."

The young man did as he was instructed. When the time came, he put the fire in his mouth and put the four masks over his face, the Masauwu mask on top. There is a great deal of symbolic meaning in these four masks. For one thing, they represent the four seasons. And the Masauwu mask on top, the fierce-looking one, represents death. It also represented the chief. And in addition to that, it was an omen of the chief's intentions. So there were several layers of meaning in the Masauwu mask alone, and the three other masks had additional meanings. The young man began running from the mountain where he was staying, and as he approached the village it was getting dark and most of the people were already in their houses. But one man was lying on the roof of one of the houses. The chief's nephew was breathing fire, and the man saw the flame approaching. He saw the chief's nephew go around the village four times and then climb to the roof of the highest house. There the young man, wearing all the masks and breathing flame, ground with the grinding stones and chanted this song:

The man who was watching him went to the kiva roof and tapped on it. He called down, "You men in the kiva! There's a strange thing going on up here! Something moves around the village breathing fire, and now it is up above grinding with grinding stones and singing!" [27] Someone answered, "Oh, is it you? You are always telling stories like that." The man said, "No, it is something ominous." They called back, "Do not disturb us. It's just your imagination again."

The following night the chief's nephew came again, running around the village four times and then going to the highest roof, where he chanted his song and ground with the grinding stones. That same man saw him, and he went to the kiva again and called down that a strange event was taking place. This time one person came up, and he saw the kikmongwi's nephew on the roof breathing fire and grinding the mealing stones together. He called into the kiva opening, saying, "Yes, it's true. There's some kind of a person or spirit breathing fire on the roof." There was laughing down below, and someone answered, "It's a ridiculous story. You two men are just alike."

On the third night the two men watched together, and this time when they called into the kiva everybody came up. They saw the fearsome figure running and breathing fire. They saw him grinding. They heard him singing.

They were worried. They wondered what it meant. Because everything came in fours, they expected that he would come the next night, and they made plans to capture the strange personage. So the next night while the kikmongwi's nephew was up on the roof grinding and singing, they blocked all the passageways in the village so that he could not get out. When he was through with his song he came down, but he could not find a way out of the village. They chased him one way and another until, finally, they caught him. They took him into the kiva, and in the light from the fire they saw the Masauwu mask. It was a terrifying sight.

They removed the Masauwu mask and laid it aside. They took off the Talavai mask and set it down. They took off the Auheulani mask, then the beautiful Kiwan mask, and at last the face of the kikmongwi's nephew was revealed. They said to him, "It appears that you are a bad omen. What is it? What is the meaning of the running, the breathing of fire, the masks?"

But the young man could not answer these questions. He said, "I don't know the meaning. I merely did what I was instructed to do."

They asked him, "Who was it that instructed you?" He answered, "My uncle, the kikmongwi."

They asked, "Why did he instruct you to do these things?"

The young man said, "Because someone seduced his wife, the mother of the village."

Now the people began to see how serious the matter was. They began to understand the meaning of the masks. They saw that the Masauwu mask was bringing a message to them. Still, they did not understand everything. They said to one another, "This young man meant to harm us. He must be killed."

The young man said, "I hope you will not kill me, because I was doing only what I was instructed to do by the kikmongwi."

They said, "Yes, we are going to kill you. That is the only thing we can do to deal with this bad omen."

The young man said, "Well, if that is how it is going to be, then this is what you are supposed to do. Bury me in the village plaza and leave my arm sticking out of the grave. This is the way it has to be done."

So they killed him immediately and buried him in the plaza with one arm protruding from the earth.[28] His thumb was folded over, so four fingers were pointed upward. Now, the next day when the people came into the plaza they saw that one of the four fingers was folded over and only three were still pointed upward. They wondered about it. The next morning they saw that the middle finger was folded down, and only two fingers were straight. The third morning only one finger was still pointing upward. The people didn't understand the meaning of it, but they were uneasy. On the fourth morning all four fingers were folded down, and the people began to understand that something awesome was about to happen.

Then the earth began to shake and the rain began to fall. Water came out of the cracks in the rocks. In the houses, water spurted out of the fireplaces. (In those days the fireplaces were in the corners of the rooms.) Where there was supposed to be fire, water was pouring out. The houses became flooded, and the people ran outside to keep from drowning. But the water was rising outside also. A large pond formed in the plaza where the young man had been buried. And from that pond Paleuleukang, the great water serpent, started to emerge. His head with the single horn came out, then his body. He raised his head high above the plaza, surveying the village.

Now, things didn't just happen by themselves. It was the kikmongwi who was responsible. He was a sorcerer or a wizard, and he had planned everything, just the way it happened. He never told his nephew why he needed the deer horns. He didn't inform him about the meaning of anything. But on that fourth day the kikmongwi took the deer horns and pushed them into the ground as if he was plowing with them. That was what disturbed the earth and caused the earthquake and the flood. And the boy who was buried in the plaza was transformed into Paleuleukang, the horned water serpent.

When the people saw him emerge they were terrified. They fled out of the village across their flooded fields until they reached high ground some distance away. They huddled together, not knowing what to do. Back in the village there were still some old people who were too feeble to run away. They remained in their houses, and as the water rose they climbed up on those high shelves that were used for storing cornmeal. The water lapped at the old people's clothes hanging down behind them. They say that some good spirit, out of compassion for those helpless old people, turned them into turkeys. Their clothing hanging down behind them became tails, and where the foam lapped at them the tails became streaked with white, just as turkey tails are today.

The people who had reached dry land were asking, "What are we going to do now?"

The elders said, "The only thing we can do to bring this catastrophe to an end is to offer Paleuleukang a young girl and a young boy as a sacrifice."

So they chose a young boy and a young girl from the Water Clan, because the kikmongwi who had caused the disaster was a Water Clan man. That was the clan that would have to make the sacrifice. They dressed the children in ceremonial clothes. The boy wore a kilt and had feathers in his hair, and they painted designs on his body. They put a wedding robe on the girl, the robe with the red and blue stripes that they call ateu'eu. They let out her hair and put eagle down on her head. Then they put prayer feathers into the children's hands and sent them back into the village. The children approached Paleuleukang. They stood at the edge of the pond and offered him the prayer feathers. Paleuleukang said, "Don't be afraid. Come closer." They waded into the pond and gave him the sacred feathers. He said, "Look here, where my skin is loose. Open it and get inside." They pulled the skin open and went in. Then Paleuleukang submerged and entered his kiva down below. That was when the earth stopped shaking and the water stopped spurting from the ground.

Now, when the people sent the boy and girl to Paleuleukang with the prayer feathers they assumed that they'd never see them again. They left their temporary camp and began to journey northward without knowing where they were supposed to go. But when the horned water snake brought the children into his kiva he removed his snakeskin and took the form of a human being. He spoke gently to them. He instructed them. He told them the things that the Water Clan and the other clans would have to know in order to survive. He instructed them about how the people from Palatkwa should live. He said, "Soon I am going to take you up and send you back to your families, and you must tell the people everything that you learn here. They will have a long journey. I will guide them by the star Suheu.[29] Let them follow that star. Tell them, 'Paleuleukang will protect you in your travels and give you a sign when it is time to build a temporary village and rest. When it is time to go on, Paleuleukang will give you another sign. Your destination is a place called Sichdukwi, Flower Mound.' "

Paleuleukang taught the children sacred chants. He made them sing the songs over and over again until they knew them by heart. He taught them the ceremonies that were to be performed once every year. He said, "I have a sacred name. I will tell it to you. But only one person of the Water Clan is to know what my sacred name is, and he will not divulge it to anyone else. When there is a ceremony and the people offer me prayer feathers, that person will face the south and say, 'Palatkwavay'ay (meaning At the Place of Palatkwa), I offer these pahos to you. Accept them. Take care of us. We need rain.' The Water Clan people must lead good lives. They must follow the way of good principles. This is what you must tell them: 'Whenever a stranger comes to the village, treat him well. Give him food to eat. When people are old and can't work hard any more, don't turn them out to shift for themselves, but take care of them as they once took care of you. Don't injure one another, because all beings deserve to live without harm being done to them. If you are attacked, defend yourselves, but don't go out seeking war.' "

After some days had gone by, Paleuleukang put on his snakeskin again and carried the boy and girl up to the plaza of the deserted village. But before he let them go he said, "There is one more thing. Take a piece of skin from the left side of my chest. This sacred piece of skin should be preserved to remind the people who I am and where they came from." The children protested. They didn't want to hurt Paleuleukang. But he insisted. So they took the skin and after that he set them on the ground and went down into his kiva. The children went looking for their families. And somewhere north of Palatkwa they found the main group, which still was not certain which way to go.[30] The children reported to the people everything that had happened and everything that Paleuleukang had said. So from there onward they were guided by the star Suheu.

They stopped at a place called Kunchalpi and remained there a number of years. After leaving Kunchalpi they went on to a place named Hohokyam, near Nuvakwiotaka (Chaves Pass). Then after some years they went on till they came to the Little Colorado River near where Winslow is today. There they built two villages, a large one called Homolovi and a small one a mile or so away called Tikri. Tikri was situated away from the water, along the edge of the cliff. (The last time I was there the walls were still visible.)

In time they had a sign from Paleuleukang and resumed their journey to the north, but some of the Water Clan branched off to the west and went on to settle where the Wupatki ruins are, north of Flagstaff. The ones who went to Wupatki didn't stay at that place very long. The main party going north followed a cloud that Paleuleukang sent to guide them. They stopped next at a place called Sikyatkiva, Yellow Bird Spring, which some people now call Bird Spring, and they built a village there and rested for a while. In time they went on north again to a spot called Little Ruin Mound, and from there the clans branched off from one another, you might say in three directions. Some went to Awatovi, some continued north toward First Mesa, and some went west toward Second Mesa.

Some of the Tobacco Clan and Rabbit Brush Clan, which are closely affiliated, must have gone to Awatovi, because at a later time a Tobacco Clan man from that village brought the rituals of three kiva societies to Walpi. I'll tell you about that later in connection with the Awatovi story. The Rabbit Brush Clan had taken its name during the journey from the south. There was a crying baby in the bunch, and its mother pulled up some rabbit brush and gave it to the baby to keep it quiet. It was from that event that the clan adoped its emblem. One group that didn't yet have a name arrived at a certain place near Shipaulovi just as the sun was rising, showing its forehead, as they say, and took the name Forehead or Sun Glow Clan.

The Water Clan and the Sand Clan, the parts that had not branched off, went to Keuchaptevela, and so did parts of the Rabbit Clan and the Tobacco Clan. Also, the Reed Clan and its affiliated Hawk and Eagle clans are supposed to have come from Palatkwa, though some people claim they originated over in the Rio Grande Valley.

As far as the Water Clan is concerned, it brought the One Horn ritual to the Hopis, the One Horn referring to the horn on Paleuleukang. This clan is supposed to have brought ritual paraphernalia from Palatkwa, including that Masauwu mask that the kikmongwi made his nephew wear on top of the three other masks. It is said that the Masauwu mask is still in the possession of the Water Clan in Walpi, but of course it has to be a copy of the original one, or maybe it actually originated here. And that piece of skin or flesh that is supposed to have been taken from Paleuleukang by the two children, they have that also. It is kept in one of the back rooms of the chief kiva. You can't tell what kind of skin it really is from looking at it. Whenever they make pahos for rain they always rub them on the skin. Then a Water Clan person takes the pahos to the Paleuleukang shrine and offers them toward Palatkwa. He is the one who knows Paleuleukang's secret name. In the midwinter ceremonies the Water Clan group—including the Sand Clan, the Tobacco Clan and the Hawk Clan—holds secret Palatkwa rituals in the back room of the kiva. Later they come out into the main part of the kiva and perform there. That's the only part of their ritual that we other clans can see.

That Auheulani mask—the one that the kikmongwi's nephew wore—they have one of those also in the midwinter ceremonies. The one who impersonates Auheulani appears in public with a female kachina on each side. He holds his thumbs folded over, and of course this relates to the folded thumbs of the kikmongwi's nephew when he was buried in the plaza at Palatkwa. He carries a long staff with feathers attached to the top. The top half of the staff is painted blue, and the bottom half is black, signifying the underworld where Paleuleukang lives.[31] This kachina person taps on the ground with the staff to let Paleuleukang know that they are performing his ritual according to his instructions. He chants by himself. When he gets to a certain part of the chant he sprinkles sacred meal. He goes through this four times, then he and the two women kachinas are led back to the kiva.

There's a young woman performing in these ceremonies. She represents the young girl who went down into Paleuleukang's kiva. There's also a personage representing the kikmongwi's nephew, the young man who could run without tiring. I speak of these things as if they were still going on. But the performance inside the kiva hasn't occurred since 1945 because they don't hold initiations for the four main kiva societies in Walpi any more.

However, they still have these initiations at Shongopovi. The Water Clan over there is still active. If the First Mesa people want to be involved in commemoration of Palatkwa they go to Shongopovi. In Walpi the Water Clan still ties sacred feathers for Paleuleukang and takes them to the shrines, but a lot of what we used to see isn't here any more. The Tobacco Clan and the Sand Clan also have rituals commemorating Palatkwa. Their ceremonials vary a little bit from those of the Water Clan.

The Basket Dancers—the women who perform the Lalakon Dance—their activities are related to those of the One Horn Society. The teachings of the One Horn are the things taught to the two young children, but primarily to the boy, by the horned water snake. But Paleuleukang taught the girl some special things that the Lalakon Society preserves. You might say that Lalakon is a women's affiliate of the One Horn.

They used to have an elaborate water snake play here on First Mesa with puppets, scenery and masks. It was called Paleuleukanti. It was a dramatic presentation depicting water snakes, Spider Grandmother and a number of other deities. Even though Paleuleukang is specifically identified with the clans that came from Palatkwa and with the One Horn Fraternity, this play wasn't put on by the One Horn group, but by several men who developed this festival presentation on their own. It was performed in the kiva, but it wasn't sacred, and anybody who wanted to could come and watch.[32]

One more thing about those Palatkwa clans. There are some Coyote Clan people here who claim their clan also came from Palatkwa. That's their claim, but the Water Clan and other Palatkwa clans don't accept it. According to my father and other members of the Water Clan, the Coyotes came from Hemis in New Mexico and don't have any part in the Paleuleukang ceremonials.

The Middle Village on First Mesa, Sichomovi, was established by the Water Clan. For a long time after the Tewas arrived here there was open space between Tewa Village and Walpi. Now Sichomovi occupies all that space. It was settled by the Water Clan as a branch-off from Walpi. Walpi didn't have any room to expand, but the Water Clan was increasing. So they asked the kikmongwi and the heads of the Snake and Bear clans, "Why can't we take over that open space and build houses there?"

The answer was, "Yes, you can take it over if you want to. But the Water Clan will have to take charge of that village and be responsible for everything. Whatever has to be done, the Water Clan will have to do it. You'll have to be responsible for the ceremonies over there, and see that things are done."

So the Water Clan moved in and started to build Sichomovi. After that, other people came in. Some of the Badger Clan came from Oraibi, and

Coyote Clan people who had been scattered from Sikyatki followed them. Their houses are over on the east side of the village. Later on, Mustard Clan people came from around Puye in New Mexico.[33] Those Puye people were T'hanos. When they left Puye to get away from the Spanish, some of them went to Laguna and Zuni, and the others came to Sichomovi. Today[1977— Ed.] a woman named Matilda Sihonka, of the Water Clan, is the mother of that village. But Sichomovi is really just an extension of Walpi.

I've given you a brief account of the Water Clan and how it came to be situated here on First Mesa. Of course, every clan has a story that tells about its wanderings. All that open country around here in all directions has evidence of the clans on their migrations. Look on the rocks where they left their signatures. Sometimes you'll find these clan marks in the middle of nowhere. Sometimes they're at the site of an old village. If you find a ruin, look around for the clan signs. Every clan has its own markings. If you see a horny toad, that's the Sand Clan. The Sun Clan is a circle with lines radiating from it and a face in the center. The Sun Glow, or Forehead, Clan just shows the top of the circle, the sun's forehead. The Water Clan draws three little half circles, concave sides down, looking like clouds, with straight lines coming straight down, meaning rain. The Horn Clan draws an antelope. Badger draws a badger footprint. Bear draws the footprint of a bear. If more than one clan stayed at a certain place, they'd all leave their markings. Of course they had no way of showing when they were at a certain place, but sometimes the sequence of markings can give a clue as to who was first and who came later.

The clans not only left their signs on the rocks, they left them on their pottery too. When a group abandoned a village to go on a journey, the pottery was too heavy to carry. They usually left the pottery behind, and when they settled at a new place they baked fresh pottery. So if you find pottery pieces at an old village site they may give you a clue as to who was there. Some of the designs on the pottery aren't clan marks, though. If you see a tadpole, that could mean that the pot was for holding ceremonial water. And of course some pots didn't have any painting on them at all. The pots used for cooking were grey, made of clay mixed with fine sand. And the grey rough surface pots, marked with thumb impressions, were for storage. They were made with a rough surface so they wouldn't slip when they were picked up. They didn't have any clan marks either. It was the smooth, decorated pots that told what clan made them.

The things I have been telling about the clans, I didn't really know much about them when I was growing up. You might say that there were different levels of knowledge in the villages. There were people like me who had picked up a little knowledge of traditions here and there, but who didn't know too much about the inner workings of things. Then there were the ones who'd been educated in the kiva societies. As I mentioned before, the individuals who had been initiated into the kiva groups, particularly the four main fraternities, were the "real" Hopis, and the rest of us were unfulfilled, like unripened corn. At least that's the way it was seen by the ones who knew the history and traditions of the clans and the mysteries of the kiva ceremonies.

If it hadn't been for my work as an interpreter at the Keam's Canyon Indian Agency I might never have become a member of the Kwakwanteu, or One Horn Lodge. Whenever Hopis came with problems, I interpreted for them and the Agency people, Hopi into English and English into Hopi. If a Hopi spokesman said something about a certain matter, I had to understand what was back of what he said and all the things that were implied but not spoken. I had to know something about the situation in his village, and how his clan stood in his village. My job was not only to translate words but to translate culture. After a while I began to feel that some of the village or clan spokesmen were holding back a little, not saying everything that was on their minds. If I asked them directly about this they were a little evasive and didn't give me good answers. But little by little I gathered that they didn't trust me to interpret faithfully for them because I didn't belong to one of the important kiva groups. Because of that, they felt I did not have an adequate understanding of a lot of things they were talking about. Because I didn't know the claims and traditions of the kiva societies, or how various persons fitted into the scheme of things, they felt I would not know what their point of view was based on or what their authority was. Once in a while one of those men told me confidentially, "If you join one of the important kiva groups and get to really know what persons and clans are significant to these questions, people will have more confidence in you."

As I said before, my father, Sitaiema, was a Water Clan man, and he was one of the top-ranking members of the Kwakwanteu, or One Horn Fraternity. He had some very important responsibilities. Among other things, he was the official Sun Watcher for the village. By his readings of the position of the sun, the village would know when all the various ceremonies were to take place. His observatory was out at the point of the mesa, at the south end. He had a notched stick, with the notches in groups of four, and he'd hold this notched stick in such a way as to measure the horizon and see exactly where the sun was coming up. There was a natural bowl in the rock, a kind of smoothed-out pothole, and he would record his readings inside that bowl. His sun readings set the calendar for all important events and indicated to the different clans when they were supposed to do various things. He'd begin in January with Pameuya.[34] They would have these free-for-all dances for a good time. Even the high muckamucks got involved, playing gambling games or doing other things to celebrate. Next the Sun Watcher would announce the date of the Bean Dance to the man in charge of the Bean Ceremony. Next, the planting season. He announced the time for planting corn in the fields from which the Niman dancers would later bring in the first corn. He announced everything through the year, and the whole cycle of ceremonial events was set by his sun readings.

Well, my father had always wanted me to be initiated into the One Horn Fraternity. (In translation, we call the kiva groups fraternities, societies or lodges.) Even before I was out of school he had called on a man named Nitioma to invite me to join and to sponsor me. There are different reasons why a certain person becomes a sponsor of a young man and sees him through an initiation. One circumstance is this: Let us say that a boy or young man had some kind of sickness. His parents would go to some elderly person with curative powers, a knowledge of "medicine," as that word is used by Indians. They would ask this man to do something for their son. The man would treat the sick boy and cure him. After that, of course, the boy owed something to the man who had made him well, but in curing the sick boy the man had assumed an obligation to him. That obligation was to sponsor the boy's initiation. The man would go to the parents and say, "I'd like to take your son into my lodge." If the parents agreed to that, and they usually did because they also had incurred an obligation, the man would become the boy's sponsor. In this kind of situation you can see another one of the invisible relationships that exist in a village. In my own case, I hadn't been sick, but my father, whom I hadn't seen much of when I was small, had it in his mind that he wanted to share his ceremonial knowledge with me and make me a true Hopi. He gave ceremonial cornmeal to Nitioma and asked him to take me in charge. The first time Nitioma approached me, I was still going to school in Keam's Canyon. He asked me if I was ready to be initiated, because the winter initiations were coming up soon. I was a little vague about it. I wasn't sure I wanted it. I told him I'd see if I could get my parents' permission.

Next time I was home in the village I let my mother and stepfather know about the invitation. But my uncles—my mother's brothers—heard about it and they were against it. They told my mother, "No, let things remain the way they are. Some of the things going on in those lodges could be dangerous to Albert. Let him just be a Tewa and stay out of those lodges. Even if his father is pushing for it, Albert shouldn't get involved. If Sitaiema comes around to talk about it, tell him we don't agree." In our Hopi and Tewa way, a boy's uncles have a lot of authority in such things, and so my mother told my father and Nitioma that I couldn't be initiated. But my father didn't let the matter die.

Now that I was finished with school and back at First Mesa, Nitioma came to me again. He said, "Son." I said, "Yes." He said, "Do you want to enter my lodge?" By this time I had already decided to go ahead with it despite the oppositon of my uncles. I realized that as translator for the Keam's Canyon Agency I had to know much more about the inner workings of Hopi life, how the people were ceremonially related, who were the moving forces. So I told Nitioma, "Yes, I'm ready now." He said, "Good, then it's settled. I'll prepare for it." By that he meant he'd start weaving a ceremonial sash and kilt for me. A person's sponsor was supposed to do that. He'd weave those complicated designs into the kilt and sash to represent elements in our present life and the life to come. Those weavings aren't just to look artistic, they are symbolic.

The initiations into the four important societies take place in November in connection with the New Fire Ceremony. The four fraternities are these: the Kwakwanteu, usually called the One Horn after the horned water snake of Palatkwa; the Aalteu, which simply means Horn, but usually called Two Horn to distinguish it from the One Horn. It's based on clans having names of animals with two horns, such as deer and antelope. Any of those clans can use the Aal kiva. The other two are the Wuwuchimteu and the Tat-aukyameu. On the day of Lalakon, the Women's Basket Dance, in September, our chakmongwi, or crier chief, made the announcement that initiations were going to be held. He said, "Everyone who has someone to be initiated, get ready."

The families that had young men who were going into one or another of the lodges made preparations. One of the things to be done was to provide for a jackrabbit feast that would be given when the first stage of the initiation was finished. There was a kind of ceremonial jackrabbit hunt in honor of each of the boys to be initiated. The boy's sponsor was usually present at the hunt, but if he couldn't be there a member of the Rabbit Clan took his place. And when they'd caught enough jackrabbits for the feast they'd bring them to the initiate's mother. The boy himself participated in the hunt, dressed up something like a kachina, and he had a rabbit stick made for him by his sponsor. All of this was what you might call a preliminary festival.

The day that Nahtna—our initiation ritual—was to take place, the boys—really young men—didn't go anywhere, just stayed home waiting for their sponsors to come and get them and take them to the kiva. It was around five in the afternoon when the sponsors started to call for their initiates. My sponsor, Nitioma, couldn't see very well and it was hard for him to get around, so he sent his nephew for me with a blanket. I had to take off all my clothes except my briefs. All I wore was the blanket, and it was the same with the other fellows who were being initiated. We went to the Wuwuchim kiva in Walpi, and Nitioma was waiting for me at the kiva entrance.

Before we went down he gave me some sacred meal and said, "Now, Albert, do you want to reconsider? This is your last chance. Are you serious about going through with it? If not, you can still turn away from it. It's up to you."

I said, "No, I don't want to turn back. I've made up my mind." He said, "All right. Sprinkle your cornmeal into the kiva." After I'd sprinkled my cornmeal into the kiva opening he took me down.

All four of the societies were gathered inside. But as I said before, the One Horn separates its rituals from those of the other three fraternities. From the top of the ladder down, a blanket hung across the kiva to divide the One Horn people off from the Two Horn, the Tataukyameu and the Wuwuchimteu. There were two men standing at the base of the ladder. If a boy belonged to the One Horn group, one of the men took him to that side, behind the blanket. If a boy belonged to one of the other groups, a man would guide him over there. Our part of the activities was completely curtained off from the other fraternities.

The first phase of the rituals was bringing the sacred fire out of the wood. That is where the New Fire Ceremony got its name. Everyone sang the sacred fire chant. Each group had its own fire stick or drill. The points were set against tinder that would catch fire when the friction generated enough heat. There were four men at each stick. One man would rotate the stick swiftly between his palms, his hands gradually moving downward. Then another man would take over at the top of the stick, keeping it rotating. When his hands had moved toward the bottom, another man would take hold. One after another they took turns, always keeping the stick in motion. When the wood underneath smouldered and sparks were visible, someone called, "The fire has come out!" Each group generated its own sacred fire this way.

The Two Horn, Tataukyam and Wuwuchim, groups took their new fire and went out, to their own kiva. We One Horn stayed where we were. After that those other three groups conducted their ceremonies separately from us. We stayed in the chief kiva till quite late. Then someone went up and looked around. He said, "Well, it looks safe. There doesn't seem to be anybody up here. Let's go." We all went from there to the One Horn Kiva with our new fire. Everyone was chanting. When we got to our own kiva my sponsor rubbed me with ice-cold water from an earthen jar. He said, "Now, Albert, I want you to drink some water, as much as you can. It's the last water you'll have for a long time. Drink slowly, don't hurry." I drank the whole jar of water. Nitioma had told me the truth. It was the last water I tasted for four days. That was part of the test they were putting us to, making us endure thirst.

There were four of us One Horn initiates, and for four days we sat in the kiva with blankets around us, mostly in one position, with hardly any breaks. They gave us white piki to eat once in a while, but no water. We couldn't eat the piki because our mouths were too dry. Some of those old-timers would bring drinking water into the kiva, but not for us. After a while we got so that we could *smell* water on the far side of the kiva. I never knew it was possible to smell water. The fellow sitting next to me said, "Albert, that man coming down the ladder is bringing water with him. Don't you smell it?" I said, "Yes, I smell it." And I really did. Another thing, those old-timers would always be talking about water, how it flowed down the Little Colorado, and what such and such a lake looked like. It was for our benefit, of course. Old man Charlie was always talking about Grand Canyon and all the water that went through there, and how he used to swim in it when he was young. It made us pretty mad.

Once a day, in the evening, we were allowed to stand up and stretch ourselves. Usually it was when the men of the other lodges arrived up above our kiva with their initiates and chanted sacred songs. After they'd gone and when there weren't many people around, our sponsors took us out of the kiva and walked us to the end of the village with blankets over our heads so that we couldn't be recognized. Then at a certain place where we couldn't be seen from the village, they took the blankets off us and rubbed us down to loosen our muscles. Now, as I said, this was in November, and it was pretty cold to be standing there without any clothes on. We felt a little better when we got back to the kiva because there was a fire down there, but then we had to get into those cramped sitting positions again. Once in a while they let us put our heads on the floor and get a little sleep, but it wasn't long before we heard someone thumping on the kiva roof and calling, "All right, time to wake up." So then we sat up again. There was always something going on. From time to time the One Horn members would gather and sing sacred chants.

The other three lodges also had something going all the time for their initiates. They had their own tests, and the Two Horn Society was in charge. Often they took the initiates here and there, made them run to distant places or do unpleasant things. The boys had to do whatever they were told, even if it was nonsensical. They were supposed to be learning discipline and how to endure hardship, like you hear about U.S. Marine training.

Of course, most of the things that happened in their initiation ceremonies were kept secret from us, just as our doings were kept secret from them. But later I learned that one of the things their initiates had to .do was to run all the way to Huckyatwi, Badger Butte, about four miles from Walpi. You can see that butte from the west side of Walpi where the Alosoka shrine is. There was an Alosoka shrine at Huckyatwi, too, and rituals were carried out at that place. Alosoka is closely connected with the New Fire Ceremony activities of those three lodges. Well, in the evening they'd make the initiates race back from Huckyatwi, and this would take place in the dark. People would be watching from the top of the mesa for fires and other signals from the valley, and they would call down into our kiva, "They're moving this way. . . . We see their light at such and such a place."

In the kiva, we One Horn people would be chanting for the welfare of the Alosoka initiates. When our watcher up above announced, "Now they're at the foot of the village," we stopped chanting. The initiate who won the race back to Walpi was met by his sponsor, who escorted him back to their kiva while chanting, "My mother is very fertile. Why is my mother fertile? Because of my father." Where the chant says "my mother" it refers to the earth, and "my father" means sun and rain, the forces that make things grow. That is what Alosoka is all about, bringing things to fruition.

We One Horn initiates had our own running ordeal. They took us northeast to that place where the Tewa inscription is on the cliff wall, telling about the battle with the Utes. A little beyond there at a place not far from the spring, they said, "Now, boys, line up. We are going to test you. Start running. Run as fast as you can. Don't stop. We older men will follow you and catch you." Well, we tried to run but we couldn't. Our legs were weak. How could we run after we'd been sitting in that cramped position so long, and without any water? We could hardly hobble. But we tried. They caught us before we'd gone very far. I don't know what the purpose of that test could have been. Maybe it was just to put us in our place and teach us young ones a little humility, I don't know. I heard a story about one of those tests that took place in the old days. There was a good strong boy, or young man, among the initiates, and when they were told to run he just took off. They couldn't catch him. He got further and further away from the village, and the men couldn't even get close to him. At last he disappeared out there in the distance somewhere, and it was the last they ever saw of him. He never came back.

When we returned to the kiva we brought lots of firewood with us to keep the main kiva fire going. It kept the kiva warm, of course, but it was also the only thing we had for light. There weren't any lamps of any kind.[35] The person who fed the fire and kept it going was called the fire chief. The sacred fire that had been brought out of the wood in the New Fire Ceremony could not be used for any utilitarian purpose. If someone wanted to light a pipe, it had to be from the main kiva fire. A Tobacco Clan man was in charge of filling the pipes. As for the New Fire, it had to be extinguished when the ceremonies ended.

Eventually the fourth day came and we initiates were liberated from our sitting position. Our sponsors said, "All right, boys, now you can get up and stretch yourselves." Well, we rolled around, rubbed our legs to get the circulation going, and looked a little more alive. However, we didn't get any water yet. Before we could drink anything they took us into the plaza, washed our bodies down with cold water and scrubbed our heads with yucca suds. You might say it was a kind of christening, because we received our new names. That was when I got the name Eutawisa, meaning Close In the Antelopes. Afterwards they took us back into the kiva and rubbed us all over with cornmeal. When that was done they offered us our first water. But they saw to it that we'd drink properly and not gulp. My sponsor said, "First thing, just rinse your mouth and spit the water out. Now let just a little trickle down your throat. All right, now take a small swallow. Take it easy. Rest for a while, then take a little more." After not having had any water for four days, it was hard to swallow. My throat didn't want to accept the water. But by taking it in easy stages I was able to drink. I don't remember any time in my whole life when water tasted so good.

The next morning our One Horn Society put on its last dance of the New Fire Ceremony in the Walpi plaza with the whole village watching. As we initiates came up from the kiva we imitated the emergence from the underworld. We had our arms locked going up the ladder (they say that's the way it was when the people came up to the Fourth World inside the bamboo), and an older man was calling, "Be careful! Be careful!" He was imitating the mockingbird who guided the people upward in the emergence. After the public dance we returned to the kiva, and in the evening they brought us all that jackrabbit food that our families had prepared for us. We had a feast.

About that name they gave me, Eutawisa—it came from my sponsor. He belonged to the Deer Clan, related to the Antelope, that came to Walpi from Tokonave or Navajo Mountain. Deer and Antelope belong to the Horn Clan group, they're affiliated. So the name that Nitioma gave me referred to his clan. But the meaning of the name can be explained another way. Nitioma told me, "When we arrived here from Tokonave, the Bear and Snake clans closed off the village to us at first, barred the path. We Deer Clan people and our relatives, the Horn, Antelope and Grass, were, you might say, closed in. So the name refers to how we were barred when we first arrived at First Mesa."

Now, that four-day ordeal I went through during Nahtna was really only the first stage of my initiation. There are four degrees you have to go through. The second stage is Soyalana, or Winter Solstice Ceremony, in December. After that, in February, comes Invaya, the Bean Planting Ceremony. On the other mesas they call it Pachaveu. Then, finally, in July, the Niman Ceremony, when the kachinas are supposed to be departing for their home over at San Francisco Peaks. All through those ceremonies your sponsor will be teaching you, as they say, mouth to ear. After the New Fire Ceremony is over he talks to you in the kiva. He explains things to you. Tells you that you must be disciplined in your behavior. "Remember that you are a Hopi. Treat everybody equally, and with respect, just the way you yourself want to be treated. If somebody comes to your home, feed him, give him something to drink. Remember that there's someone watching you, the Great Spirit. He's here with you. Conduct yourself as you should. When you get up in the morning, look towards the east where the light comes from. Pray that you'll live like a decent person and have a long life. You're a Hopi now."

What they mean when they say "You're a Hopi now" is that you're obligated to try to conduct yourself without any flaws. Of course we all have flaws, but we're supposed to make every effort to be models of decent behavior. When you've gone through all four of the ceremonies you're regarded as a full-fledged Hopi. But the teaching goes on. Your sponsor continues through the years teaching you traditions and stressing good behavior. Without going through these initiations with a "godfather," or sponsor, informing and teaching a young person, how can the generation coming up now learn standards of good living and be educated in the traditions? The prospects don't look very good, because the initiations into the main kiva societies here on First Mesa have ended. They still have initiations in Shongopovi, but they came to an end in Oraibi in 1906, when the village broke in two. The Oraibis are trying to revive the ceremonies and the initiations, but they really can't do it, and I'll explain about this a little later in connection with the Oraibi affair.

Most of the year I'm not here on First Mesa, because I have a place down at Parker on the Colorado River Reservation, but many times when I've come here for a visit or for ceremonial reasons I've asked the head of our One Horn Society, "When are you going to have initiations?" He usually

said, "Well, we've been talking about it, but we've been waiting for the
Wuwuchim Society to get together with us and agree on a time. But they've
got no headman any more and no one wants to take the responsibility." The
last leader of the Wuwuchim was Namoki, and he's dead now. You see how
it is. The clans or persons who are supposed to lead things don't want to
take the responsibility. The last initiation I attended was in 1939, when I
was sponsoring a young man for membership. He's gone now too. He was
digging ditches one time when the land caved in on him and killed him.

Of course there is a lot about our One Horn rituals that I can't reveal,
because I'm honor bound to keep these things secret. But I'll tell you one
thing. That anthropologist [Jesse Walter] Fewkes has described some of our
One Horn ceremonies,[36] and I can say he was a remarkable man. To my
knowledge, he was the only white man they ever allowed to come into the
kiva during the rituals. In fact, he became an initiate. None of us in the One
Horn can find any fault with the way he described the initiations and other
ceremonies. I had his book once. I showed it to some of our One Horn
people, and they said to get rid of it because it was too accurate and told
too much about what went on in the kiva. Fewkes had a brilliant mind. He
even drew a picture of the One Horn altar from memory and described all
of our sacred paraphernalia. I wish I still had that book.

I've seen other books written about Hopi sacred life, and many of them
aren't worth the paper they're printed on. There's one book called *The
Book of the Hopi*, by White Bear Fredericks and Frank Waters. It's really a
hodgepodge of misinformation. Quite a few Hopis were upset by that book,
but their reasons weren't the same ones that applied to Fewkes's writings. In
this case a lot of people felt that the book was full of inaccuracies and
sometimes was pretty farfetched. As I heard it, White Bear went around
getting information from different people, recording it on tape. Then this
stuff was turned over to Waters. In the first place, White Bear was never
initiated into any of the four important kiva societies, so he didn't have the
knowledge firsthand. He just went to the old-timers around Oraibi and got
them to tell him things. A lot of what they told him just isn't so, but he
wasn't in a position to know whether the information was true or false.
They must have told him this and that just to get rid of him. Some of the
stuff sounds like pure invention on the part of whoever he was talking to.
Then there were things that, if true, weren't familiar at all to people in my
One Horn group at Walpi. The book talks about three stone tablets with
pictographs, supposedly given to the Bear Clan by their protective spirit.
Maybe there are such tablets, since Waters claims to have seen one of them
at Oraibi. All I can say is that I never heard of them. And I believe that if
genuine Bear Clan tablets really exist, our Bear Clan people on First Mesa

would have wanted to give that information to members of the kiva societies. Of course, there are plenty of contradictions in the Hopi traditions. There have been many discussions and arguments in the kivas about them. Nevertheless, quite a few things in the Waters–White Bear book are so ridiculous that no knowledgeable person can accept them.

Then there's a personal narrative by Don Talayesva, called *Sun Chief*. It is all about his life and experiences. I knew Don when we were boys at the Keam's Canyon school. That was the last I saw of him for a long while. After Keam's Canyon, he went off to the Sherman Indian School at Riverside, California. He told a lot of things in his book that were true in his experience among the Oraibis. If there's any fault to find with the book it's that he talked about a lot of personal things, like his adventures with women, that most Indians wouldn't want to drag out in public. I think those editors at Yale who worked with him on the book must have pushed him into it. "Tell us about this, tell us about that," and so on. Maybe I am too old fashioned, but I find these things kind of embarrassing and not very illuminating. Another book that gave me the same feeling was *Son of Old Man Hat*. That one was by a Navajo.[37] Maybe my reactions are just a matter of taste. But the main thing I want to say is that if you really want to know something about Hopi ceremonial life and traditions, you have to go to Fewkes.[38]

There was an anthropologist working here around 1920, a woman, and she was supposed to know a lot about Pueblo Indians. The way she saw it, we Hopis and Tewas were just more Pueblos to her. I guess we really are, but our traditions can't be dumped in the same pot with the traditions of the Rio Grande people. Her name was Parsons, and I can't speak with authority on all the things she wrote about our eastern cousins. But she wrote one article about us that I've heard of. She had somebody who claimed to be a Tewa-Hopi, called Crow Wing, put down on paper all the things he did from the time he got up till the time he went to sleep. He must have given her a lot of misinformation over a period of time, according to what I've been told about the piece. For one thing, none of us here on this mesa ever heard of anybody by the name of Crow Wing living in Sichomovi. Another thing, this fellow claimed to be the keeper of one of the sacred old Tewa masks. There's nothing to that claim at all. There were four keepers of the old Tewa masks at that time, four men named Laylo, Ta'ay, Cochaase and Naylay. Nobody else.[39]

Well, after I passed through all the stages of my initiation into the One Horn, the Hopis came to know that I had a good understanding of who played what part in the ceremonial scheme of things, which men were the sources of authority or knowledge in the villages, and they became more trustful of me as translator for the Agency. Sometimes a person would ask me what kiva society I belonged to, and when I said "One Horn," that ended any doubts they might have had. They realized that I was a full-fledged Hopi as well as a Tewa, and that I was an "insider" in the ceremonial life of the villages. I acted as interpreter from 1914 to 1945. I did other work too, like shovelling coal and driving wagons, but whenever they needed a translator they sent for me.

In that job I learned a lot about the Hopi language. For one thing, it isn't spoken quite the same in the different villages. It varies from place to place. Even villages on the same mesa, such as Shongopovi, Shipaulovi and Mishongnovi, used to have their own speaking styles. You might call them dialects. Oraibis speak a kind of singsong Hopi. Second Mesa speaks kind of gruff, their inflections are different. People at the Keam's Canyon Agency accepted First Mesa as standard, and they liked to have a First Mesa person translating for them. Some of those Oraibis who'd been to school spoke better English than I did, but they weren't in demand as interpreters because of their dialect. Some people wonder why the language should be spoken a little differently in the various villages. One reason is that in the old days the villages on the three mesas were somewhat isolated from one another. Each village thought of the others as foreign tribes.

Don't forget that non-Hopi tribes actually settled around here at different times. Most of them were Eastern Pueblos who spoke Keresan, Zunian, Tiwa or Tewa. Over on Second Mesa, and here on First Mesa too, we had several Eastern Pueblo villages. Also on Third Mesa. The Awatovis had a good many Lagunas and Hemis people mixed in. Those groups could have affected Hopi speech on the three mesas.

Then there were the clans that actually joined the Hopi villages. Those clans brought different idioms and languages with them, and it stands to reason that some of the characteristics of their speech were absorbed into the Hopi way of talking. It wasn't just the Eastern Pueblos, either. There were Shoshonean speakers from up north, like the Snake and Horn clans. Where the Water, Tobacco and Sand clans really came from we don't know, but we're told they came from far to the south. It would be reasonable to expect that they didn't talk Hopi. According to what we've been told, the Hopis absorbed Pimas, Yumas, Coconinos, Apaches, Paiutes, Utes, Navajos and even some Sioux. Most of that took place in the distant past when the clans were coming in. I think it must have had an influence on the speech of the various villages so that they handled the Hopi language a little differently.

While I was working at the Agency I had to work with Navajos frequently, so over a period of time I picked up quite a bit of the Navajo

Nᴜᴠᴀʏᴏɪʏᴀᴠᴀ, Bɪɢ Fᴀʟʟɪɴɢ Sɴᴏᴡ. "When I was initiated into the One Horn Society they gave me a ceremonial name, Eutawisa, meaning Close In the Antelopes."

WALPI, SEEN FROM THE NORTHEAST, AT THE TURN OF THE CENTURY. "The main body [of the Snake Clan] came to First Mesa. . . . Masauwu, the original owner of the land, was said to be living up on top of the mesa where Walpi is today."—*Photo by Edward S. Curtis, copyright 1907. From the manuscript collection of the Museum of Northern Arizona.*

WALPI, LOOKING TOWARD THE SOUTHERN POINT OF FIRST MESA, IN THE 1890s. "Life will be hard in this place, but no one will envy us. No one will try to take our land away. This is the place where we will stay."—*Photo by J. W. Hildebrand, probably taken in February 1896. From the manuscript collection of the Museum of Northern Arizona.*

Tewa Village in the 1880s, Looking North. "You'll notice that quite a few of the houses had second stories up above. . . . I myself was born in an upper level house." The highest roof in the background group of houses was the signal and watch tower, from which could be observed the progress of ceremonial events south of the plaza, and signals sent to the other First Mesa villages. In the center of the plaza can be seen a stone shrine.—*From the collection of the National Anthropological Archives. Photo by John K. Hillers of the Bureau of American Ethnology, exact date not recorded, but prior to 1891.*

Tewa Village Today, Facing the Same Direction but at Ground Level. The upper-tier houses are gone, some old buildings have cement-block front walls, and electricity has invaded the plaza. But the signal and watch tower, though shrunken, is visible, and the stone shrine remains, reinforced with concrete.

Tsewageh, the Rio Grande Village from Which the Tewas Came to First Mesa, Once Stood on This Ground. Nothing but pottery fragments now remain visible. Across the dale is the low ridge with a stratum of white rock running through it, from which Tsewageh took its name.

Opposite:
The Shrine Which Marks the Southern Boundary of Tewa Village. It was at this place that the leader of the Tewas prophesied that they would keep their identity and not become Hopis. The centerpiece of the shrine is a large chunk of petrified wood. (The stacked wood just happened to be there when this picture was taken.)

SITE OF THE FIRST TEWA SETTLEMENT AFTER THEIR ARRIVAL IN HOPI COUNTRY. "They weren't welcomed immediately. The Walpis let them settle a little below the mesa on that low ridge on the east side, but wouldn't let them come any closer." In the background on the right is the southern tip of First Mesa where Walpi is situated.

First Mesa's Original Day School. "I was five or six when I first went to the day school below the mesa at Polacca. It was a small stone building that belonged to an uncle of mine, of the Tobacco Clan, and it was used as a temporary school until they finished building the new day school. The old building is still there, and now it's gone back to the Tobacco Clan."

ALBERT YAVA AND HIS HALF SISTER, PININI. "My half sister, Pinini (her married name is Chloris Anah), still has my diploma hanging in her house in Tewa Village."

ALBERT YAVA WITH HIS SON-IN-LAW, DEWEY HEALING, WHO ASSISTED IN THE PREPARATION OF THIS BOOK OF RECOLLECTIONS. As chairman of the Hopi Tribal Council in 1958, his name appears as a litigant in the *Healing* v. *Jones* suit against the Navajos over disputed land.

ALBERT YAVA'S FATHER, SITAIEMA. "Among other things, he was the official Sun Watcher for the village. By his readings of the position of the sun, the village would know when all the various ceremonies were to take place."—*Photo by Walter Collins O'Kane, by permission of Mrs. Henry S. Bothfeld.*

ALBERT YAVA AT AGE 65.—*Photo by Walter Collins O'Kane, by permission of Mrs. Henry S. Bothfeld.*

Lamehva, a Spring Below the Second Mesa Village of Shipaulovi. Here, according to some traditions, the Reed Clan people were created by Spider Grandmother and her grandsons, the Warrior Brothers.

Eroded Walls of Masipa, Where the Bear Clan Migrations Came to an End. "Shongopovi is supposed to have been our first village—the old Shongopovi, that is, built down below the mesa at the place called Masipa. But from the evidence, you'd have to say that those Bear Clan people weren't actually the first to settle in this region."

YAVA'S SHEEP CAMP SPRING. The stone retaining wall had been built by people who once lived on a nearby knoll. "It was a gift from those old-timers who had lived in the village up above before it became a ruin."

YAVA AT HIS SHEEP CAMP. "In my spare time I built a stone house and a storage building near the spring."

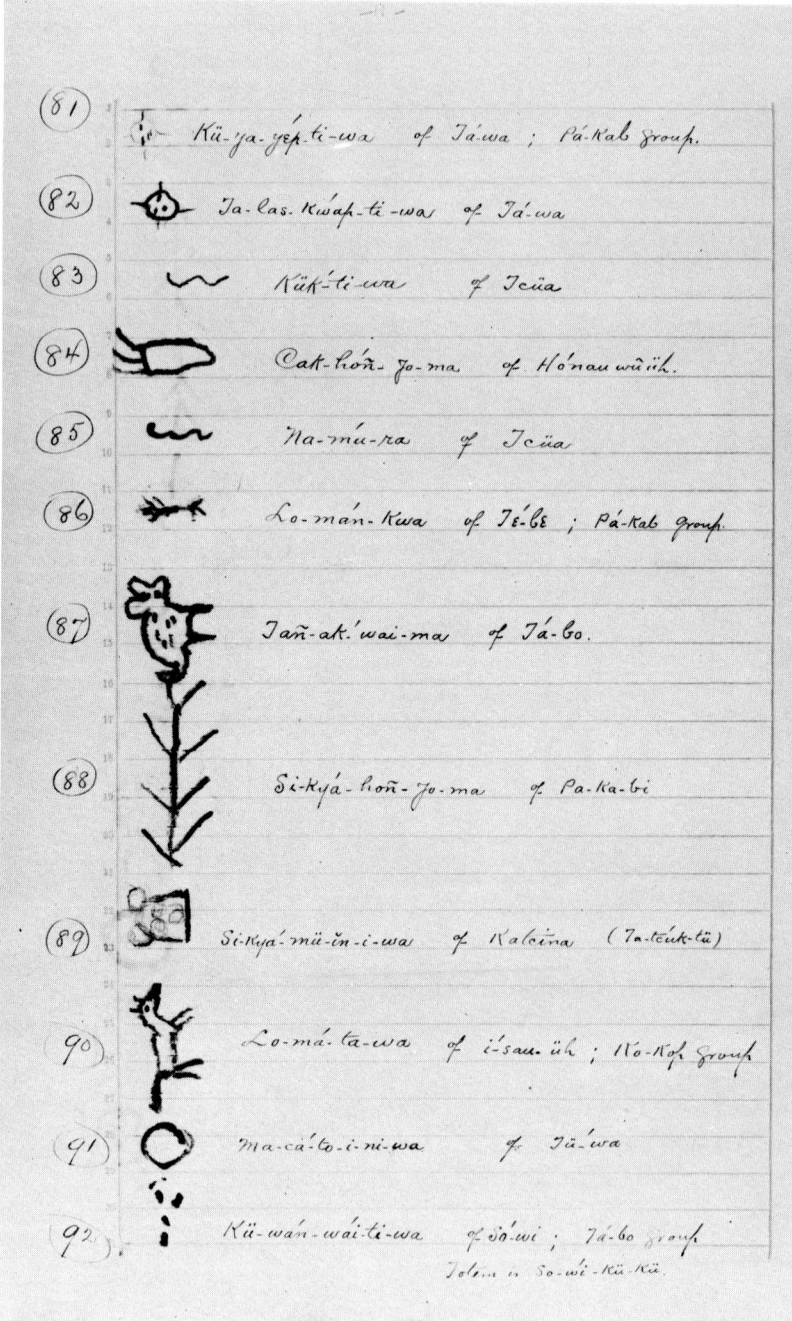

(81) Kü-ya-yép-ti-wa   of Tá-wa ; Pá-Kab group.

(82) Ta-las-Kwáp-ti-wa   of Tá-wa

(83) Kük-ti-wa   of Icüa

(84) Cak-hoñ-jo-ma   of Hó-nau wüüh.

(85) Na-mú-ra   of Icüa

(86) Lo-mán-Kwa   of Té-bɛ ; Pá-Kab group.

(87) Tañ-ak-'wai-ma   of Tá-bo.

(88) Si-Kyá-hoñ-jo-ma   of Pa-Ka-bi

(89) Si-Kyá-mü-in-i-wa   of Kalcina   (Ta-tcük-tü)

(90) Lo-má-ta-wa   of i-sau-üh ; Kó-Kof group

(91) ma-cá-to-i-ni-wa   of Tá-wa

(92) Kü-wán-wái-ti-wa   of Sö-wi ; Tá-bo group
Totem in So-wi-Kü-Kü.

Two Pages of Signatures from the Hopi Petition of 1894 to "The Washington Chiefs." (Text on pp. 165.) The "marks" or drawings represent specific clans or, sometimes, clan groupings: 81, 82, Sun Clan; 83, Snake Clan; 84, Bear Clan; 85, Snake Clan; 86, Reed Clan; 87, Rabbit Clan; 88, Reed Clan; 89, Kachina Clan; 90, Coyote Clan; 91, Sand, or Earth, Clan; 92, Rabbit Clan; 113,

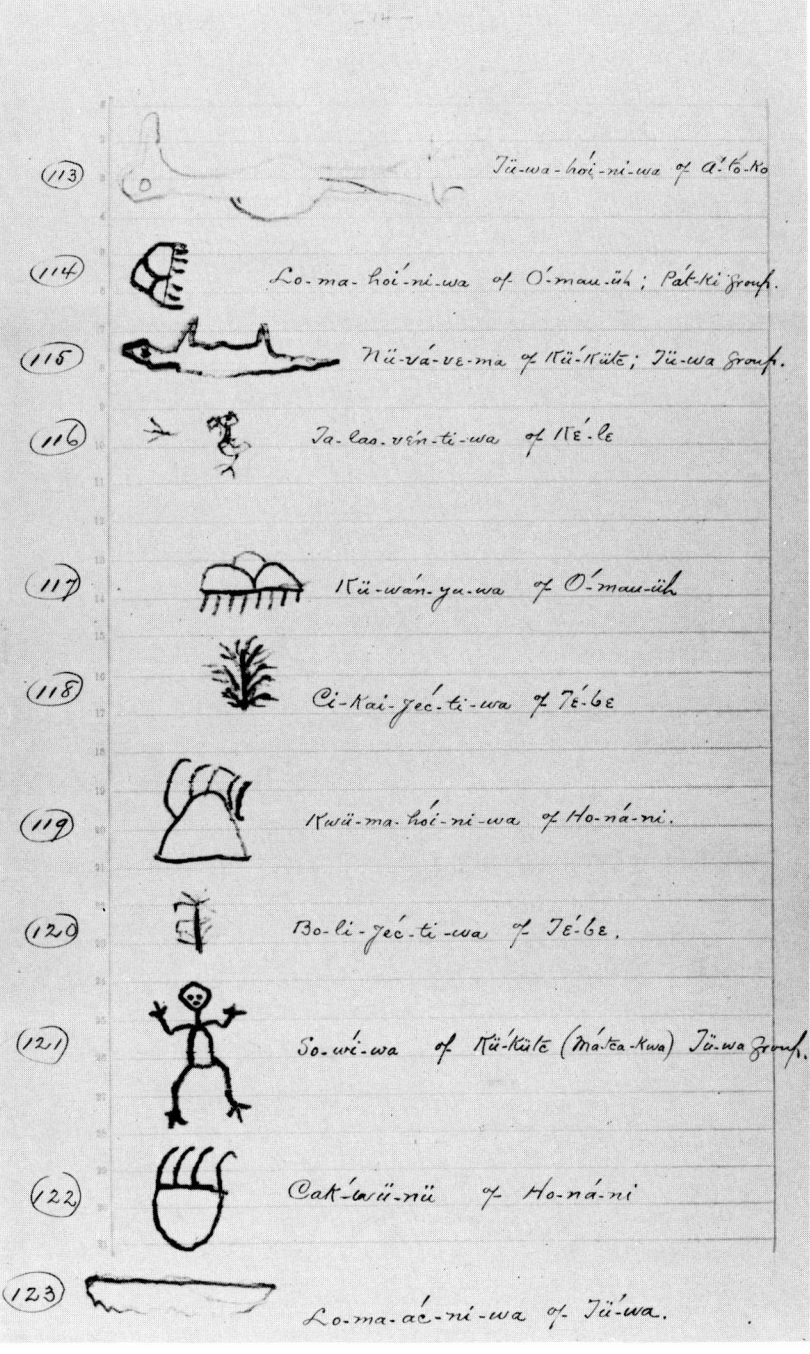

(113) Tü-wa-hoí-ni-wa of A·´ó·Ko

(114) Lo-ma-hoí-ni-wa of O·´mau-üh; Pat-ki group.

(115) Nü-vá-ve-ma of Kü-´Kütc; Tü-wa group.

(116) Ja-lao-vén-ti-wa of Ké·´le

(117) Kü-wán-yu-wa of O·´mau-üh

(118) Ci-Kai-jéc-ti-wa of Té-´be

(119) Kwü-ma-hoí-ni-wa of Ho-ná-ni.

(120) Bo-li-jéc-ti-wa of Té-´be.

(121) So-wí-wa of Kü-´Kütc (Má·ta-Kwa) Tü-wa group.

(122) Cak-´wü-nü of Ho-ná-ni

(123) Lo-ma-ác-ni-wa of Tü-´wa.

Crane Clan; 114, Water, or Rain-Cloud, Clan; 115, Lizard Clan; 116, Pigeon Hawk Clan; 117, Water, or Rain-Cloud, Clan; 118, Reed Clan; 119, Badger Clan; 120, Reed Clan; 121, Lizard Clan; 122, Badger Clan; 123, Sand, or Earth, Clan. The Hopi Petition is in the care of the National Archives.—*Smithsonian Institution photos.*

"Look on the Rocks Where They Left Their Signatures." This rock inscription on the cliffside below Walpi represents the Star Deity (Heart-of-the-Sky). The crescent-shaped face, representing the moon, is surmounted by a four-pointed star. In one hand he holds clouds and rain, in the other, lightning. On the right, above the lightning, is a symbol of the four sacred directions. This deity is sometimes personated as a kachina.

language. Also, some Mexican Spanish. Over in Oklahoma I'd worked for a
German harness maker, and I learned some German from him, but that
language wasn't of any use at Keam's Canyon.

I don't think I've said much about the Coyote Clan, only that those
people originally came to Hopi country from Hemis over on the Rio
Grande. You have to keep in mind that the Coyote and Water Coyote are
really separate groups. The Water Coyotes came from the north. The
Coyotes and the affiliated Fire Clan were the ones that settled Sikyatki, a
large village at the base of First Mesa, on the east side, about a mile north
of Tewa Village and Walpi. There's nothing but ruins there now, but you
can still see that it was an extensive settlement. Sikyatki was on the high
ground, and down below you can see the fields, thirteen of them, marked off
by neat parallel rows of stones. If you are coming from the east on the
blacktop road, just before you get to Polacca you will notice twin mounds
on top of the mesa. There was a village up there called Kukeuchomo.
Directly below that, close to the mesa wall, is where Sikyatki was. We were
told by our old people that Sikyatki and Kukeuchomo were related villages.
Kukeuchomo was a kind of guard post for Sikyatki. Those people seem to
have been Coyotes and Fire Clan also, with some Corn Clan people mixed
in. Of course, Sikyatki must have contained a number of clans, but it was
the Coyote and Fire groups that established it, and they were the ruling
clans. The guard-post village, Kukeuchomo, could spot strangers coming on
either side of the mesa, and it was so situated that it also offered some
protection from a possible attack from the Keuchaptevela side. There were
houses on both of the twin mounds. On one mound the houses were facing
east, and on the other they were facing west. South of this mesa-top village,
there was another one a little closer to the gap. It was called Terkinovi, and
was a Bear Clan settlement that might have been there before Sikyatki
came into being. They had terraced gardens on the west side of the mesa.
Possibly those Bear Clan people eventually went to Keuchaptevela.

But Sikyatki was the main settlement over there. It was built and possibly
it died long before the Spanish arrived in Hopi country. The Spanish
explorers and the Catholic missionaries never mentioned Sikyatki in their
historical writings, though they mentioned all the other main Hopi villages.
So I think Sikyatki was gone by that time. There are quite a few different
stories about Sikyatki and how it came to an end, but many of them are just
not true, and some are silly.

There were a number of anthropologists around here in the 1890s and the
early 1900s. They got information from various persons that Sikyatki was

destroyed by the Keuchaptevela people. That story is false. Whoever told it that way had got Sikyatki mixed up with Awatovi. There's always some of this confusion, with people telling things they don't really know or understand. Awatovi was destroyed, but Sikyatki wasn't destroyed by anybody, just the elements. It was abandoned. Those houses stood there a long time. It was the abandonment that dispersed the Coyote Clan to the other villages. I will give you the Sikyatki story as it was given to us First Mesa people, who were the ones immediately involved. I believe this version is nearer the truth than any of the others, though there may be details here and there that were added by an enthusiastic narrator somewhere along the line.[40]

The way the story goes—I'm going to tell it briefly—the people here were still living down in Keuchaptevela. They hadn't yet moved to the top of the mesa. There was a lot of visiting back and forth with Sikyatki. Young men in Sikyatki who were looking for wives would come to Keuchaptevela in the evening and watch the girls and try to get acquainted. There was one beautiful girl in Keuchaptevela who was the daughter of the chakmongwi, or village crier. A number of Sikyatki boys were attracted to her, but she wasn't interested in any of them.

One particular Sikyatki boy was so taken with her that he couldn't leave her alone. He kept following her. As the custom was, he went to that little window or porthole that opened from the girl's corn-grinding room and tried to talk to her while she was working there, but she didn't give him any encouragement. He said he wanted to court her, but she said, "No, I'm not ready to become a woman. I have an old father and mother to take care of. They need me. So I don't want to be courted." The boy persisted, wouldn't go away, so at last she hung her winnowing basket over the little window and cut him off.

Well, that young man wouldn't let things lie. He came back the next evening, and the evening after that, trying to wear her down. Finally the girl became exasperated and threw a handful of ground corn through the window into his face. He went back to Sikyatki in an angry mood. He spoke to some of his friends about the girl. He said, "That chakmongwi's daughter over in Keuchaptevela doesn't want to have anything to do with us. I think we ought to see to it that nobody else will get her." They understood what he was hinting at. They said, "No, we aren't going to do anything like that. It doesn't matter so much to us. There are other girls. If you do anything foolish it will make trouble between the villages. You'd better forget about her."

But the boy refused to let himself get turned back. The next evening he took his bow and some arrows and returned to Keuchaptevela. He went to the little window of the girl's grinding room. He saw her working grinding corn. He put an arrow in his bow and shot her. She fell dead against the wall. Then he ran back to Sikyatki. The girl's father and mother didn't hear the sound of grinding. When they called to her there wasn't any answer. So they went to the grinding room and found her lying dead with an arrow in her back. They cried out, and the girl's brother came. He saw his sister lying dead. He examined the arrow. On the shaft where the feathers were attached there was a painted mark. Every village had a different way of marking its arrows. When the boy saw the markings he said, "That arrow comes from Sikyatki."

Word travelled around the villages that the crier chief's daughter had been killed. Feelings ran high, but nothing happened out in the open. The father of the girl, the chakmongwi of Keuchaptevela, told his son, "I want you to practice running. I want you to run toward Star Butte every morning. Run as hard as you can. In time you will be able to get to the butte and back before the sun comes up. Then I will know you are ready." (This episode, the running practice, as you remember, also appears in the Palatkwa story. I don't know which borrowed from which.) So the young man went running every morning until he was able to get to Star Butte and back before the sun rose. Then his father said, "Good, I think you are swift enough now. Listen to me carefully. I will announce that in four days our Racer Kachinas are going to Sikyatki. You will participate as a Haircutter Kachina. Take some baked corn, some red and yellow piki, and other things like that as prizes. When all the prizes have been given out and the races are coming to an end, then you will carry out instructions that I will give you before you leave Keuchaptevela."

The day of the race came. The young men in Keuchaptevela who were going to compete put on their kachina costumes and ran to Sikyatki. The races began. The Racer Kachinas ran against whatever young men of Sikyatki challenged them. The son of the Keuchaptevela crier chief won many races. Whenever he beat a Sikyatki runner, he took tribute, the way all Haircutter Kachinas do, by cutting off a handful of the loser's hair with his flint knife. When it was getting late, he ran his last race. He caught his opponent just as they were coming into the plaza, and cut off some of his hair. Then he turned and climbed the ladder to the roof of the house belonging to the crier chief of Sikyatki. Arriving on the roof, he saw a group of girls standing there. He saw the daughter of the Sikyatki crier chief. He ran to where she was standing, threw her down and cut off her head. Holding the head by the hair, he jumped to the ground on the far side of the houses. The Sikyatki people were stunned. When they realized what had happened, the young men began to pursue the Haircutter Kachina up the stairway to the top of the cliff and across the sand hill on the west side. When he came within sight of Keuchaptevela he turned and waved the head at his pursuers. That was a challenge, you might say a taunt, for them to come after him. But they didn't dare to follow him into Keuchaptevela.

So now the feelings between the two villages became very hard. Tensions were high, and both villages understood that there couldn't be any peace between them. The chief of Keuchaptevela told the chief of Sikyatki, "Now it is even. You people killed our daughter, and in return we killed your daughter. How the matter will go from here, it will be up to you. If you want war we will give you war. But if you don't want war, the best thing is for you to move away."

The leaders in Sikyatki thought about it for a while, then they decided to abandon their village. They packed what they could carry and went away. The Coyote people went out into the valley, and there they broke up into groups. One group went to Oraibi and was accepted there. Some went to the Second Mesa villages. And one group went back to Hemis in New Mexico, the place they came from in the beginning. After a little time had passed, some of the Coyotes drifted back here and were accepted in Keuchaptevela. Sikyatki was a ghost village. No one was supposed to go over there. The Keuchaptevela leaders said that the walls of Sikyatki were doomed to erode and return to the earth. There was a prophecy—I don't know where it started—that one day the cliff wall would collapse and cover Sikyatki. Nowadays people think there was something to it, because the cliff edge up there at Kukeuchomo broke off, taking part of the kiva with it, and fell into the Sikyatki spring. That spring is pretty choked up now. People sometimes ask, "How in the world could those old timers know that the mesa wall would collapse on Sikyatki?"

Well, that is the basic story about the abandonment of Sikyatki. It's told in different versions, some of them very elaborate, and there are details in some that you won't hear in others. For example, one version says that the two girls who were killed were daughters of the chiefs, not the town criers. But the essential facts are generally the same in all of them. Over in Oraibi the story has got pretty messed up, but they acknowledge that people on First Mesa can give a more authentic account. It's the same way with us. Sometimes we say that people over in Oraibi can give a more reliable account of a certain event than we can.

One thing I didn't mention about the Coyote Clan is how it was supposed to have gotten its name. It's similar to the story of how the Rabbit Brush Clan took a name for itself. They say that one time when these people were on their migrations, there was a baby that never stopped crying. Its mother didn't know what to do for it. She tried everything. Then one day a man found a coyote den with puppies in it. He took one of the cubs and gave it to the baby to play with. The baby stopped crying immediately, and the people accepted this as a good omen. So they adopted the name Coyote for their clan.

In the Sikyatki story, the boy who wanted the Keuchaptevela girl and eventually killed her wasn't doing anything wrong by going to the window of the corn-grinding room—it's not really a window, just a vent in the wall for air—and talking to her. Actually, it was a customary thing when a boy was courting a girl and didn't have any opportunity of meeting with her somewhere. It wasn't disapproved of by the old people. However, there was a traditional way for young people to get together and become acquainted. After the kachina dances were over for the season, the boys and girls would go together in a group to a place on the other side of the gap. It was something like a picnic. The girls would make somiviki (something like a tamale tied up in two places), and the boys would bring some kind of meat, maybe jerky. The usual spot for this gathering was Sheep Spring. An elder person would come along as a sort of chaperon to see that the young people didn't get out of line. As I remember it, we young ones were pretty well behaved.

Sometimes on those occasions something would get started between certain boys and girls. If a boy wanted to follow up on it and keep in touch with the girl, he would go to her house at night, and if she was grinding corn he would talk to her through that vent in the wall.

If both of them were pretty serious, he would say, "I'm going to announce myself to your parents. Would that be all right with you?"

If she was agreeable she would say, "Yes, if you want to." She would let him into the house and he would let her parents know he wanted to marry her.

They would ask him questions like, "Are you serious about marrying our daughter?" And if they were satisfied with his answers and were willing to go along, they would say, "Well, you'll have to find out if your parents will accept our daughter. Let them say yes or no."

If it turned out that both families were agreeable, the girl and her mother would grind corn and make piki. They would take it to the boy's parents to show their approval of the marriage. If the boy's parents accepted this symbolic gift in a good way, it indicated that they also were agreeable. But if they refused to accept the ground corn and piki it meant that they didn't want the match to take place, and they'd explain their feelings. Naturally, if it turned out that the boy's clan and the girl's clan were related, the marriage would have to be called off. A girl and boy of the same clan group couldn't marry each other. In the old days it was unheard of that young people of the same clan or affiliated clans should marry. But this is another of our old ways that young people are rejecting. The younger generation says that all this clan business is outmoded, something out of the ancient past. They say it is a tradition without any meaning in modern life. They don't want it. I wouldn't be surprised if a day should come when a young man or a young woman won't even know what clan he or she belongs to.

Awatovi, that ruins over on Antelope Mesa, was an important village in its time. It was already there when the Bear Clan arrived in Hopi country, and it contributed a great deal to Hopi ceremonialism. When it was destroyed by Hopis it affected the way Hopis regarded themselves. They had always been the Peaceful People, but after the destruction they had to live with guilt feelings for violating their principles. To understand what the Awatovi affair was all about, you have to go back to when the Spanish were establishing their control over the Eastern Pueblos in the middle of the sixteenth century. The Spanish gave those Eastern Pueblos a pretty hard time—made them perform forced labor, tried to kill off their religious beliefs, and compelled them to convert to Catholicism. They attacked villages that wouldn't cooperate and destroyed them. They took some of the Pueblo people to Santa Fe and to Old Mexico as slaves. They heard rumors about these western villages out this way, and a Spaniard named [Pedro de] Tovar led an expedition over here. He had horse soldiers and Catholic padres with him.

The first place he arrived at was Antelope Mesa. At that time there were a number of villages on the mesa and along Jeddito Wash. The main village was Awatovi. The other villages had been settled by Kawaikas—that is, Laguna people—who had been coming in for some time. A number of the Lagunas had come to get away from the Spanish and the Catholic Church in New Mexico. One Laguna village on Antelope Mesa was called Kawaika. Chakpahu, that was another Laguna village. And there was Akokavi, a settlement of Hemis people. The name means Place of Sunflowers. A little to the northeast above the Jeddito Wash was Meusiptanga, meaning Place of Wild Gourds. You can see the ruins of all those villages up there today.

Awatovi was originally a Hopi village, according to what the old people told us, but they must have taken in a lot of Kawaikas, Payupkis and other Eastern Pueblos, because the ceremonies we inherited from them have a good many songs that are not in the Hopi language. Awatovi was founded by the Bow Clan. Awat means Bow, and Awatovi signifies Bow Place. The name proclaimed the village as under the leadership of the Bow Clan. But of course there were other clans there too—the Tobacco, Blue Horn, Sun, Sand, Parrot, Bluebird, Strap and Corn groups, and some others as well. Well, Tovar arrived on Antelope Mesa, but before he reached Awatovi he came to Kawaika. The Kawaikas didn't accept him, so he attacked that village and destroyed it. I suppose the people scattered to the nearby villages. Tovar and his bunch then went on to Awatovi. The Awatovis were of two minds about him. Some of the people wanted to resist, but they were uncertain about the outcome, so they received him peacefully.

After that, Tovar went west to Keuchaptevela, Shongopovi, Mishongnovi and Oraibi. That was the beginning. The Spanish and their Catholic Church officials began to squeeze the Hopis. They built churches in all those five villages. According to the way it was told to us, some of the big beams for the churches had to be brought from forty to fifty miles away, where there were large trees. Hopi men were conscripted by the Catholic priests to do this work. I suppose the beams were actually pulled to the villages by oxen. In Oraibi they can show you some long, worn grooves in the rocks that they say were made by dragging the logs.

The padres were pretty successful at converting people in Awatovi. The way it is told, eventually more than half the population allowed itself to be baptized, and the ones that resisted were a minority. The padres were quite severe with everybody and tried to get everyone to give up their old traditions and ceremonies. Awatovi was a big village. I think it had four rows of terraced houses, three plazas or courts, and five or six kivas. After a while, the converts began moving to the north side to be near the church buildings, and so you might say that Awatovi was broken into two halves. There are a lot of stories about the padres and their doings. It is said that they frequently took women and young girls into their quarters and seduced them. In order to get the women they sometimes had to dispose of their menfolk. Often the men just disappeared. One story says that the padres would send a young man to some distant place to get sacred water from a certain spring, and while he was gone they would take his wife. Some of these young men never returned because they were killed by enemies. Whatever the real truth of these stories, there's no doubt that the padres gave the Awatovis a rough life. The people had to haul stones and timbers, construct the church buildings, and do everything they were told to do. It was also like that in the other villages.

The village leaders and the people were always thinking about how they might get rid of the Castillas—that's what they called the Spanish. Then one time they got word from the Eastern Pueblos that some kind of uprising was being planned. They sent a delegation over there, representing the main Hopi villages, and found out that the Eastern Pueblos had gotten together and were preparing a revolt under the leadership of a Tewa named Popay, who came from San Juan or Santa Clara, which had been called Kapo until the Spanish renamed it. In Tewa, Popay means water bug—mosquito larva—and they say he was called that because he was always in motion. In Hopi they call him Pa'ateu. He was probably a Water Clan man. He was the driving force of the revolt. After he got the Tewas to back him up, he went to the other pueblos organizing and getting support.

Well, the Hopis joined forces with the Eastern Pueblos. A particular day had been set for the beginning of the attack against the Castillas. The Hopi delegation brought back a buckskin thong with a number of knots in it, indicating the number of days to go before the uprising. The last knot on the thong represented the day when all the villages on the Rio Grande side and the Hopi side were supposed to go into action. But after the Hopi delegation returned home, Popay learned that someone had revealed plans for the uprising to the Spanish, and so he moved the date of the attack ahead. As a result, the uprising along the Rio Grande began before the Hopis came to the last knot in the thong. The date was August 10, 1680. The Eastern Pueblos struck hard, killed a lot of Spaniards, and drove the rest of them south into Mexico. Of course, all that didn't happen on the first day. After the first attack, the Indians just kept pressing the Castillas until they were gone from Pueblo country.

Back here in the Hopi villages, the revolt started a couple of days later. In Oraibi, a war party attacked the church and the outbuildings. It seems that some of the padres and their assistants were away at the time, having gone somewhere for supplies. They say over there that the Badger Clan warriors took the lead. They killed two padres, their Indian assistants, and a few Spanish soldiers who were stationed in the village. They dragged the bodies away and threw them in deep washes. After that they looted the church, stripping out all the paraphernalia. The church livestock was divided among the clans. The One Horn Society took the steel lances of the Castilla soldiers and put them in the kiva as a record of the event. After that, the people razed the church to the ground, stone by stone and beam by beam. They scattered the stones in all directions, and stacked up the beams for future use. The large church bells were hauled away and sealed up in a secret crypt.

At Keuchaptevela, over here on First Mesa, the church was torn down the same way, and the big bells were taken out in the valley and buried at a place of drifting sand. On top of the mesa they laid out a line of stones pointing to where the bells were buried. In later years, people sometimes went to the line of stones and sighted along it to see whether the sand might have drifted away and uncovered the bells. Our One Horn Society on

First Mesa has several souvenirs of the church, for example, some small bells that look like sleigh bells. We ring those bells on certain occasions when we are chanting in a ceremony. All the villages tore down their churches. In Awatovi everything was torn down except a few of the outbuildings, which were later converted into living quarters by some of the families. Of course, the Hopis didn't have to confront Spanish military forces, but what they did took some courage because it invited reprisals by the Spaniards. After that they waited, expecting that one day or another the Castillas would arrive to punish them. The Keuchaptevela people moved their village to the top of the mesa, where Walpi is today, for more security. Other villages also moved to higher ground. Awatovi already was on top of Antelope Mesa. In time it began to look as if the Castillas weren't coming back. They were gradually resuming their control over the Eastern Pueblos, and I guess they were too preoccupied with that to think much about the Hopi villages.

Eventually, in the early 1690s, the military governor of New Mexico [Don Diego de Vargas] showed up in Hopi country with mounted troops. All he was after was for the Hopis to agree that they were still under the authority of the Spanish Crown. I don't know what they agreed to, but the Spanish troops stayed awhile and then returned to Santa Fé. Nothing more happened until the Catholic padres [41] turned up again in the year 1700. First they came to Awatovi. Some of the people welcomed them because they had already been baptized as Catholics. Others in Awatovi didn't want them. One of the first things the padres did was to begin the reconstruction of the church. Word filtered out that the Catholics were planning to return to the other villages too. The people in Walpi, Shongopovi and Oraibi had hard feelings about it. They were saying, "Is this how it is going? Is it starting all over again?" According to the way our old people told the story, when the padres came back to Awatovi they made the Catholic converts feel bold again. Ever since the uprising they had been kind of quiet, but now they had more courage and were showing themselves and acting in a contentious way. There was a lot of friction in Awatovi.

The kikmongwi of Awatovi, a Bow Clan man, was having a pretty hard time controlling things. Young people were not paying much attention to the religious traditions and were getting out of hand. There was constant trouble between the traditionals and the Catholics, who were in the majority. People were getting hurt. The Catholics were ridiculing and interfering with the Hopi religious ceremonies. The kikmongwi saw that everything was falling apart, but he couldn't stop it. He decided that the only thing that could be done was to destroy the village and wipe the slate clean. The basic story they tell says that the Awatovi chief was really responsible for everything that happened after that. I can't tell you if it's true or not. It could be that the other villages added that part to take some of the responsibility off themselves.

What happened was this. The chief of Awatovi went to Walpi and spoke to the kikmongwi there. He said, "Things are very bad in my village. It is full of evil. The Castilla sorcerers are doing bad things. Women are being raped. People are killing each other. We can't carry on the ceremonies properly. Everything is disrupted. It's like it was before we came out of the underworld."

The Walpi chief asked, "What is it you want us to do?"

The Awatovi chief said, "I want you to send warriors over there to destroy Awatovi."

The chief of Walpi said, "Yes, I see that things are bad. But why should my village be involved? We can't make war on another Hopi village. You are asking too much." [42]

So the Awatovi chief left Walpi and went to Oraibi. He told the Oraibi chief the same thing, asking him to send Oraibi warriors to destroy Awatovi. The Oraibi chief hesitated. At first he said, "Why should Oraibi be involved?"

·But then the Awatovi chief said, "I only want you to kill the men. You can take the women and children as prisoners. They will help to keep your population flourishing."

At last the Oraibi chief said, "It's too big a thing for Oraibi to take on alone. Other villages ought to be involved."

The Awatovi chief said, "I've already been talking to the chief of Walpi. He refused."

The Oraibi chief said, "Let us go together and try them again."

So they went together to Walpi, and this time they didn't approach the village chief but the kaletakmongwi, the war chief, who was of the Reed Clan. He was more willing than the village chief had been. The chief of Awatovi said, "I promised that the Oraibis can take all the women. You Walpi Reed Clan people, you can have all the land and the fields, because they are too far away from the Oraibis. The land is yours, the women are theirs."

The Walpi kaletakmongwi said, "Yes, that is all right."

He went to the kikmongwi and told him what had been agreed to. The kikmongwi said to him, "I can't stop you from taking your Reed Clan warriors on this expedition. If you are determined to fight the Awatovis, that's up to you. You'll have to take the responsibility. But what you have agreed to do isn't good. It's not the Hopi way. I won't have anything to do with it."

It was arranged that in four days the Oraibi and Walpi war party would position itself for the attack. The Awatovi chief would stand on a high rooftop and give a signal when all the people were asleep in the kivas and the houses. On the fourth day the Oraibi group started out. It stopped at Mishongnovi[43] and gathered a number of recruits there, then went on. Somewhere along the line they met up with the Walpis. The united war party arrived undetected at Antelope Mesa and hid close to the village. While they were waiting for the signal they rehearsed what they were going to do. They stayed at their hiding place all night, and just before daybreak the Awatovi chief signalled them with a firebrand. That was when the attack began. They stormed into Awatovi, and the first thing they did was to pull the ladders out of all the kivas, trapping the men who were sleeping or having ceremonies down there. They threw burning cedar bark, firewood and crushed chili peppers into the kivas, so that everyone down below was suffocated. They also did this to many of the houses, which had their entrances through the roofs. They killed anyone they caught, men or old women. They herded the young women and children out of the village and took them to a place that's now called Skull Ridge or Skull Mound. There they killed quite a few of their captives. This spot is called Skull Mound because after the Awatovi affair people used to find a lot of skulls there.

After leaving Skull Mound, the war party marched its captives to another place. There was some more killing there. They killed any old men or old women who happened to be among the prisoners. There was a lot of dissension between the Oraibis and the Walpis, because the Walpis had captured many young women, and the Oraibis said that all the young women had been pledged to them. Eventually they agreed to divide up the young women, boys and girls. So some of the captives were taken to Oraibi, some to Walpi and some to Mishongnovi. This is how the Awatovi clans came to be represented in these three villages. There are long stories about this destruction containing a great many details, but I have indicated the main events.

One thing that some of the stories forget to mention is that a number of people escaped from the massacre. It seems that the plans for the attack leaked out. Don't forget that there were people in Walpi and Oraibi who had clan relatives in Awatovi. I suppose some of these people got word to their relatives in Awatovi. There's one story, which could be a true one, telling how a Two Horn priest dressed up in an Alosoka costume wandered through Awatovi chanting a song with hints of the tragedy to come. He was singing:

> *Listen to me! Listen to me!*
> *Somebody says that we mustn't stay here any more!*

We must go away,
That's what Sakieva said from the fiery pit!

What this Two Horn priest was singing about was what some Hopi
converts to the Catholic Church had done to his three sons. The oldest son
was Sakieva, and his two brothers were Momo'a and Pakushkasha. A gang of
hooligans had built a big fire in a pit—maybe a corn-roasting pit—and
thrown the three brothers into it, killing them. The song was a long one:

No one should stay here!
Let everyone go!
Don't let anyone remain behind!
That's what Sakieva is telling us!
That's what Momo'a is telling us!
That's what Pakushkasha is telling us
From the fiery pit!
Something is going to happen
And everyone will be moaning and crying! 44

Those three young men who'd been murdered, their bodies had been
rubbed with cornmeal before they were thrown into the fire. The symbolic
meaning of that was that whatever might be planted in Awatovi would
never grow. So the murder and the way it was carried out were also a kind of
warning to people who could grasp it.

The Bow Clan chief managed to get out of the village before the attack,
along with some of his clan relatives. And the leader of the Tobacco Clan
and some of his people got out. A number of Tobacco Clan members found
sanctuary among the Navajos and intermarried with them. It's their
descendants—all Navajos now—who came back later and made terrace
gardens up on the mesa. Some of those Navajos up there today claim to
belong to the Tobacco Clan. But the Tobacco Clan leader in Awatovi
didn't join the Navajos. One night before the attack he went down in the
kivas and gathered the most important paraphernalia of the three big kiva
societies of the village—the Two Horn, the Wuwuchim and the Tataukyam—and carried it all away in the dark and hid it in one of the
canyons.

Then, some time after the destruction, when all the excitement had
subsided, he went to the Snake Clan house in Walpi. It was on the
southeast side, not far from the point of the mesa, close to that Snake Rock
where Masauwu was supposed to have lived. In those days they didn't have

doors like now, they usually had rabbitskin quilts hanging over the entrances. He announced himself through the quilt. They told him to come in, and they gave him a pipe to smoke. After that they said, "Who is it? Who are you?"

He said, "I'm from Awatovi."

They said, "What's the purpose of your visit?"

He said, "I've brought a lot of things to Walpi."

They asked, "What did you bring?"

He said, "I've brought the altars and paraphernalia that we used in our rituals. Can I be accepted here?"

The Snake Clan discussed it, then they said, "Yes, we accept you."

According to the Snake Clan tradition, that was how those three societies—the Aal, the Wuwuchim and the Tataukyam—came to Walpi. They were transplanted here from Awatovi. Eventually the other Hopi villages took up these ceremonies and performed them. The One Horn fraternity is the only one of the major kiva societies that didn't come from Awatovi. How did Awatovi get those three kiva societies? They must have been brought there by the Acomas or Lagunas. To this day, all the songs those three societies sing in their initiations in Walpi are in the Laguna language, not Hopi. In their New Fire Ceremony also, it is the Laguna language that you hear.[45]

Nowadays the Hopis want to forget that whole Awatovi affair. They're ashamed of what happened, because they were supposed to be the Peaceful People. But I believe that when the destruction actually took place they were mortally afraid of letting that Catholic thing grow and spread. Some people regarded the padres as sorcerers, men who were performing witchcraft. You get that belief in one version of the Awatovi story, which doesn't even mention the Catholics by name, but says that half the village had taken up witchcraft and other evil practices. Another version says that what went wrong was a fall of morals. Anyway, most Hopis look at it as a dark day in their history. They don't want to be reminded of it. I happened to be over there at Awatovi one time when Joe Brew and a team of archeologists were excavating a part of the ruins. A Hopi complained to me about what they were doing, and I said, "What are you kicking about? They're just tearing down the walls. Isn't that what you Hopis wanted?" Of course they were really just taking out the debris to find out what was underneath.

Once when I was over at Keam's Canyon a Catholic father came to the Agency to talk about restoring Awatovi as a national monument. Awatovi was an important village historically, and I could understand why someone might want to have it restored. But the Catholics were interested mainly because it was there that they had their big church and converted so many people. Anyway, the Agency wanted to know which person among the Hopis had the authority to talk about Awatovi. I told them I knew the man who had the authority. I took the padre to see a person named Nahee, who was chief of the Reed Clan. As I mentioned in the story, the Reed Clan was the owner of Awatovi and all the lands around it, under the agreement made with the Awatovi kikmongwi at the time of the destruction.

I said to Nahee, "A Catholic padre wants to speak to you."

He said, "What about?"

I said, "He wants to talk about getting the government to restore the walls of Awatovi and make it a national monument."

He said, "No, I don't want to talk about it. Awatovi should stay the way it is. We don't want to revive it after all the things that happened there."

The priest said, "Well, those things happened a long time ago."

The Reed Clan chief said, "Yes, it happened a long time ago and we don't want to remember it. I don't want my people to know anything about it. Leave Awatovi alone till it disappears."

That expedition of archeologists—Joe Brew's outfit—that was excavating in Awatovi [46] uncovered a big tunnel pointing west, a little distance away from the convent building they were working on. They found a lot of skeletons in there in rows, so they filled the tunnel in again without disturbing the remains. Hopis who seem to know something about Awatovi said that the skeletons belonged to the young men who were killed off so that the padres could get their women. Whether that is true or untrue I can't say. The archeologists also excavated one of the big kivas. The convent had been built on top of it as a symbol that the Catholics had been victorious over the pagans. The walls of the kiva were covered with beautiful ceremonial paintings. Some young women on the archeological team, probably students at the university, traced the designs so that they could be transferred to the Northern Arizona Museum at Flagstaff.

I don't know if the other kivas at Awatovi were decorated with murals the same way, but we Hopis and Tewas here on First Mesa didn't have that tradition of putting permanent paintings on the kiva walls. I can't say if this applies to all the kivas in the other Hopi villages, but usually the walls are white. The only time the walls are decorated is at the Bean Planting Ceremony in February. That event is under the direction of the Kachina Society. They have a young woman who's going to participate in the dance, and for long stretches of time she has to sit on that curb or bench along the wall in the kiva. In order for things not to be too monotonous for her they paint some kind of a design on the wall near where she's sitting, maybe a rainbow. After the Bean Planting Ceremony is finished, they paint over the design with whitewash.

One more thing, about the colors that were used in the Awatovi kiva paintings. The knowledge of how to make those colors was a kiva secret. They used all kinds of things for pigments—earth, stone, vegetables, roots, bark, even saliva. That knowledge has been handed down from generation to generation. It was taught to the members of our kiva societies here on First Mesa.

East of the trading post at Piñon there's an old ruins that belonged to the Kachina Clan. There were other clans living there, of course, but the Kachina Clan was the ruling group in that place. It's called Burnt Corn Ruins. The village was destroyed by fire, it seems. I went over there one time to look at it. The upper part of the walls has disappeared, but the foundations are visible, and if you dig around a little you can expose the storage rooms where they kept the corn. A lot of the corn is still there, and it is burnt. Only the Kachina Clan has the details of what happened. They lived in that place before they came here to First Mesa. There used to be a lot of turquoise and arrowheads scattered around Burnt Corn Ruins, but after the Navajos moved in around there they began picking all this stuff up. They even took a lot of corn out of the storage pits. That pilfering came to a sudden stop when some of the Navajos died. They began to believe that the deaths were caused by their taking things from the ruins, so they stopped that business. They let Burnt Corn Ruins alone.

When the initiation takes place in the Kachina Fraternity they repeat the tradition of how the Kachina Clan people came here to Flower Mound, to the old village of Keuchaptevela. According to the way they tell it, the Kachina Clan was invited to come to initiate the young men into their kiva society. There's a man in a white robe down in the kiva during the initiation who recites the events connected with the Kachina Clan's arrival. Of course, the actual details of the Kachina initiations are known only to members of that fraternity. Since I am not a member, I am not an authority on these matters.[47] However, I think most Hopis know about the Whipper Kachinas who come into the kiva and give whippings to the initiates. Those Whippers are pretty fearsome looking. One kind is called Tunwup, and another, a female, is called Tumas.[48]

According to general belief among the Hopis, Nuvatikyao—San Francisco Peaks—down south near Flagstaff is where the kachinas have their real home. They come to the villages for half a year, then after the Niman or Going Home Ceremony they are supposed to go back to Nuvatikyao. You hear some stories that say the kachinas live up north at Navajo Mountain, but most people believe it's at Nuvatikyao that they stay. Now, this is what you get in the stories, but the best informed and qualified Hopis—the ones most involved in the kiva ceremonies—tell us that the kachinas live in springs. They have this connection in their minds between kachinas and water, and numerous springs are called "kachina homes." In each village the Kachina Clan has a somewhat different story regarding the origin of the kachinas. If they ever get together maybe they can agree on a single explanation, but their stories are contradictory. I knew an old blind man of the Kachina Clan whom I used to talk to a great deal whenever we met in the kiva. He told me what he knew of the kachinas the way he had heard it from his elders. According to him, the kachinas all emerged from springs. And if I understood him correctly, the members of his clan claim to be kachinas or descended from kachinas.

Over near Piñon there's a spring called Kisiwu, or Kisiwuva, that's claimed to be a "kachina home." There's a shrine there. They say that whenever you take prayer feathers to the shrine, from a distance you can hear the kachinas chanting and making kachina sounds. Many of the shrines scattered all over this country are at springs. There is a Hopi shrine over in the San Francisco Mountains that is sacred to the kachinas. Sometimes they carry prayer feathers over there. It isn't the mountains that are sacred "kachina homes" but the spring. I've never seen that shrine, so I can't say exactly where it is.

All the different groups that came here to live as Hopis brought their own ideas about a good many things. You can't always trace where those ideas came from. Some of them have caused endless discussions and arguments in the kivas because they contradict one another. For example, there are conflicting ideas about where people go when they die. One idea is that spirits of the dead return to the underworld, from which the people originally came, through the sipapuni. Over here on First Mesa the people don't claim to know where the sipapuni is located. For them the location is lost to memory. But the Oraibis claim that the sipapuni is in the bottom of the Grand Canyon, and they'll tell you exactly where it is. Whenever the Oraibis go to the Canyon on a ceremonial salt-gathering expedition—there's a big salt deposit there—they stop at the place where the sipapuni is supposed to be. I think it is a marshy spot that is usually covered with muddy water.[49]

The concept that spirits or souls of the dead go back to the underworld through the sipapuni comes from that original story of the emergence from down below. The sorcerer or evil one that escaped from the Third World without being recognized seems to have played a big part in educating the people. I told you how he was responsible for making the sun, moon and stars and getting them placed in the sky. (Of course, in another version of the story it's Spider Grandmother who does these things.)

Well, the evil one also educated the people about death. Before the people discovered that he was up in the Fourth World with them, the child of some important person died. That was when they began to look around for a sorcerer or witch, because they were certain that the child had died from witchcraft. They looked here and there and finally they identified the evil one. They accused him of responsibility for the child's death and he acknowledged it. So some of them grabbed him and wanted to throw him back into the Third World. But he said to them, "Wait, there's no need to mourn about this. The child is not gone forever. Come over here and look down through the sipapuni."

They crowded around and looked down, and they saw that child, the one who had died, walking around and playing in the Third World. The sorcerer said, "You see, he is alive. Even if you put a body in a grave up here, its breath of life goes down below and lives on."

They asked him, "Well, if a person goes on living down there, why couldn't he go on living up here?"

The evil one told them, "No, it wouldn't be good for the spirits of the dead to stay here with us. When a person dies he leaves his stalk where you bury him, and his spirit goes elsewhere to live. That is the way it is."

So the people accepted what he told them. Of course, the story doesn't explain why anyone would want to go back to the underworld after everybody had tried so hard to get out of that place.

The belief that dead spirits reenter the sipapuni is familiar to most Hopis, but there is also belief in a place called Maski, the House of the Dead or the Place of the Dead. It is generally described as being in the west, but over here on First Mesa we don't have any particular knowledge of where it is supposed to be located. Some of the Oraibis believe that the entrance to Maski is in the Grand Canyon in the general vicinity of the sipapuni. There is a shrine to Masauwu over there. Because they believe this, the Oraibis generally bury their dead facing west, toward the Canyon to which their dead spirits have to go. We First Mesa people don't hold to that belief. We generally bury our dead facing east, and I'll tell you about our burial traditions later.

There are quite a few stories about Maski. The details vary from story to story, but the descriptions of Maski are quite similar. They say that the spirits of the dead have the same human forms in Maski that the people did when they were living. Their houses resemble the ones that they left behind. The dead spirits take care of their fields, make pottery and do things that living people do. But everything in Maski has a kind of shadowy substance. You might say everything is made of eeksi, breath. Also, everything is reversed, because death is the opposite to life. For example, the spirits of the dead consider themselves to be *alive*, and they look on living people as masauwus, or dead spirits. One of the Oraibi stories about a living person who made a journey to Maski and returned again to the living world is this one:

There was a young man who married a young widow. They were deeply in love. But there was a group of sorcerers in the village who wanted that young woman for one of their own members. So they challenged the young man to a gambling contest. They said that if he and his wife could go for four days and nights without sleeping, then he could have her and they would leave him alone. But if the young man and his wife couldn't make it, he would lose her. They said, "If you win the contest you won't hear from us any more."

The young man and his wife kept awake for three days and nights, but when the fourth night came they were hardly able to keep their eyes open. They were sitting at their fireplace, and it was beginning to look as if they were not going to get through the night without falling asleep. Then an old woman came into the house. It was Spider Grandmother. She said to them, "I know what is going on. I came to help you." She put some piñon pitch on their eyelids, made the lids stick so they wouldn't close. Then she put something in the fire and said, "Just watch that fire, it will help to keep you awake." Spider Grandmother had put something mysterious in there. A glowing wheel was spinning around. It would go dim, then flare up again. They stayed in front of the fire, watching the spinning object. The young man sat behind his wife so that he could shake her every so often to prevent her from going to sleep. They were all right almost till the break of day. But just before the sun rose, the girl fell asleep. Her husband shook her, but it was too late, and she went from sleep into death. Her people buried her.

The young man was lonely and full of grief because he had loved his wife a great deal. So he often went out and sat by her grave so that he could be close to her. And one time while he was sitting there he saw a glow coming from the grave. He could see right through the earth that covered his wife. There was a kind of fire inside the grave. He saw his wife sitting there, her face turned away from the fire, combing her hair. She looked up and saw her husband. She said, "Why did you come?"

He said, "I can't help it. I keep thinking about you."

She said, "What do you want?"

He said, "I want to come down where you are."

She said, "No, you can't come down because you are a masauwu, a dead spirit, to me." You see, she called the live person a dead spirit because

everything is reversed for the dead. She said, "In four days I am leaving."
That is, her spirit was going to leave the earth and go down to Maski.

He said, "I'll go with you."

She answered, "No, you're a masauwu. You can't come with me."

He insisted, but she kept saying no. He said, "We've got some deer meat
in our house. Can I bring you some?"

She said, "I can't eat meat. I can only inhale the fumes."

He went for the deer meat and when he returned he handed it down to
her. She threw it into the fire, and when it was roasted she took it out and
placed it in front of her. She inhaled the fumes from the meat. That's how
she took nourishment. The boy kept insisting that he was going with her to
Maski, and at last she gave in.

She said, "All right, then, if you are so determined. This is what you have
to do to get ready. Make four buckskin shirts for yourself, four pairs of
buckskin leggings, and four pairs of moccasins. Also, bring your chijro, the
bird robe that your father made for you when you were small. I left some
baked cornmeal on the top shelf in our house. Bring that. Be sure to bring a
gourd of water. You'll need all those things. On the fourth day I'll start my
journey to the spirit world. You'll see me in the air with this eagle-down on
my head. You'll have to follow on the ground. I'll be like a cloud guiding
you. You'll have to run hard to keep up with me. You'll have to go through
four cactus fields. That's what your four sets of buckskin clothes are for.
After that you'll come to a deep abyss. You won't be able to cross it on foot.
Sit on your bird robe, it will carry you across. Don't waste any time, because
I can't go slow for you. I have to get where I am going in just one day."

So the young man did all the things she told him to do—made four sets of
buckskin clothing, and on the fourth day came to the grave with his bird
robe, food and water. And on that day the spirit of his wife left the grave
and went soaring into the air. The young man followed her, running as fast
as he could so that he wouldn't fall behind. In time he came to a huge
cactus field. The cactus spikes tore his shirt, his leggings and his moccasins
to shreds. He had to change to another set of clothes. Soon after that he
came to another cactus field, and when he had come through that he had to
change again. He went through four cactus fields, and each time it was the
same. After going through the fourth field he came to a deep, wide chasm.
He threw down the bird robe his father had made for him and lay on it. It
soared up and carried him across the chasm.

The place where the bird robe brought him down was the afterworld,
Maski, the Place of the Dead. Evil people were getting their punishment for
bad things they had done when they were alive. There was a long sloping
sand hill, and the young man saw a line of women trying to walk to the top.

They were all carrying their grinding stones, which were very heavy, and they were slipping in the loose sand. Whenever a woman almost got to the top she would slip back, slide all the way down again. What those women were being punished for was being too free when they were alive, not putting any restraint on their intercourse. They had slept with many men other than their husbands. At another place, men were trying to climb the sand hill the same way. They were carrying strings of vaginas around their necks. Just like the women, they couldn't get to the top. That was their punishment for all the times they had had intercourse with other men's wives. The young man saw all these things. He kept running, following his wife who was floating up above with eagle-down in her hair. (Sometimes we call that eagle-down "breath feathers.") He saw other men and women being punished in different ways for bad things they had done when they were alive.[50]

The young man came to a fork in the trail. On one side, the trail led to a fiery pit, on the other side to a village. There were two guards standing at the fork. One wore a Kwakwan helmet, and the other wore an Aal helmet with mountain sheep horns on it. They had sacred feathers hanging over their faces, and each one held a staff. They stopped the young man, said to him, "Where are you going?"

He said, "I'm following my wife."

They said, "Who is your wife?"

He said, "She just died recently. She's up there, floating on her bridal robe, and I'm following her."

They said, "Oh, well, but you can't come into this place. Your time hasn't come yet, so you'd better turn back."

Just then someone came along the trail toward the fork. They asked the young man, "You recognize that person?"

He said yes, he recognized him.

They said, "He was a mean, wicked man when he was alive."

The young man said, "Yes, I know it."

They said, "Well, now, watch what we do to people like that." And when the dead spirit of that man arrived at the fork, the Kwakwan and Aal guards grabbed him, carried him to the flaming pit and threw him in. They came back and said, "You see what it's like here for bad people?"

He said, "Yes."

They said, "We advise you to turn back. The people over there in the village won't accept you. You're a dead spirit to them. They'll reject you. But if you're determined, we'll let you go over there a little while. Then you'll have to come back." They motioned him on, and he went to the village of the dead.

From the trail he saw a lot of children and young people on a rabbit hunt, but instead of hunting rabbits they were hunting crickets and grasshoppers. They were having a good time, but when they saw the young man approaching they turned and ran away, shouting, "Here comes a masauwu!" He arrived in the village. He saw his wife climbing up the ladder of a certain house. On the roof a man was welcoming her. It was her former husband, the first one she'd been married to. They went into the house together. The young man tried to climb the ladder, but it wouldn't hold his weight because it was made out of sunflower stalks. The rungs broke under him. Only the spirit of a dead person could climb that ladder.

He was feeling very bad because of the way things had turned out, but there wasn't anything that he could do. So he turned back, went home the way he had come, past those guards and the people being punished, across the chasm and through the cactus fields. When he was approaching his village, he met Spider Grandmother. She was at the trail waiting for him. She said, "Now you've learned something, haven't you? You had to learn the hard way. Not till you die can you make that trip. Only your spirit will be accepted in Maski."

Spider Grandmother took him to her house to purify him. She said, "I have gotten everything ready. I have to remove your outer skin because it is contaminated with death. When you return home, don't tell the people where you've been. Say that you've been on a hunting trip. Then they won't be fearful of you." She made the young man stand in a basin and she poured boiling water over him. Then she took a piece of devil's claw cactus—it is shaped with two prongs—and stuck it into his scalp. She put a stick between the prongs and twisted, kept twisting, till the soles of his feet split. She kept twisting and wrenching and finally the whole skin came off over his head, and she threw it into the fire. Of course, he had another complete skin underneath, the way snakes do. After that, Spider Grandmother painted his face red, the way hunters do when they are going out for game. She gave him a bow and some arrows, and also the carcass of a deer. She said, "Now, as I told you, pretend that you are coming home from a hunting expedition. Don't tell anyone where you've really been or they'll reject you. When you get to your house, call for your father and mother. They both think that you are dead."

So the young man took the deer carcass and went to his village. He came to his mother's house. He called out, "Ha'u! Here I am, Talahoyema!" [51]

They called back, "No, do not tease us. Talahoyema is dead."

He said, "Truly, I am your son, Talahoyema." They came out of the house. They saw him carrying the deer carcass. He said, "I need water to wash my hands." (After hunting, before entering his house a man always washes to purify himself of the scent of game.) They brought him water and poured it for him. He washed and went into his house.

That is the end of the story about the man who went to Maski and returned. I have shortened it quite a bit, because it's quite long, one of those drawn-out stories they tell in the winter, which is the proper storytelling season. The moral points in this tale are apparent. All those punishments given to people in Maski are reminders that there are approved ways of living, that in this world no one can go around doing whatever comes into his head.[52] There is another idea there, too. A person shouldn't go where he is not wanted. He shouldn't go anywhere before he is welcome. Everything should be done in its proper season.

About the young man's bird robe that we call chijro, it's supposed to represent a bird or flight. Hopi fathers make these robes for their male children. Chijros are believed to carry their owners across the great chasm when the time comes. Women have something comparable. When a young woman is about to be married, several robes are given to her. (In the old days, the father wove all of them, but men don't have much time or inclination for weaving any more, and so these robes may be acquired from someone else.) The large white one, called kwatskiaveu, is supposed to carry her up above like a cloud when she dies. Dead people are believed to send rain in answer to the prayers of the living, so this robe is woven loosely to allow the rain to come through. If the weaving is too tight, the rain can't penetrate. There's another woman's robe with many designs woven in— butterflies and, down at the bottom, streaks meaning long life. These designs symbolize the present world. There is a third robe, or shawl, white with red and indigo stripes at the ends representing rainbows. When the spirit of a dead woman is sitting up there in the clouds, she wears it like a manta.

As I mentioned before, the Oraibis and the First Mesa people don't follow the same burial traditions. The Oraibis bury their dead facing west, and the Walpis and Tewas over here bury their dead facing east. The Oraibis base their custom on something said to have occurred at the time of the emergence. So do the First Mesa people. When the people came out of the underworld there was a prophecy that a Good Bahana, or white man, would some day come to the Hopis from the east to guide them and bring harmony and a good life. I can't say what clan brought that tradition, but it is particularly strong in the Fire Clan, which owns the broken stone tablet that's supposed to key in with the Good Bahana's broken stone tablet. Whoever may have contributed that belief, the idea is widely accepted among the Hopis. The Water Clan old ones sometimes say that they were the ones who were intended to bring harmony.

Anyway, that special Bahana never arrived.[53] He is still expected, though, especially among old, tradition-minded people. For this reason, important personages—village officials, clan chiefs and leaders in the kiva societies— usually are buried facing the east so that they can recognize and welcome the Good Bahana when he makes his appearance. Their bodies are dressed in the proper ceremonial costumes to explain who they were when they were living. Sometimes they are buried sitting up. Or they can be buried lying with their feet toward the east, so that if they were to sit up they would be looking eastward. Even people who aren't important personages can be buried this way if it is known that they wanted it, or if their families want it. Hopis and Tewas alike on First Mesa follow this tradition. However, like other aspects of our ceremonial life, the custom is often ignored among younger people.

I remember that when my stepfather Peki died, I came home from Keam's Canyon to bury him. We placed him in his grave sitting up, facing toward the east. We didn't have any caskets in those days. He only had a blanket around him. The same way with Peki's sister. When she died, I carried her down to the burial place from the mesa top on my back. We buried her right next to Peki, facing in the same direction.

Of course there was always a ritual in the house before the body was taken to the graveyard. The main part of it was the headwashing of the corpse with yucca suds. People used to undergo headwashing at all the critical points in their lives—when they were given their first names, when they were married, when they were initiated into fraternities and so on. This was the last headwashing. It was done by the grandmother, you might say the oldest woman in the clan, and after she was finished she whispered a secret name into the dead person's ear. That was the name he or she would take into the next world, wherever that is. They placed cotton over the dead person's face—not cloth, but raw unspun cotton—with two holes for the eyes and one for the mouth. It was a cotton mask, you might say, tied with a cord around the forehead. The cord also held four turkey feathers pointing downward over the masked face. The reason for the white cotton was to make the person appear as white and unblemished as possible before the Great Spirit.

After the burial there was a feast, and the choicest part of the food, usually the heart, was put in a bowl and taken down to the grave and placed on top. Another bowl with yucca roots, which had been used in the headwashing, was also placed on the grave. Before my time they may have buried a lot of pottery in people's graves, because anthropologists and archeologists have dug up numerous pots from ancient burial sites. But in my generation it was just those two bowls.

Our First Mesa Tewa tradition about where we go when we die is a little vague. I am told that the Eastern Tewas along the Rio Grande have the belief that when they die they return to Sibopay, the place from which they emerged. That is similar to the Hopi idea of going back through the sipapuni. But First Mesa Tewas have a tradition that the spirits of the dead go to a place called Kwaiyegeh, over in Grand Canyon. The name of the place suggests a downward movement, probably meaning below the surface. Maybe we got that idea of the Grand Canyon from the Oraibis, or maybe we brought it with us when we first came here, I can't say for sure.

Eagles also have some connection with Hopi ideas about death. Eagles are killed by some Hopis just after the Niman ceremonies are over. Men go out and capture fledgling eagles by climbing down from the cliffs. They take them home, sometimes carrying them in cradleboards as if they were babies. The eagles are kept tied by the feet on roofs. The people who catch them take good care of them, hunt rabbits for them to eat. After the Niman Dance they kill the eagles by putting a finger in their throats and pressing on their windpipes. Then they remove the feathers and down, which are used for sacred rituals. That down is considered specially important. When the feathers have been removed, the eagle has a ceremonial burial. They give it a carved doll as a present to take up to the eagle afterworld. Tradition says that there is another land up there in the sky, with tall mountains. Eagles are supposed to go there, breed to replenish their numbers, and after that return to the earth. Behind all this is the belief that human children were once transformed into eagles and cared for by eagle mothers and fathers. This explains why young eagles are carried in cradleboards when they are captured, and given dolls as presents. According to this belief it is human children in the form of eagles who provide the Hopis with feathers for their rituals. Over in Shongopovi and some of the other villages they still go out to capture young eagles for this purpose, but it's not done on First Mesa.

I never liked this mistreatment of eagles. It is cruel. Somebody ought to put a stop to it. Our eagles are vanishing. It won't be long before they are gone. We Tewas never catch eagles. The Zunis and Lagunas capture them, but they don't kill them, just keep them tied by one foot until they die of old age. That is pretty cruel too. But I think this capturing of eagles is dying out. The question is whether the eagle rituals or the eagles will die out first. I suppose that tradition came in here with one of those clan migrations and belongs only to certain groups, because it wasn't followed by a good many people.

Of course, you can't talk about death without considering Masauwu. Even though the Fire Clan claims Masauwu as their relative, people of other clans believe in him. You can't say he's evil, even though he's feared.

It seems that he is a benefactor to people who lead decent lives, but a destroyer to the bad ones. Why a spirit that represents death was in charge of the land up here in the Fourth World is hard to explain. I have heard some people say that he was merely an ordinary masauwu, or dead spirit, who somehow came to life again, and that it was in this way that he got his name, Masauwu. There are stories that this dead spirit was thrown into that pit of flames for punishment down in Maski, but that he escaped from it and returned to the land of living things.

It was the fire in the pit, they say, that burned off his hair and made horrible scars all over his body, and that put flames in his mouth. If you see a flame or a kind of a flare moving in the dark, that's Masauwu's breath, and you'd better get away from there as fast as you can. That's in the tradition. That missionary Voth who set down all the stories he heard over there in Oraibi translated masauwu as "skeleton." [54] I think that the man who translated for him probably didn't know English too well. A masauwu isn't a skeleton, but the breath or spirit of a person who has died. Masauwu as a proper name means the Death Personage who owned all the land in this Fourth World when the people emerged from down below.

I myself heard a lot of talk about Masauwu when I was growing up, but I never paid much attention to it. I think my mother believed there was something to it, though. I remember one time when I was a young man. I was helping my uncle, and I had to take some horses from his sheep camp over to Second Mesa. It was late, and I decided to stop off at Tewa Village for the night. I came to the place where the Walpi trail goes down to the spring. It was pretty dark. I happened to glance toward where another trail goes to the day school, and I saw a flare or a spot of light down there. I thought it was probably someone riding along there and lighting a cigarette, and so I waited where I was, but I didn't hear any hoofbeats and nobody came along.

When I got to my mother's house I told her about it. She said, "You mustn't look around at night." I said it must have been someone smoking, but she was very concerned. She said, "If you see a flare at night, that's an evil omen." I didn't take much stock in that, but the next morning after I left First Mesa my horse stepped into a badger hole and fell on me. She was kicking around and got her foot caught in one of the stirrups and couldn't get up. When I finally got out from under, my leg was pretty badly hurt. Later that day when I got back to Tewa Village, my mother made a connection between my accident and the flare I had seen the night before. Well, I really don't believe in omens, but I have to admit I saw that flare. Nobody mentioned Masauwu by name, but I know that was what they were thinking about.

People describe Masauwu's head as shining red, no hair on it, just red and glistening. And that reminds me of something that happened one night. I was married and living with Taiyomana in Walpi at that time. I've told you about her. It was pretty hot, and we were sleeping on the roof. Well, about midnight she hit me across the back, said, "Get up!"

I said, "What is it? What's the matter?"

She said, "There goes that Red Headed Man!"

I got up and looked over the edge of the roof. Somebody was walking along. He was naked except for a flapping manta partly covering his head, and he carried a basket. His body was mottled grey. No hair on his head. It just shone red. He was walking out there toward the point of the mesa where the kachinas rest between dances, saying, "Honai!" My wife said, "Do something! Go after him! Didn't you see him?"

I said yes, I'd seen him. Her brother came up from another house, stood in a corner watching. He said, "I saw him too." She wanted me to do something, but I don't know what. I was sleepy.

I said, "Agh, somebody else can do it."

She said, "Albert, don't you believe in anything?"

That person who went by resembled Masauwu, all right. There must have been some kind of a ritual going on, possibly a purification ceremony. If you believed in Masauwu you had to take that Masauwu personage seriously. He was a terrifying sight. One thing was sure, the dogs let him go by without making a sound. I guess they didn't have the nerve. They didn't have enough courage to bark until he had gone through the village and disappeared out at the point of the mesa.

There are things in our traditions that I've not taken as literally as I might have, but just the same they've made a deep impression on me. For example, where a person goes when he dies. Our Tewa tradition is "downward," and the Hopi tradition, for some people, is back through the sipapuni into the underworld. I mention it in connection with an experience I had down on the Colorado River Reservation. A few years ago I had a heart attack and they rushed me to the hospital. I was unconscious, and before I came out of it I had a dream.

I seemed to be in a room, solid walls all around me and no doors or windows. I was sitting there saying to myself, "Which way can I go? How can I get out?" And I said, "Look down below, there's an opening in the floor." And I asked, "How can I get down in there?" I was asking the questions and answering them too. I said, "Just put your right foot in there. It'll open for you." I stuck my foot down in that place and pushed, but it didn't open. I said, "Well, it doesn't open, so I think it isn't time for me to go down there. Anyway, I'm not ready for that." Then I woke up. I was really sweating. I said, "Where am I?" They said, "In Parker, in bed." I didn't think of it at the time, but that passageway in the floor that wouldn't open for me in my dream surely had to have something to do with the sipapuni idea.

There was another thing that happened since I moved down to Parker. I won't try to explain it, and you can make whatever you want out of it. I'd been reading a Jehovah's Witnesses paper called *Awake*. It was interesting to me because it was explaining various verses of the Bible. It was late and I should have been asleep, but I kept reading until I finished the article. Then I turned out the light and lay down. It was dark, but I saw a man and a woman standing there and I thought somebody had come in from the front room. I thought, "Gee whiz, I didn't hear anyone come in." I said, "What is it, folks? What is it you want?" They didn't say anything, but the man was smiling and waving his hand from side to side. Then I saw another man, a tall one with long hair, standing in the corner. He was smiling at me too. I turned the light on. There wasn't anybody there.

I said, "What's the matter with me? Am I going crazy?" That's what it seemed like. I thought that after reading the Jehovah's Witnesses paper I wasn't in my right mind. So I turned the light off, and there those three people were again. I got out of bed and put out my hand to touch them. Nothing there. I was talking. I said, "What do you folks want?"

My son-in-law, Jesse, Estelle's husband, heard me and thought I had visitors. I called out, "Jesse."

He said, "What is it?" and I told him to come in. He came in and stood by the door. The lights were off.

I said, "You see anybody standing there?"

He said, "No, I don't see anybody."

I said, "Well, there's a couple standing by the bed and a man in the corner."

Jesse said, "You been drinking something?"

I said, "No, I've been reading this Jehovah's Witnesses pamphlet. When I turned out the light I saw those people standing there."

He said, "Turn the light on again." I turned it on. Nobody was there.

A man named Dan Welch was living in the house next door. I called him and he came over. I told him what was going on. He had a German Shepherd dog, and he said, "Let me bring the dog in." He brought the dog. It just went around the room, didn't notice anything. Well, the three of us were there talking till almost six in the morning, then Dan and Jesse left. It was winter and it was still dark. I went into the living room, put some wood in the stove and sat there till daybreak wondering what in the world was going on.

The next night when I went to bed and turned off the light there were two women instead of the couple, and also that man with the long hair standing in the corner. The two women were sitting on the bed. They were wearing Apache squaw dresses, shirtwaist style, all checkered. So I sent somebody to get Estelle's uncle, John Scott. He was a kind of medicine man. He came and I told him what was happening.

I said, "One of the men who was here last night didn't come tonight. There's a woman in his place. The two women are sitting on the bed."

He said, "Right by you?"

I said, "Yes."

So he held out a string of beads to where the women were, but they wouldn't take them. They were motioning with their hands but I didn't know what they meant. John said to them, "Here, take the beads and go away." But they wouldn't take the beads.

John said, "Well, Albert, I'll stay here with you for a while."

We turned on the lights. John had some Indian tobacco with him. He rolled it in a cornhusk and lighted it. He blew four times and gave it to me. I smoked with him. He said, "This will send those spirits away." Also, he got some piñon pitch and burned it. Carried it all through the house, left piñon smoke everywhere. Then he took it outside and circled the house.

After that he said, "Well, they wouldn't accept my present so I'll go home now."

I said, "Okay."

Of course, those three people were still there when I turned the light off. So I got to thinking about something I had learned in the One Horn Society. I said to myself, "Well, John couldn't do anything, so I'll try something myself." I got some turkey and bluebird feathers and some eagle-down, also some string. Then I went out and cut a willow stick. I tied the turkey and bluebird feathers to two short lengths of the willow stick and made two pahos representing male and female, with a little bit of eagle-down hanging from the bottom. I took them outside and stuck them into the pathway to the house. Then I took some cornmeal and sprinkled it forward. When that was done, I went in and hit the hay. Just like that I went to sleep. Those visitors were gone. In the morning I went out, took the prayer sticks and buried them. I was never bothered by those visitors again, or any others.

How can you describe that experience? Imagination? I don't believe so, but I can't tell you what to think about it. I know I wasn't drinking. All I had been doing was reading the Jehovah's Witnesses stuff. What the pamphlet said was that when a person dies, he is dead, and there is nothing more until the resurrection. After that his soul goes to heaven or hell. That is their story, and you can add it to all the other stories about what happens when you die. But what it has to do with those night visitors of mine, I can't tell you.

I don't know all the answers, but one thing I do believe in is the Great Spirit. I believe that the Great Spirit is holding this universe together and renewing life. I have a friend who doesn't go along with this way of thinking. He argues with me. He says, "Albert, let it go. They'll make you crazy with this kind of talk." I tell him, "No, I don't think they'll make me grow crazy. I've been looking around me all my life at the way things grow and the way our world is ordered, and I really believe a Great Spirit is behind everything we see and know."

One of the important events that took place in Hopi country during my lifetime was the fragmenting of Oraibi. Oraibi is said in the guidebooks to be the "oldest continually inhabited village in the United States," dating from around the thirteenth century. Well, we know that Shongopovi was the first Hopi village, and if you don't take into account the fact that it had an earlier site down below Second Mesa, you can say that it is the oldest. But for a long time Oraibi was very important ceremonially. The Oraibis always thought of themselves as the center of everything, and they sort of looked at the other villages as outlying provinces. Anyway, circumstances eventually caught up with them. For a long time there had been friction between certain clans. Basically it was the Bear Clan against the Fire Clan. As I mentioned before, Oraibi was settled by the Bear Clan and it was therefore a Bear Clan village. But the Fire Clan, which arrived later than the Bear Clan, always claimed to be paramount because Masauwu was their relative. The argument about who should lead the village went on without end. The Water Coyote Clan supported the Fire Clan in this quarrel. I don't know how those Water Coyotes got their name. They came from the north, not the south. The Coyote Clan immigrated from the Rio Grande pueblos. I don't understand where the word "water" in Water Coyote comes from. It doesn't have anything to do with the Water Clan group that originated at Palatkwa. We have discussed this in the kiva, and some of us think that the "water" part of the name is a mistranslation. Originally it must have meant something else.

Well, when the white people began coming in from the east, the Government started pressing the villages to cooperate with modernization. Of course, the Government did not really understand the Hopi way of life, and it did a lot of things that were disruptive and even silly. It did not understand about the Hopi system of landholding, that certain lands belonged to certain clans, and it caused a lot of confusion and anxiety when it tried to survey all the land and reallocate it to individuals. It seems that they couldn't comprehend anything but individual ownership, or they thought clan ownership was an alien way of life that ought not to be allowed in the United States.[55] The Government also wanted to put all the Hopi children in school, but the conservative factions in the various villages resisted this as long as they could. These problems came to a head in Oraibi when Lololoma of the Bear Clan was chief, and he was followed by Tawaquaptewa. Both of these chiefs wanted to cooperate with the whites, because they understood that times had changed since the old days, and that now they would have to learn to live with the white man's Government in Washington.

Nobody in any of the factions wanted the silly land reallocation, but there were big differences over the school question. Both Lololoma and Tawaquaptewa were in favor of sending Hopi children to school. The people who supported them were known as the Friendlies because they were for cooperation with the whites. The ones that wanted the Government to keep out of all Hopi affairs were known as the Hostiles. Later on the two groups came to be called Progressives and Traditionals.

During Tawaquaptewa's time the leader of the Oraibi Hostiles was Yukioma of the Fire Clan. He maintained, "The Fire Clan is the preserver of the Hopi way of life." He told the Bear Clan, "Masauwu named us your elder brothers. We were supposed to be acknowledged when we arrived here, but you refused. This is why Oraibi is suffering. You people who want to live the life of the white man, go somewhere else if you want to give up your traditions."

And the Bear Clan people were saying, "You Masauwus (the Fire Clan was also called the Masauwu Clan) and you [Water] Coyotes, if you can't live in peace, if you can't stop disrupting everything, go back to your own village in Kalewistema." That was where the two clans had come from, Kalewistema, those cliff ruins near Kayenta.[56] You see how it was getting to be in Oraibi, the Fire Clan and its supporters against the Bear Clan and its supporters, the same old confrontation.

Even the ceremonies were disrupted. The Hostiles refused to participate in the important kiva rituals. So the Friendlies held the ceremonies without them on the days when they were supposed to take place, and afterwards the Hostiles held their own ceremonies. The important kiva societies were broken in two, and it was impossible to carry out the rituals properly. The Hostiles kept saying, "You people want to follow the white man. Then follow him. But he isn't the Bahana we have been waiting for, and we aren't going along with you."

It was 1906 when Oraibi came to the end of the trail. Some families wouldn't talk to other families. There were fights in the streets, and some men took to carrying weapons. Yukioma felt he needed reinforcements, so he sent a message to Shongopovi and other villages asking for Fire and [Water] Coyote Clan people to come to Oraibi to back him up. To balance that off, Tawaquaptewa asked for Friendlies to come to Oraibi from Moencopi, which was an Oraibi satellite village. Things kept building up that way. It came time for the Niman Ceremony—the Home Dance. That was in July. The Hostiles refused to participate. They held their own Niman Ceremonies. Tawaquaptewa kept telling the Fire and Coyote Clans that they would have to leave and go back to their old cliff villages at Kalewistema. Yukioma said no, that it was the Bear Clan and its people that would have to go.

So it came to the point of no return, and finally, on September 8, 1906, the Friendlies went from house to house and kiva to kiva rounding up the Hostiles and their families. Took them all over to the west side, maybe a little north of the village where there's a flat rocky place. When they got all the Hostiles together at that spot they said, "Well, now, it's all over. Now you people can go back to Kalewistema. You weren't supposed to come here in the first place, because Masauwu assigned all these lands to us, the Bear Clan."

Yukioma said, "No, we aren't going anywhere. We belong here. It's you Bear Clan people and your relatives who have to go."

There was a lot of angry shouting back and forth, and it was getting to look as if there was going to be a big fight. Some of those men who had come from Shongopovi and Moencopi were carrying weapons and were ready to use them.

When the situation was getting to look pretty bad, someone suggested a contest to decide who should go and who should stay. I don't know whose idea that was. Some people say it was Yukioma's idea. Anyway, they agreed to have a pushing contest, the Hostiles on one side and the Friendlies on the other. Yukioma and Tawaquaptewa stood face to face, with their supporters behind them. Yukioma said, "Here is the line, and if you Friendlies can push us across it, then we'll leave Oraibi. If you can't do it, then you are the ones to leave." So Yukioma and Tawaquaptewa began pushing, and Yukioma's people were pushing him from behind and Tawaquaptewa's people were pushing him from behind. Those two leaders were crushed in the middle. It was a hard struggle. At last Yukioma called out for the pushing to stop. He said, "Now it's done, I've been pushed across the line." So the contest was over. The Fire Clan and the Water Coyote Clan and all their followers got ready to leave. They went to their houses to collect their things, whatever they could carry. After that they went a little distance out of Oraibi and stayed there for the night. The next morning they went away.[57]

Of course, when we say that the Fire Clan and the Water Coyote Clan left and the Bear Clan stayed, that is only a way of generalizing. The ones who left and the ones who stayed were mixed clans. Remember that the wife of a Fire Clan or Coyote Clan person had to be from a different clan group, maybe Bear Clan; and the wife of a Bear Clan or Strap Clan man had to be from a different group, perhaps Badger Clan or Fire Clan. So when the Hostiles went away they had members of a number of clans among them, even though the Fire Clan was leading. In this way, clans and families were broken up. A father could be on one side and his son on the other. Brothers and sisters were separated. Some people didn't know which way to go because their families were split two ways. They had hard choices to make.

Where that big push took place there's a mark on the rock with Yukioma's words, "Well it have to be this way now that when you pass me over this line it will be done," and the date is engraved there too. Yukioma and his bunch camped at several different places on the mesa. I think they stopped for a short time at the ruins of Huckovi, that village that was destroyed by fire. But they didn't have any intention of going to Kalewistema. Instead, they finally settled just a few miles north of Oraibi, on the west side of the mesa, near Hotevilla Spring.

They had a hard time that winter. The Government arrested some of their men for refusing to send their children to school. Then a group under the leadership of the Sand Clan chief decided to break away from Hotevilla. Some of the group wanted to go back to Oraibi. They tried, but the Oraibis didn't want them, so they went a little east of Hotevilla to Bakavi, Reed Spring, and built a village there. The Government gave some help to the Bakavis, who were more on the side of the Friendlies than they had been before. The Sand Clan chief was recognized as the leader of Bakavi, and the Government made him a policeman. Over in Hotevilla, those people regarded themselves as the mainstay of traditional Hopi life, and they continued to resist sending their kids to school. Eventually the Government sent troops to Hotevilla to take the children to school. That was in 1911. As I said earlier, I had a small part in that. I drove a wagon from Keam's Canyon to get a load of children and bring them back to the Agency school.

That is the main line of the story about the Oraibi split, but there are a lot of details that you can get only from Third Mesa people. I warn you again, though, that you are going to get details that conflict with one another, because every clan interprets events according to how events are seen by them. But one thing is certain. The breakup of Oraibi brought an end to all the important rituals and kiva organizations there. The Hotevillas claim that they took the rituals with them, but they left all the ritual paraphernalia behind in Oraibi when they went away.

Eventually all the paraphernalia was destroyed by a Bow Clan man named Johnson, a convert to the Mennonite Church. His Indian name was Tawaletstiwa. He was in charge of those objects, and when he became a Christian he took the Wuwuchim and Two Horn altars and all the other ritual objects of those two kiva societies and burned them. He made a big public display of it, announcing in advance what he was going to do. Quite a few people assembled and watched the bonfire. I was in New Oraibi the day it happened. I had to take a wagonload of supplies to New Oraibi from Keam's, and when I arrived I saw the crowd over on the north side watching Johnson destroy the altars and other paraphernalia. He took the responsibility on himself because it was his people, the Bow Clan, who had brought those traditions from Awatovi. The paraphernalia that he burned must have been copies of the originals—that is what First Mesa people believe, because First Mesa traditions say that the altars and other sacred things were brought from Awatovi to Walpi by a Tobacco Clan man. But whether the sacred objects were originals or copies, they were accepted in Oraibi as the real thing and they were essential to the proper carrying out of rituals.

So neither the Oraibis nor the Hotevillas had the sacred objects any more. But it was not just the burning of the altars that doomed the rituals in Oraibi. Some of the people who had gone to Hotevilla were leaders in the kiva societies. They had a lot of the knowledge and secrets in their heads. The continuity was broken.

After the Hostiles departed, the Oraibi chief, Tawaquaptewa, understood that the old life was gone for good. He said, "We can't live in those old ways any more. Now we have to look to the white man's ways. Our rituals are gone, our clan system is gone. The clan landholdings are finished. If people need land for their gardens, let them take fields that aren't being used by someone else." Tawaquaptewa was the last real chief of Oraibi. I think I've already said that he was buried in his Eototo Kachina costume. Eototo is supposed to represent the Fire, or Masauwu, Clan.[58] Burying the chief in that costume meant the end of Oraibi's history and rituals, and an end of the clans' control over the fields and lands around Oraibi. Masauwu had given out those lands, and the chief being buried that way signified that the gift was revoked, that henceforth the Oraibis were on their own without any ceremonial connections to the past. Tawaquaptewa made his meaning clear before he died. Shortly before his death I heard him say to a group of elders, "Now anyone can select his land anywhere he wants. The clans don't control the land any more." In those days the words of the kikmongwi were law. He said that the chieftainship was coming to an end.

He designated Myron Poliquaptewa of the Parrot Clan to perform the duties of the chief for four more years, and after that Oraibi wasn't supposed to have a traditional kikmongwi. I know this to be true because I was present when he made this declaration. But Myron's sister, Mina Lansa, also of the Parrot Clan, took over as chief of Oraibi, and she's been asserting that authority ever since, even though the Tribal Council recognizes Myron as the rightful chief. The main thing is that Tawaquaptewa proclaimed the end of Oraibi's ceremonial life. They've tried to revive the ceremonies in recent years, but if they succeed it will only be on a superficial level because it just can't be done in a meaningful way.[59]

Even before the breakup in 1906 people had been moving down from the mesa top to lower ground on the east side, where New Oraibi is today. The name of that spot is Kikeuchmovi, meaning Old Ruins Mound. There was an ancient settlement there, but how far back it goes I don't know. After the breakup a lot more people came down, not wanting to stay in a ghost village. They wanted to get away from all the reminders of what had taken place. I think six or seven families stayed on in Oraibi. There are still some families living there, and some of them have been rebuilding their broken walls, but for the most part old Oraibi is just another of the old Hopi ruins. The active life is in Kikeuchmovi. That's where the general store, the library, the school and the Tribal Council are located. Old Oraibi isn't anything any more. It lost its claim to be anything, but some of those people are still stirring the pot, trying to be keepers of the old traditions. I told Myron many times, "You Oraibis don't have anything to preserve. You threw it all away." You'd have to say that the Second Mesa villages are the center of the important ceremonies now.

Hotevilla and Bakavi were not the only offshoots of Oraibi. There was an earlier one, Moencopi. In the old days the Hopis grew a lot of cotton around there. That's what they used for all their weaving before the Spanish arrived and introduced wool. Moencopi is only a short distance, maybe half a mile, from Tuba City, which the Hopis used to call Keuchatewa, meaning White Sand. There are some fertile little canyons around Moencopi, and flowing water. That area is part of Bear Clan history. The Bear Clan is supposed to have come through there on their migrations before they settled at Shongopovi. A number of Oraibis had fields around Moencopi and they would go down there in the summer to cultivate. (I already mentioned how they ran all the way to Moencopi and back.) But there was no permanent settlement until an Oraibi man named Teuvi of the Corn Clan took his family and went there to live. That was late in the 1800s. I always understood it to be the result of some kind of a quarrel between clans in Oraibi, but I never heard any details. The name Teuvi means Throw Away, and they may have called him that because he was "thrown away" by the Oraibis and had to leave the village.[60] After a while the Young Corn Clan followed him from Oraibi, and later other clans came.

When the Mormons showed up, Teuvi became a Mormon and looked to them for protection from the Navajos who were moving in. I was about nine or ten years old when the Government made the Mormons get out of there. I was at the Keam's Canyon school at the time, and I saw the Mormons passing through on their way out. They were driving schooner wagons, and some of them were walking along behind. I think they were going to Bluff, Utah, which was Mormon country.

Moencopi is not inside the Hopi Reservation. It is inside territory that the Government gave to the Navajos. Just the same, that land traditionally belonged to the Hopis. West of Tuba going towards Grand Canyon along the old trail there are many pictographs showing that this country was an old Hopi region. Oraibi people went along this trail on their ceremonial salt-gathering expeditions. There's a big flat rock at a place called Teuteuveni where men on these expeditions made their clan signs after getting their salt. The Oraibis went there, but the Walpis went on their salt-gathering expeditions to Zuni Lake in New Mexico. They used to have a big ceremony in Walpi in connection with those expeditions.[61]

Anyway, when Oraibi was in contention between the Friendlies and the Traditionalists, the same thing was taking place in Moencopi. Even today you can see how those two groups stand off from each other. The Friendlies now call themselves Progressives. They are the ones the Government deals with, under the Indian Reorganization Act of 1934, because the Traditionalists stood back and would not have anything to do with the new constitution. They said they already had their own governing system, and they didn't want the Government to set one political system on top of another. The Traditionalists didn't bother to vote on the constitution, and the Progressives won hands down. Those two groups continue to have hard feelings toward each other.

With all the difficulties the Hopis have had among themselves and with the whites through the years, you might say that they didn't need the Navajos pushing in on them. The Hopis suffered from the Navajos a long time, beginning back when the Navajos began floating in here from the north. It wasn't just Navajos we had to contend with, either. There were Comanches and Apaches also, but the Navajos were the main ones. I never thought the Navajos were bad people. They have had their problems too, and still do. But they had the same idea that the whites had about land. If they wanted it and no one seemed to be living there, they just moved in. With us Hopis and Tewas, we have always respected the land claims of other people. But the Navajos were basically migrators who moved around a lot until the Government drew a line around them and made them stay in one place. Before that, they didn't stay fixed on the land anywhere. They followed the game. If they ran out of corn and didn't have any reserve supplies, they attacked a village or raided a cornfield to get something to eat.

From the Hopi point of view, the Navajos were not good neighbors because they were aggressive and warlike whenever they needed something. They not only took food in their raids, but women and children too. You can say that they believed aggressive action was the way to survive, in contrast to the Hopi concept of hard work and restrained behavior. Even after the Navajos were more or less settled on their reservation, they still had that aggressiveness in them. They stopped being a wandering people, but we Hopis were outsiders to them and fair game if they needed something we had. Horses, for example. It was as if the Navajo men were pretending it was still the old days, when a brave went out and got a horse wherever he could find it.

When the white people started coming in around here they found Hopi ruins all through this region. They asked the Navajos who the ruins belonged to, and the Navajos said Anasazi. Well, the white people wanted to know, who were the Anasazi? And the Navajos said, "It means the Old Ones, or the Ancient People." They never acknowledged that these ruins were left by Hopi clans in the old days, because they didn't want the Hopis to have any claim to land the Navajos wanted to use. I heard from someone who seems to know what he is talking about that the word Anasazi properly translated really means Old Enemy. One thing is certain, that practically up to the present time the Navajos have thought of Hopis as the offspring of Old Enemy. When Hopis see Navajos occupying land that is traditional Hopi land, some of it designated by the Government as Hopi territory, they can't help but feel that the Navajos still have that old predatory attitude.

Still, quite a few Hopis have Navajo friends, and some have intermarried. You will find some pretty conservative Hopi families here and there whose sons or daughters are married to Navajos. That could be a trend of the future, when all our hard feelings will be washed out. I myself have been welcomed into Navajo hogans as a clan relative. Even someone I didn't know might ask me, "What clan are you?" And I would say, "Spruce Clan, related to Bear and Spider." He'd say, "You are my clan brother. I am Bear Clan." I can count many times that I have eaten and slept in a Navajo hogan.

And you have to remember that not only our Indian neighbors, but the Spanish too gave us hard times. They captured Hopi women and children and made slaves out of them. You can see that documented in books. When the Spanish were operating around here and in New Mexico, even after the revolt of 1680, sometimes they carried off some children and young women and took them to Santa Fé or Mexico and forced them to work, that is, made slaves out of them. This isn't a make-believe story, it is true. I believe the Spanish used to do that right down to the time of the Treaty of Guadalupe Hidalgo in 1848, maybe even later. Of course the white man still had his own slaves, and he didn't worry too much about Indians being carried off by Spaniards or Mexicans. (We call them both, Spaniards and white Mexicans, Castillas. We call Mexican Indians Síu Castillas, meaning Onion Castillas, because they eat so much chili and onions.)

One of my cousins who died not long ago had an uncle—his father's brother—who was sold to the Castillas by Hopis when he was quite young. His name was Weupa, meaning Tall or Long. He was taken down into Mexico and nobody around here expected to ever hear from him again. But one day he reappeared. I was herding sheep out there in the valley, and out of nowhere Weupa showed up. He told me who he was, that he was my cousin's uncle, and I invited him to stay with me at the sheep camp for a while. After we ate our dinner that night I asked him, "Now, where have you been all this time?"

He said, "Way down in Chihuahua, also in Sonora. I've been in many parts of Mexico."

I asked him what he was doing down there.

He said, "I herded sheep for my Papá. The man I worked for, I called him that. He took good care of me. He didn't treat me like a slave, but like one of the family. When I worked for him I wasn't a slave any more."

I asked him how he got captured by the Castillas.

He said, "They didn't capture me. I was sold by my own people when I was still small. The village was having a famine at the time, and I guess it was hard to get enough to eat. So my family sold me to the Castillas. That's how it was. I was taken by a rich man down there who had lots of sheep in different parts of the country. When I was grown and in my prime he asked me if I wanted to go back to my people. So eventually I left him, moved around a lot, herded sheep here and there, and drifted north till I got home."

He told me about his experiences in Mexico, said he had met other Indians who had been sold to the Castillas. He said he knew some Hopi women in Sonora who had been captured, but they didn't want to come back. They had lived there so long they felt they were Mexicans.

Well, as you can see, the Hopis have had their share of problems for a long while. They have had the Navajos squeezing them from all sides. They have had the Government making decisions for them without really understanding Hopi traditions and, I might say, the difficulties of surviving in the desert and getting a living out of sand. And they have had the problem of establishing their claim to lands they held long before the white man arrived on the scene. If the Government ever seriously considered the plight of the Hopis living in a territory completely surrounded by Navajos, it never did go all the way and fix a boundary to stop Navajo encroachments. If you look at a map of the Hopi area the way it has been drawn in recent years you will see a section of about 630,000 acres reserved for exclusive Hopi use, and around it in a rectangle an area of about 1,800,000 acres known as Joint Use land. That center section is sometimes called District 6. The Joint Use land is really Hopi territory, always was before the Navajos moved in and before the white man began divvying it up according to his own ideas of how it should be. Traditionally, Hopi lands extended hundreds of miles in all directions. They went north to the San Juan River and south to well below Winslow. On the west side they went to the Little Colorado River, and on the east they went beyond Jeddito and White Cone. There are still sacred Hopi shrines at Grand Canyon and in the San Francisco Mountains.

In 1882 President Chester Arthur set off two and a half million acres for the Hopis, and the Navajos were not supposed to come into that area. It was supposed to be exclusively for the Hopis and maybe some other Indians that the Secretary of the Interior might want to settle in it. But the Navajos kept coming in. They swarmed all over it, and the Government let them do it. Some of our old-timers took it that the Chester Arthur Reservation settled our boundaries, but it never did. It didn't have the force of law. That's why it was possible later for Federal officials to cut the whole territory up into so-called grazing districts and let the Navajos settle down everywhere but District 6, which wasn't anything more than the core of the territory specified by President Arthur. No, we Hopis and Tewas never had any agreement or hard commitment on the Government side.[62] Still, there were a lot of stubborn minds among the Hopis who insisted that the Government had recognized our boundaries.

My friend Dutch [H. C.] Diehl, who lived in Colorado Springs, did a lot of research for us at the National Archives and the BIA in Washington. Went through all the documents. I went up to see him one time to find out if there was any record of what happened when our Hopi delegation went to Washington in 1890. I thought there ought to be some indication of what the Government might have agreed to. Dutch showed me all the documents that he had found, and there wasn't a thing among all those papers about a land agreement. He said, "Albert, I've showed you everything there is. You have to accept it. No matter what your old people told you, there was no land treaty in any form. All there is on paper is that executive order of President Arthur." I was sorry to hear it, but what he told me was in line with what a good many of us already knew.

Another time, before the passage of the Indian Reorganization Bill in 1934, some of us Hopis and Tewas met with a Senator named Cameron down in Winslow about the land. We were representing a group we called the Hopi Federal Organization. We asked the Senator point blank, "Is there any agreement in existence between the Hopis and the Government to confirm the 1882 executive order of President Arthur?" He said, "None. There isn't any such agreement. You Hopis are at the mercy of the Government. Nobody is bound by that executive order. It isn't a treaty and it isn't law." Just the same, some wishful Hopis kept saying, "We don't have to do anything. It's already agreed with the Government." It isn't so. They hate to hear it, but it isn't so.

Old-timers told us that back in the 1800s some representative from Washington came out here to talk about a land agreement. He didn't make much progress on it. He said, "Don't you people want to have something on paper, an agreement showing what you are claiming?"

The Hopi chiefs said, "No, we don't have to have an agreement. This is our land. Always was our land. Why do we have to negotiate for our own land? We were here first. Why do we have to have some kind of paper to show?"

The Government representative said, "Well, we want to have some kind of understanding with you."

The Hopis said, "We don't need any agreement like that. We were here long before you people came, living right here, so we don't need to sign any paper."

The man said, "It's got to be done or you'll have lots of difficulties."

The Hopis answered, "If we had been at war with you it would be different. Then we'd have to make an agreement to settle it. But we weren't fighting each other. We're just sitting here at peace, the way we've always been, so what good is a paper?"

The man from Washington looked around. He said, "Well, now, I could go up on top of that house and knock the smokestack over, or go over there and tear the door off the building. Or I could go inside and get somebody by the ear and shake him. Then we could say we have been at war and could sign a peace agreement spelling out where all your lands are."

The Hopis told him, "No, we don't need any peace treaty. This land is already ours."

They wouldn't agree to sign anything. After President Arthur's executive order, as I said, quite a number of Hopis maintained that everything was settled, which it wasn't, and they had to learn the truth through hard experience. I can't say it was altogether their fault though. The Government had a lot of mouthpieces, and you'd hear one thing from one and another thing from another. The Indians didn't know how the white man's Government worked, or who was who. They had to be educated to it through experience, the same way that I had to learn who was who in the villages by going into the One Horn Society.

I mentioned that a Hopi delegation went to Washington in 1890 to talk about our land problem and the inroads of the Navajos. At that time we had a BIA agent named Vandever. When our people talked to him at Keam's Canyon they frequently indicated they wanted to go to Washington to get a pledge from the Great White Father that their lands would be protected.

But the main thing on Vandever's mind was the new Keam's Canyon boarding school for Indians. The Hopis resisted sending their children to the school. So there was a new school there and only three kids in it. Vandever was always pressing the chiefs to let the children come and fill up the school.

Tom Keam also was trying to persuade the chiefs on this. He owned the trading post at Keam's Canyon. You could say he was merely a private citizen, but he really had the interests of the Hopis and Tewas in his mind, and he was always working for them. He kept saying, "Now, you are going to have to deal with the white man for the rest of your lives. He isn't going to leave. And the best way for you to deal with him in years to come is for your children to get a good education and learn how to read and write the English language. Without that, you aren't going to get anywhere."

The Hopis trusted Tom Keam, but they still were not ready to let their children go to the Keam's Canyon school. They felt that there was something more important to talk about than the school. They wanted to go to Washington and talk to the Big White Chief, the President, about the land and the Navajos. Vandever kept asking them for a promise to send their kids to school. They said they wanted to talk to the Big White Chief first, and after that they might be willing. Vandever said no, they had to agree first about the school. Somehow or other they struck a bargain. Some of the chiefs agreed to send enough children to fill the school and Vandever got permission from the Indian Commissioner to send the Hopi delegation to Washington. Tom Keam had a lot to do with this. He personally had talked to the Commissioner—his name was Morgan—and written some letters. He also recommended who was to be on the delegation. They were

Lololoma, kikmongwi of Oraibi, Polaccaca, Anawita of Sichomovi, Simo, kikmongwi of Walpi, and Honani of Shongopovi.[63] So this was the group that went east to see the Big White Chief. That is what they thought, but they never got further than the Commissioner. They had their meeting with Commissioner Morgan, along with Vandever and Tom Keam. Tom Polaccaca was the interpreter.

From what I've heard, and from the evidence, I would say there wasn't much discussion of the land question.[64] Unfortunately, in those days we Tewas and Hopis weren't able to keep records and minutes of meetings. Everything we knew was mouth to ear. When the men in the delegation got back to their villages they told the people that they had made their points about the land problem, but they didn't say anything about what the Commissioner had answered. I think you have to sympathize with the leaders who tried to deal with the Government in those days. They knew what they had on their minds to say, but the white man's voice was always louder. They were nervous talking to the spokesman for the Big White Chief in Washington because they didn't know what new trick he was going to pull on them. I think that when they came home from some of those meetings they might have been pretty vague about what the white man had told them. They didn't want the villages to know that they had come back empty handed.

I already mentioned the Government's effort to carve up the clan lands and redistribute them to individuals. That came out of a plan thought up by Senator [Henry L.] Dawes in 1890. It was adopted by the Congress and called the General Allotment Act. I don't know where Dawes got his knowledge of Indian ways, but he was dead set against a tribe or clan owning communal lands. The 1890 law said that clan lands and tribal lands should be abolished and every individual given a plot for himself. A couple of years after that the Government began to survey the Hopi lands to divide them up, and they did all this without any consultations with responsible Hopi leaders. They started around Oraibi and ran into difficulties when they tried to allot one clan's land to individuals outside that clan. They only stirred up confusion and resentment by what they were doing.

Old Tom Keam was very concerned about the whole land question, the lack of an officially designated Hopi reservation and the carving up of the clan lands as well. He thought that the Hopis had better get together and do something to keep their lands and landholding system intact. In 1894 he went around urging the village and ceremonial leaders to unite and write a petition asking that the Government protect the Hopi claims. He talked with the leaders a good long time before he convinced them that it was important to put up a solid front. The villages had never had a tradition of working together. Each one considered itself to be an independent group. The Hopis had never seen themselves as a single tribe that could act in a unified way, but rather as separate village communities, you might say separate political entities.

Tom Keam persuaded them to send an appeal from the Hopi people to Washington. He drew up the letter in his own handwriting and had it taken to all the important men in the villages and read to them. After that they signed. On First Mesa, representatives of Walpi, Sichomovi and Tewa Village signed. On Second Mesa he got signatures of people living in Shongopovi, Shipaulovi and Mishongnovi, and on Third Mesa from Oraibi. Practically every clan and family was represented. One hundred and twenty-three men in all signed by making their clan marks.

The petition went into great detail explaining the traditional system of clan landholding, and why so much land was required by a family to keep it alive in this desert country.[65] Although the petition was received in Washington, there never was a reply to it, and on the Hopi side there was no follow-up. The Government continued to carve up the clan lands, but finally, about fifteen or sixteen years later, it gave up on this because there was so much confusion and resistance. However, there are still some fields over in Oraibi and Moencopi that are known as allotment lands.

The question of Hopi boundaries has been confusing in lots of ways. Part of the trouble has been bad communications. The Hopis often didn't know what the Government was thinking and the Government didn't know what the Hopis were thinking. The Hopis didn't understand their status under law and assumed some things that weren't so. The Government didn't understand too much about Hopi traditions and claims and didn't make great efforts to learn about them. One thing the Hopis wanted, though, was clear-cut boundaries to their reservation that would include lands set aside in the Chester Arthur executive order. But somehow they never got around to stating exactly what they claimed. It seems that many times the Government asked, "What do you actually claim? Tell us exactly from where to where." The Hopis never did that officially, or if they did no one can say where and when.

I remember one time when there was a big discussion going on in the kiva a fellow named Dingavay said, "Why do you people keep thrashing around with this land question? When our delegation went to Washington and came back here they told us all we have to do is to motion to where our land is, so you people are talking nonsense." The Hopis never motioned.

Over a period of time quite a few Government representatives came out here to look around and find out what our complaints were, but most of them did not listen very hard, or look very hard either. It appeared to us that all they wanted to do was to confirm their own ideas. Most of the time they would be well dressed, follow a few good roads here and there, then go home and make their reports. But they hardly ever went out in the back country to see what they were supposed to see.

When our Hopi Tribal Council was first set up under the 1934 Constitution, it asked the Government to extend District 6, which was supposed to be for exclusive Hopi use. The Government representative—I forget this one's name, because there've been quite a few—who came to get details followed the same pattern. We met him at the Jeddito Trading Post. From there we went toward the Holbrook Road, followed it a little way to Tallahogan Road at the southern end, then took the road to Hotevilla. That's as much as he saw. We told him we wanted to extend the District a little and told him what areas we had in mind. He said, "Yes, but there are Navajos living there." We said yes, we knew it, but the Navajos had come in just recently and we were trying to keep our lands from being taken over by them. That conversation didn't go anywhere. Still, over a period of years, a few corners were added to the Reservation [i.e., to District 6], but they were just token and didn't add up to anything. I think that the land problem had got so fouled up through Government failure to deal with it that it was like moving a mountain to get anything straightened out. Hardly any Government people wanted to take the responsibility.

I must say that some Agency representatives tried to help. One thing they did was to get a number of Hopis to go and settle on the Colorado River Reservation. That took place under Commissioner Beatty. I was one of the group that went down there. Another thing they did was to urge Hopis to go out and settle in the outlying areas of the Chester Arthur Reservation as a means of holding the land against Navajo infiltration, but I don't think they appreciated the risks that the Hopis had to take in doing this. If a Hopi went out there to build a house or set up a sheep camp, the Navajos did whatever they could to discourage him and make him go back where he came from. I knew a number of people who had that experience. One was a man named Naheu. He went to Cow Springs, at the northern part of the Arthur Reservation. And there was Wupatka, he went over to Jeddito Valley to settle with his livestock. And a woman, Weupawuhti, also went there. When there were ceremonial activities in the villages those people came home to participate, leaving their places unattended. When they got back afterwards they found that their houses had been knocked down and their property destroyed. This was the way the Navajos tried to prevent the Hopis from utilizing the land.

A man named George Lomayesva was homesteading at Echo Springs. He built a house out there and planted fruit trees. One day he came to the BIA office and said someone had broken into his house and smashed everything up—doors, windows and anything else that was breakable. Also, they had pulled up all his fruit trees. I went with the Superintendent, Leo Crane, in his Model T Ford to see what had happened. What we saw was just the way George had described it. Later, after we got back to Keam's Canyon, we had the situation checked out by an Agency policeman. Many of the police were Navajos, and we rarely had any satisfaction when they went out to investigate these cases. They didn't want to do or say anything against their Navajo brothers. This time we sent a Tewa policeman. He established that it was George Lomayesva's Navajo neighbors who had done that damage. All these things were pretty discouraging, because in former times, before the Navajos came in, the Hopis had homesteads and small settlements all through those places.

I had some discouraging experiences of my own with the Navajos. While I was still working with the BIA, my uncle Irving Pawbinele and I decided to build a house out in the back country where we were grazing our stock. Whenever we had time we went out there to do some work on the house. One day I found the house, as much as we had built, smashed to bits. The foundations were pounded to powder. Another time, I moved away from the village to take care of some of my own stock. I put in a farm and had some horses. But my horses kept disappearing. The Navajos ran off with them whenever they had a chance. I had one particular horse, a sorrel, that I got from a man who had a range near Winslow. I really cared for that horse. One day he was gone. Later on, a Navajo policeman, someone I knew, dropped by and said, "That sorrel you spoke about, I saw him in a corral in Ganado. They're using him for a racing pony." I said, "Who has it?" But he wouldn't tell me who it was.

Some time after that, a cousin of mine—we were working together in a field I'd planted some distance from my sheep camp—said, "Say, there's a horse out there. Doesn't it look like your sorrel?"

I said, "Yes, it looks like him. Go and see."

He went to investigate, and when he returned he said, "It's your horse, all right."

That sorrel had broken loose somehow and come home all the way from Ganado. But he was the only one I ever got back. The others I lost to the Navajos, I never saw them again.

I think you can understand why we Hopis and Tewas have been so concerned about getting the land question settled. We've never been able to look to the Navajos for restraint. They've just kept coming and coming, and up to recent times the whites have looked the other way. I'm not saying that the Navajos are all well off. There are some pretty poor ones living out there in their hogans, and as individuals they may be pretty decent people. But as a group they've been pushing us hard. For more than a century we have been looking to the whites for justice, but they have always had the attitude that if they let the problem alone it would go away. Despite our difficult experiences, there have been a lot of Hopis who never lost faith that the whites would help them get back their lost lands.

That idea of the Joint Use areas doesn't go back very far. As I said, the Government divided the Chester Arthur Reservation into grazing districts. Supposedly that was just for the purpose of regulating the grazing, keeping the livestock down to manageable numbers so they wouldn't eat off all the grass. In 1958 the U.S. Congress authorized the Hopi and Navajo Tribal councils to initiate court action to get a decision. My son-in-law Dewey Healing was chairman of the Hopi Tribal Council at the time. On behalf of the Hopis and Tewas he filed suit against the Navajos in the Arizona District Court. What came out of that suit was that the Hopis had exclusive use of District 6, but the Hopis and Navajos had equal and undivided interests in all the other districts. Of course there never was a chance that Hopis and Navajos could share the land on that basis. There never could be anything but conflict and friction. The only thing left for us was to get that area partitioned, and that's what we've been trying to do ever since.

I haven't been directly involved in the fight over the disputed land for quite a while, because I've been living on the Colorado River Reservation since 1952, a good four hundred miles from all the discussions and action. Of course, people have consulted me from time to time about what I know of how this mess developed, because a good part of the history of the dispute is buried in the minds of old-timers like myself. And my son-in-law, Dewey Healing, has been in the thick of it and has always kept me informed of the goings on in the Hopi villages.

On the whole, though, I've been content to let the younger people and the Hopi Tribal Government do as they think best about these matters. I enjoy sitting down and taking it easy in my house, which is just a few miles from Parker. I don't even want to get involved too much in kiva affairs, and I'm satisfied to let the people in Tewa Village and Walpi hash out ceremonial problems without me. I am eighty-nine now, and I don't mind sitting out most of these mind-joggling activities.

I haven't said anything about how I came to be in Parker instead of in Tewa Village, and so I will explain about that as briefly as I can. During World War II there was a Japanese internment camp at this place. The Government was recruiting people from the whole Colorado River area to colonize the land along the river. It sent men to the Navajos, the Hopis and

Tewas, and a half dozen other tribal groups to offer them good fields for farming. A big feature of the settlement was to be irrigation. A Navajo party went down to look the place over, but it turned the Government proposition down. When those Navajos got home they said, "That land isn't good for anything. You can't graze sheep in that country. It's all desert." There's only one Navajo I personally know about who accepted land and settled.

I went down with a group of Hopis. I think we were all pretty impressed with what the Japanese internees had been able to accomplish with the land. A number of us agreed to become settlers. I selected some ground right where the Japanese had a hog farm before the internment camp was dispersed. I still had my job at Keam's Canyon, so I couldn't actually move in until I was retired. I bought an old barrack from the Government and they brought it to my place. I converted it into a house. It was pretty good sized, about twenty by sixty, but later half of it burned down, so my house shrank. I have a new house there now, built with Government help. I was still married to Virginia Scott at the time, and she lived with me on the Colorado River Reservation until she abandoned me and the children. I am living alone now, but I have a lot of friends, and my daughter Estelle and her family are only twenty miles or so away.

The Colorado River Reservation isn't anything like the Hopi Reservation. It has all kinds of Indians—Apaches, Supais, Mojaves, Cocopahs, Chemehuevis, Yumas and Pimas, as well as Hopis. From an Indian viewpoint, it is pretty cosmopolitan. It is warmer there in the winter than the Hopi mesas are, and that is one of the reasons I like it. I make trips up to Hopi country sometimes for important ceremonies or when someone in the family is sick, but I am usually glad to get back. Once in a while Dewey and Juanita come down to visit me.

Some absurd things have happened over the years. For example, over on Second Mesa some members of the kiva fraternities revealed certain sacred activities to whites. Now, it is against our traditions to reveal the secrets of the four societies. Why in the world did those men do it? I spoke to some of them once about this question. I said, "These things are sacred, why are you telling them to outsiders the way you are doing? What is the white man going to do with this information? He doesn't have the background to understand what it's all about." They said, "Well, we tell them these things because when the time comes maybe they'll help us to get our land back."

There is a Hopi kiva in Mesa, near Phoenix. A man named Billingsly is the head of it. That Mesa group has initiated a number of whites into the

Hopi religious societies. Billingsly is a Hopi, and he also belongs to the
Masons. Some folks on Second Mesa don't like what he's been doing, and
they have been asking him questions. I was there one time when he was
explaining about the initiations. He said the same thing, that they had been
adopting the white people as Hopis thinking that they might help to get the
land back. At the same time, he acknowledged that the sacred rituals should
not have been exposed that way. On one occasion, four of us who were
members of the main kiva societies went to Mesa to look at Billingsly's kiva
and investigate what was going on. It was a proper, traditional kiva, all right.
It had a sipapuni in the floor, a little opening where they kept a lot of ritual
paraphernalia. This was the place where they initiated the whites. I don't
know how many whites were initiated. But here and there I have run into
white men who told me they were initiated Hopis. I said, "Where were you
initiated?" They said, "In Mesa, Arizona." For my part, I don't see how
those men can be considered Hopis, and I don't see how revealing ritual
secrets to them can ever help solve the land question.

In any case, I expect that the land conflict is going to be settled one of
these days, maybe while I am still around to see it. The Congress and the
courts finally have had to face up to the situation. I think that what remains
to be seen is merely how those so-called Joint Use lands will be divided
between us and the Navajos. You can put it another way and say we will
have to see how much more Hopi land has to be given up before we get
legal reservation boundaries. There is a kind of irony in it. Most of the other
Indians have had to stand by and watch their territory being taken over by
the white man. In our case the white man is in the background, and it is a
group of fellow Indians who have been taking from us.

As to how we Tewas have fared here, living among the Hopis, I think we
have done all right in the long haul. When we came, the Hopis expected us
to be totally absorbed like all the clans that drifted in from time to time.
But we have managed to maintain our own traditions and our own language
for almost three hundred years. All those Lagunas, Payupkis and other
Eastern Pueblo people who came from the Rio Grande country are gone,
except for the ones who intermarried and blended into the Hopi culture.
Even though we maintained many of our own ways, we have shared the
Hopi life and taken in a good deal of it. Whenever the welfare of the Hopi
people has been at stake we have stood shoulder to shoulder with them. We
are interrelated with Hopi families in all the villages. Many of us have
become members of the various Hopi kiva societies. We share dances and
festival days with the Hopis. We belong to the same clans. We are usually

represented on the Hopi Tribal Council. We have fought side by side with the Hopis on all the survival questions, stood solid with them facing the Navajos and the white man. In many ways we are indistinguishable from them, and often you hear us say in conversation, "we Hopis," not because we have forgotten that we are Tewas but because we identify with the Hopis in facing the outside world. In fact, in many ways we are closer to the Hopis than to our Tewa brothers and sisters in New Mexico.

We have been in the forefront of many progressive changes that have taken place here on the Hopi mesas. Regarding education, for example, we Tewas were for getting the children into school when conservative Hopis were fighting against it back in Tom Polaccaca's time. Tom Polaccaca pushed hard for education and other modernizations and took a lot of abuse for it. Some Hopi conservatives have never stopped being resentful about how the Tewas stood on these issues. Also, I think that they never gave up their expectations that the Tewas would blend and disappear as a separate group.

You probably remember the story of how the Tewas, when they settled here, didn't accept the offer of the Walpi people to intermarry with them. The reason the Tewas gave for this was that goodwill between the two villages had not yet been tested. They didn't know how Tewas and Hopis were going to get along. I believe that the Hopi high muckamucks always felt that if the villages intermarried, the Tewas would be absorbed. Eventually Hopis and Tewas did intermarry. I remember some of the Hopi men who were married into our village when I was young. A man named Yoyowaya married one of our great-aunts. His grandfather, Lesso, had married into the Tewa Corn Clan. A Hopi named Mungwe married into the Tewa Tobacco Clan. Lechioma married into the Tewa Parrot and Cottonwood Clan. Namingaha married the sister of Lechioma's wife. Sikyapiki was married into the Tewas and lived right across the court from where my daughter Juanita lives now. Hung'i, the head of the Hopi Snake Clan, and Coóyawaima, a Snake Clan priest, married into Tewa clans. So did Lomaventiwa, Ngeuatewa, Anghah, Chilveh, Kwajuh and Duwakuku. However, that was no way to swallow us up, because their children were all Tewas. As I told you, my father was a Hopi, but because my mother was Tewa I am Tewa.

I think it is generally recognized that we Tewas have pushed hard to get things done even when some of the Hopi leaders were pulling back. It has seemed to us that many of the Hopis were willing to let us take the risks, so that if something went wrong in our dealings with the Government, the Hopis wouldn't have to take the responsibility. We have also noticed that some of those Hopis who strongly opposed following the white man's way were the first to take advantage of the gains that were achieved. Some didn't want the blacktop road that now goes close to all the villages, but when the road was completed they used it as much as anyone else. It was that way also with the water when it was brought to the top of First Mesa. Then there was that lawsuit against the Navajos, *Healing* v. *Jones*, that finally broke open the land controversy. Dewey Healing is a Tewa. He is a nephew of Tom Polaccaca.

There may be some Hopis who think we Tewas are too aggressive, that we try too hard to be out in front. I don't think that is really the case, though it may be true that we are a little more outgoing by nature and temperament than Hopis are. Hopis tend to draw back. Traditionally they have taken their blows and waited for prophecies to be fulfilled. That is one reason they had such a hard time in their dealings with the white man. Things that had to be done to cope with the sudden changes around us could not wait for the fulfillment of prophecies.

On the Tewa side, our old-timers had a sense of commitment to the compact that was made when we came here to defend Walpi from the Utes, Paiutes and Apaches. The Tewas pledged themselves to be protectors and watchdogs against any kind of threats to the Hopis. They believed they were expected to stand up front in critical times, and they have done this. You can call this "pushing" or "leading" if you want to. I know that some Hopis resent it. But the Tewas, particularly the older generation, see it as an obligation undertaken when our people came here from Tsewageh.

I am sorry to say I don't think that the commitment is felt as strongly by some of the Hopis around here. Every so often you may hear one of them say that the lands assigned to the Tewas by the Bear and Snake clans were not really given but merely loaned. I have even heard it said that the Tewas weren't supposed to stay here permanently, that they were supposed to move on to Keuchatewa, Tuba City. Where in the world that nonsense came from I can't tell you. The Tewa lands were clearly specified. They were to belong to the Tewas as long as the sun would shine in the sky. Old-time Hopi leaders never questioned that pledge, they never went back on it. But those leaders passed away, and then another generation passed away, and after a while it was all in the ancient past and there were quite a few people who did not know the true story any more. Even after nearly three hundred years, there are some Hopis who have the idea that we are just visitors here on First Mesa. From time to time we have had incidents in which Hopis have ignored our rights to certain lands, and it has made for hard feelings.[66]

It is too bad that this kind of contention should exist today when it is so important for us to be pulling together, because we have a long way to go if we are going to get our children educated in the right way and make a better life for ourselves. We know that we are not yet in a position to go it alone without the help of the Government. We need to work together. But maybe contention is an elemental aspect of Hopi culture, which some observer, probably an anthropologist, called "regulated anarchy." It seems as though dissension and internal conflicts have been with us as far back as our traditions go, beginning with emergence from the underworld. The Hopis call themselves Hopitu, the Peaceful People, and they have a pretty good record of not going out to make war on other tribes. Of course there have been raids by one Hopi village against another, and there was that massacre at Awatovi that everyone wants to forget. On the whole, considering the kind of times they lived through, the Hopis deserve a reputation for peacefulness. However, they have always been prone to quarrel among themselves. Village quarrelled with village until one or another of them had to pick up and move on. Clans quarrelled with clans, as happened at Oraibi. So I think it is too much to expect that at least some Hopis would not quarrel with the Tewas.

You sometimes hear Hopis disparaging the Tewas as pottery makers. They say the Tewas never made pottery till they learned from the Hopis. That is obvious nonsense. We were making pottery way back in Tsewageh long before we ever came here. According to people who have been there, our old village site back in New Mexico still has pottery shards scattered all around the place. The fact is that pottery making tapered off to almost nothing here on First Mesa at one time, then it revived again. Dewey Healing's great-grandmother, White Corn, a Tewa woman, was still making pottery when a lot of Hopi women had given it up. White Corn's daughter was Nampeyo. She was Dewey's grandmother. You may have heard about her. She became famous for pottery. She and her husband used to go together to the Sikyatki ruins—also to other ruins beyond, towards Keam's Canyon—and find pottery fragments. She would incorporate the old designs into her own work. It was the recognition her work received that stimulated a revival of pottery making on First Mesa. Hopi potters, also, began to go back to the Sikyatki designs for decorating their pots.[67]

It's pretty evident that things have changed a great deal around here since I was a boy. If you look at those photos taken by old-time photographers in the 1890s you'll get a good idea of how big the change has been. I think we have lost some of our old values that gave our lives meaning through many centuries. I am sorry for that. Those values helped us see what was right and what was wrong, and to walk a straight trail in this wilderness. The younger generations will never know what it was like. There are young people who have suddenly become interested in the old traditions. That is good, as far as it goes. But they can never really get back to where we were, and they will never fully understand what the traditions meant to their ancestors who were moving here and there and struggling for survival and balance with the land and the elements. There is no doubt that when the white man showed up here in the Southwest the old ways were doomed. We were a small stream overtaken by a great flood. There is no way to turn time back. People who do not recognize that are lost.

Ever since the white man appeared, we have been changing, adapting to new ideas and ways of bettering our condition. It has been pretty painful at times. The white man brought, you might say, a new order of nature. It was as if our whole environment, the things we had to contend with, had turned into something new. To survive, we had to do things we never did before. We had to reorganize our thinking, and while we were doing this we lost a firm grip on our old traditions. For a while we were halfway there and halfway here. We wanted to cope with a new culture without giving up our old one. Some of those old traditionalist leaders thought we could stay the way we used to be. I have always thought that the only way we can save the old traditions is to recognize the new forces at work in our lives, accept that times have changed, and become part of the modern world. That way we can survive and preserve a part of our minds for the old values. If you don't survive, you don't have anything.

The Hopi Constitution that came into force under the Reorganization Bill of 1934 caused us a lot of problems. For one thing, it widened the split between the progressives and the conservatives. But I don't think that this situation will go on forever. Actually, the Hopis gained quite a bit in ratifying the Constitution. It gave them a chance to deal with problems in a unified way through an elected Tribal Council. Even with considerable opposition from conservative elements,[68] the Council has been able to do things that the villages could never do separately.

Traditionally, every village was a separate unit. Even though the people said they were Hopis, first allegiance was to a person's own village, and each village was a kind of miniature republic, you might call it a village-state. It had its own traditions, its own rules for living and its own ceremonial structure. The ceremonial base for running a village was not a political structure as we understand the term today. The village life was governed, or you might say controlled, by the kikmongwi and the ceremonial chiefs—the important men in the kiva societies and the clans. They were the ones who guided everything by traditional—you could call them religious—ideas. The ceremonial structure did not provide any practical way of dealing with modern problems. The men responsible for ceremonial life had all they could handle. Add to that the fact that the different villages had contrary ideas about many things, and that if a certain clan asserted one thing, another clan might deny it and say the contrary.

There had to be a unified political structure. Even though leaders in some of the villages were conservative in their ideas, still I believe many of them were glad to have a Tribal Council to talk to the Government and deal with some of the special problems that arose with the coming of the white man. We began to get some kind of a grip on the land question only when we had the Tribal Council to speak for all of us. There are still a number of Hopis who detest the Council. But how do they think the separate villages could ever have gotten together on such things as roads and mining leases? You can't say that the tribal reorganization and constitution didn't put us ahead of where we used to be.

As for religious beliefs, we old-timers can see that there has been a steady drift away from our traditional attitude toward nature and the universe. What I'm talking about is not the dancing and the kiva paraphernalia, all those visible things. They are only a means of expressing what we feel about the world. I am talking about the feelings and attitudes behind the kiva rituals. We feel that the world is good. We are grateful to be alive. We are conscious that all men are brothers. We sense that we are related to other living creatures. Life is to be valued and preserved. If you see a grain of corn on the ground, pick it up and take care of it, because it has life inside. When you go out of your house in the morning and see the sun rising, pause a moment to think about it. That sun brings warmth to the things that grow in the fields. If there's a cloud in the sky, look at it and remember that it brings rain to a dry land. When you take water from a spring, be aware that it is a gift of nature.

All those stories we tell about men changing into bears or deer, and then changing back, you can look at them as primitive ideas if you want to, but they really express our certainty that the dividing line between humans and animals is very slim, and that we are here to share what is given to us. We seek a way of communicating with the source of life, so we have prayers and kachinas. I think we are probably as successful at this effort to communicate as Christians are. You don't hear as much about the Great Spirit in our traditions as you do about those lesser spirits that are sacred to particular clans and kiva societies, but I believe we are constantly aware that it exists, and that without it we would not be here. You can say that we have not lost our sense of wonder about the universe and existence.

This knowledge is supposed to be translated into personal good behavior, into the way we act toward other individuals, our clan and our village. If you meet a person, you greet him. If he is a stranger or someone you know it is all the same. If someone comes to the village from another place, even if he belongs to a different tribe, feed him. Keep your mind cleansed of evil thoughts against people. We have purification rituals to accomplish this. Be generous with whatever you have. Avoid injuring others. Respect older people. No matter how they appear to you, they have had hard experiences and have acquired knowledge from living. Do not injure others by violence or gossip. Now, if all these ideas don't meet the highest standards of the different Christian churches that have been busy trying to convert us, I'd like to know why.

Still, we have had a long line of missionaries parading through the villages. First were the Catholics, but they were thrown out—unfortunately not without some sad events, such as the massacre and destruction at Awatovi. Then there were Mennonites, Mormons, Jehovah's Witnesses, Seventh Day Adventists and Baptists. You will find churches in or close to all the villages now. The missionaries came telling the Hopis and the Tewas that the old traditional ways were barbaric, and each one claimed to have the true faith, the only one that paid respect to the Great Spirit. Because of that old tradition that a Good Bahana would come some day, the Hopis and Tewas listened, some of them wondering if this missionary or that missionary was the right one.

I remember a man who was in charge of the Sunlight Mission, back around 1912. He approached me and said, "Say, Yava, what do you think about all these things that are going on in the villages?"

I said, "What kind of things do you mean?"

He said, "Well, all those things that are going on in the kivas. Don't you think they are pretty bad?"

I said, "I know that you are trying to convert me to your church. Maybe that would be all right, I can't say. Maybe you have a good church. But I have been doing a lot of thinking about what you missionaries are doing, and the way you are doing it. The first thing you do is to say that the Hopi and Tewa religious practices are barbaric, and after that you convince a few people here and there that they have to become Christians so as not to go to hell. But I don't think you are doing very well. You don't catch more than a few stragglers. One reason for that is that you really don't know anything about what Hopis and Tewas believe in. You just assume that they don't know the difference between right and wrong. I thought that Christians were supposed to have humility, but I don't see any humility in that. How can you just assume that we're barbaric? Have you ever taken the trouble to study our ways and find out what our religious beliefs are? If you are ever going to be successful with your converting of Hopis and Tewas, you are going to have to know a lot more about us."

He said, "Yava, I believe you're right about that."

I suppose he and some other missionaries made an effort to know more about us, but they all came with that fixed idea that the poor barbaric Indians had to be saved, so they only learned what they wanted to.

I myself have listened to these missionaries. They come to my house sometimes, and I invite them in and hear everything they have to say. Sometimes I have gone to one church or another on Sunday. Of course, a great deal of what they say is interesting. But I have not heard anything yet to persuade me that what they have is superior to what we Tewas and Hopis have. All I can tell those missionaries is that it is a matter of conscience. I tell them that if a person believes in the Indian way and lives according to what Indians believe is a good way of life, that is okay. And if a person is a Baptist or a Mormon and lives according to what Baptists and Mormons believe is a good way of life, that is okay too. That is the choice everybody should have, and the missionaries should stop putting themselves forward as the only ones who know the difference between good and evil.

I don't believe any of the Christian denominations has something valuable that we don't already have. "If a man falls down, help him to get up." That is our belief. Do the Christian churches have anything better than that? I don't think so. In fact, you have to judge those churches by the way Christians act in their everyday lives. And too often we have seen a man fall down and a Christian walk right by, in a way of speaking. "Share what you have." We believe in that, but we have had a long experience with the white man. Sometimes he has shared what he has, other times he has taken away what we have. "If you see something edible, take a part of it, only what you need." Too often the white man has eaten everything up.

One thing is clear. The Hopis and Tewas who convert from our traditional religion have taken themselves out of our traditional ways. The missionaries have had a great deal to do with the destruction of Hopi-Tewa religion. In a way, they are competing with each other to see who can do the most destruction. I guess you can't blame the missionaries too much. They are doing what they believe they are supposed to do. If our traditional religion is passing, you have to blame the Hopis and Tewas themselves. There is one fellow over in Oraibi who was lamenting that the Hopi religious beliefs were disappearing. I said to him, "Why are you crying? You yourself joined the Mennonites a long time ago. You talk about the Hopi way, but you deserted it. So who are the people who should be blamed? The ones who stayed or the ones who left?"

However, there is no doubt in my mind that the white man brought good as well as bad to these villages. You see poverty on the mesas, but you also see new houses better than the old ones, water tanks, electricity, roads, and other such things. In the old days no one had much of anything and life was hard. People shared the hard life on an equal basis. We shared our poverty. We are still in some kind of transition from the old way to the new way. It is painful to some of the old ones to see the things they valued slipping away, even though they are living better and don't have to struggle so hard. The children are getting schooling and they are learning what they have to do to achieve and compete in the modern white world. Part of our problems can be the result of the confrontation between two ways of life, the Indian and the white. However, now and then I hear white people making the same complaints as the elder Hopis and Tewas: "The young generation does not listen to us. They don't pay attention to our values." At this point you have to say whites and Indians are on the same trail. We sometimes cuss and praise the white man in the same breath, yet I think that here on the Hopi mesas we have done better than some of our Indian cousins. There are quite a few tribes that have lost more and fared far worse than we have.

To measure where we Hopis and Tewas are today, I suppose we have to measure against the white man's level of living, and that will show how far we have to go to catch up. Many of our younger people are getting college educations and financial help that we ourselves never had. A lot depends on individuals and how much they want to take advantage of opportunities to get ahead. You can see reflections of the mainstream white culture in the development of a kind of Hopi middle class. Some of those people are economically better off than the average villager. They own businesses or have substantial livestock investments. I think I have to say that this introduces a new element into Hopi-Tewa life—a new grouping. We used to have groupings by clans and families and kiva lodges, and now we have to add a grouping by wealth. The well-off Hopi has special interests. If he owns a lot of cattle, for example, that land we have been contesting with the Navajos is much more important to him than to a poor family in Shipaulovi. The average Hopi isn't going to benefit very much from the land settlement.

What more available opportunities will do to Hopi-Tewa society as a whole, it is hard to know. While there will be benefits to individuals, I think that many of us are going to be scattered from the Reservation. As the people get more and more education there will be a drift into the outside world. Of course there will be some who will stay behind out of their own choice, but the Reservation will become more and more like any other place. White culture will wash out mostly everything else. I have seen it happening all my life. I think that what we old-timers want most to do is to prepare the younger generations to cope and take care of themselves. The

Reservation as you see it now will disappear, and I believe it will be for the good, because the old traditions will be diluted or gone anyway. There are groups, like over at Oraibi, who are organizing an attempt to bring back the old ways, but those little organizations are not taking root.

Assimilating into the mainstream will probably be something like it was for European immigrants. Those people formed their own communities at first, kept themselves kind of clannish for a while, then they moved on. Maybe it will be the same story for us Hopis and Tewas from these Arizona mesas. It will be up to the individual which way he goes. Time is changing everything. That's what I keep telling my children and grandchildren down on the Colorado River Reservation. "If you acquire a good education instead of fooling away your time you will be able to take care of yourselves in a decent way. Whatever white people do, you are capable of doing it too. Get to know them and understand them and they'll get to understand you and what you are worth as a person."

As to intermarriage, it's happening all around us. My boy Aaron is married to a white woman in California, and my daughter Pat is married to a doctor in Gallup. Aaron is going to school and paints in his spare time, so he usually has a little money in his pocket, but if he's up against it he lets me know and I help him out. I sent my daughter Pat to California to learn to be a medical technican. She went to Gallup to finish her studies, that's how she met the doctor and married him. They wanted me to come and stay with them, but I said no, I have my own place and that's where I ought to be.

I see all kinds of changes on the Colorado River Reservation. Many Indians are marrying outsiders—Mexicans and white Americans. We've got some old-timers on the Reservation who are worried about this intermarriage. They say, "What are we going to do about those whites and Mexicans coming here and living on our land?"

I say, "Accept them, of course. Adopt them."

They say, "Aah, we can't do it. We can't have them here."

I say, "Get rid of that notion! You've got to accept people as people, no matter where they come from. If they'll stay and work in this hot place, what's the complaint?"

Looking back, I can remember when one Hopi village didn't want to intermarry with another Hopi village. That's a measure of how things have changed with the years. Now Hopis are marrying with whites and with other Indians, including Navajos, their traditional enemies.

I think it is inevitable that we are going along with the big flood. In one or two hundred years you won't find a full-blooded Indian anywhere. We will all be in the same pot.

I believe that this is about as far as I can go. What I have told you may not seem to be anything more than a lot of recollections, traditions, opinions and observations. Maybe that's all a person is, a collection of these things. I tried not to put myself forward too much, though I am sure some people will think I did not talk about myself enough. In our Indian way of looking at the world the individual isn't important, only the group. We forget the names of our heroes and villains, while remembering what the group did, for good or evil, and how it met challenges and dangers, and how it lived in balance with nature. Anyway, these recollections will tell people something about what life was like during my times. For some Hopis and Tewas now growing up, what I have said may make the gap between where we were and where they are now more understandable. As for myself, I am just one more person in that long line of people stretching back to Sibopay, the place of emergence.

Back Notes

1. An "official" spelling commonly used is Kyakotsmovi.

2. This concept that the first husband is the "true" husband with whom a woman will be reunited in death is reflected in the Maski story told by Mr. Yava. A young man marries a widow, and when she dies he pursues her to the afterworld, only to discover that she is once again living with her first husband. See pp. 99–104.

3. Although Mr. Yava did not know any stories about the more serious Oraibi raids against Walpi, he recalled the following, which is "documented" by a pictograph on the shelf of First Mesa:

"There was a young married couple who were tending their field in the valley. They were newlyweds, and they were sort of playing around, doing silly things. The woman was fixing the man's hair to look like a girl's. Then she fixed her hair to look like a man's. She put some of her clothes on her husband, and took some of her husband's clothing for herself. So she looked like a man and he looked like a woman. That was when a party of Oraibis came on a raid, a small party. The Walpi man did not run, but picked up his bow to fight. The woman stood aside. To the Oraibis it appeared that a woman was fighting while the man did nothing. It seemed as if the woman was shooting arrows, and it puzzled them.

"But of course things weren't good for the Walpi couple because they were outnumbered. The man had a dog up in the village and he called him. The dog was up on top of the houses when he heard the call. He jumped down and ran out to the field and attacked the Oraibis. He was pretty fierce, and they backed off and went away. To commemorate that event, someone drew a picture of a dog on the rocks right where it happened. People call the place Puweuvetaka, The Dog Chased Them Away. Oraibis don't like to hear the story or the name of the place. The rock is near the ruins of Keuchaptevela. In those days Oraibis and Walpis didn't consider themselves to be the same people. Every village was a kind of city-state. This particular raid was only a small one, but some of the others were pretty serious."

4. John P. Harrington, *The Ethnogeography of the Tewa Indians*, p. 254, describes the site of Tsewageh (or Tsewari) as it appeared early in this century: "The ruin consists of low mounds of disintegrated adobe, lying on a low bluff on the south side of Santa Cruz Creek, a short distance west of the Mexican settlement of Puebla. It is strewn with fragments of pottery." The Editor of this volume of Mr. Yava's recollections visited the Tsewageh site in 1976, locating it from a sketch map in the Harrington book. By this time all indications of walls had disappeared, though numerous pottery fragments were still to be found.

5. In his first telling of this story, Mr. Yava identified the expedition leader as Agayoping (Aguayaping), Oak Mountain. Later he corrected the name to Agaiotsay, as given here.

6. Harrington, *ibid.*, pp. 255–56, quotes several authorities as stating that Tsewageh was finally deserted in 1696. Mr. Yava's estimated date for the Tewa arrival in Hopi country is 1702. If correct, this would mean a lapse of six years. It is possible that the Tewas actually spent considerable time in their westward migration. First Mesa

Tewas say that the group from Tsewageh made four "stops" en route, but how long the Tsewageh people remained at these stops is not clear. It is possible that each stop was for a season or part of a season, and that temporary houses were built at each place. Note Mr. Yava's statement that the Tsewageh people had to build temporary houses below First Mesa before finally being allowed to proceed to the top, and that the ruins of those houses are still visible. However, the actual year of arrival is not certain.

7. Though it is contended by some that scalping was learned from the whites, Mr. Yava says the tradition is that the first to practice scalping in the Southwest were the Zunis. Some of the myth-legends of the Warrior Brothers, the Pokangs, involve scalping incidents. See for example Courlander, *The Fourth World of the Hopis*, pp. 74–75.

8. In her 1925 *Pueblo Indian Journal*, p. 7, Elsie Clews Parsons makes a reference to this site based on garbled information from one of her sources, possibly her main informant, Crow Wing, as follows: "On a slope below First Mesa under a conspicuous old cedar there is buried the heart of a Navajo chief, which is deemed a protection for First Mesa."

9. The significance of the petrified wood was not indicated. However, in Tewa the word for petrified wood is kaiyeh, and the word for shrine is kaiyehtay, meaning the structure around the petrified wood, suggesting a traditional linkage.

10. According to custom, the children of a Hopi mother and a Tewa father would belong to the mother's clan and be considered Hopis. Therefore, they would have to be left behind if the Tewas were to move away.

11. The institution of village chief has disappeared from Tewa Village. Informants could not say whether the First Mesa Tewas had any village chiefs after the time of Agaiotsay. The nearest thing the Tewas have to a headman or spokesman is the chief of their Tobacco Clan.

12. Hopi tradition supports the Tewa account of how Walpi asked the people of Tsewageh for help. An account given to the editor in 1969 by a Hopi informant, Powtiwa, Tobacco Clan in Walpi, also speaks of four requests. But it states that the Tsewagehs were Hanos (T'hanos), not Tewas, explaining why Hopis called the new settlement on First Mesa Hano. T'hanos, or Tanos, were actually southern Tewas, but the population of Tewa Village has always rejected the designation Hano. The Hopi version given by Powtiwa differs from the Tewa account in that it ascribes to the Tsewageh people a desire "to become Hopis." It says: "The Hopi delegation . . . offered them a place to stay, and said they would permit the Hanos to become Hopis. . . . The Hanos wanted to become Hopis." Mr. Yava stresses that, contrary to this Hopi contention, the Tewas insisted on retaining their own traditions.

13. See back note no. 6.

14. Different renditions of this myth frequently name birds other than those specified here.

15. For variants of the creation myth, see H. R. Voth, *The Traditions of the Hopi*, pp. 1–21. Another variant is to be found in Courlander, *The Fourth World of the Hopis*, pp. 17–33.

16. Harrington, *ibid.*, p. 567, says: "The human race and animals [according to some Eastern Tewa traditions] were born in the underworld. They climbed up a great Douglas spruce tree and entered this world through a lake called Sipop'e, a word of obscure etymology. . . . Sipop'e was like an entrance into this world. When people die, their spirits go to Sipop'e, through which they pass into the underworld. There are many spirits in the waters of Sipop'e. [It] is a brackish lake situated in the sand dunes north of Alamosa, Colorado."

17. For music notation of this song, see Appendix IV, p. 168.

18. Inasmuch as this prophecy seems to be free-floating, without any apparent connection to existing clan traditions, there is room for the question as to whether it may be spillover from Christian missionary teachings. In Water Clan traditions, some versions of the destruction of Palatkwa attribute the disaster to earthquake, while others say the destruction was caused by flood.

19. See "The Lamehva People" in Courlander, *ibid.*, p. 43 ff.

20. In a number of Oraibi stories, the Yayas (or Yayaponchatu, or Yayatu) are spoken of as a separate ethnic group rather than as a kiva society of the Reed Clan. In Voth, *ibid.*, p. 241, the story of the destruction of Pivanhonkapi begins: "A long time ago, there lived some people north of the place where the Oraibis at present dry their peaches. They were called Yayaponchatu. There was only one village of them, probably a small one. . . ." The chief of Pivanhonkapi wants to have his village destroyed because the people have become corrupt, so he goes to the Yayas, "who were known to have special influence over and with storms and fire, and who, in fact, were looked upon as being in league with supernatural forces." He asks the Yayas to destroy his village by fire. They perform a ceremony that brings a distant fire to Pivanhonkapi. Another Oraibi story set down by Voth, *ibid.*, pp. 123–24, locates the Yaya village much at the same place, north of the peach orchards. It describes the Yayas in this way: "They are not Hopi, but they are beings something like the skeletons. [Voth here refers to masauwus, spirits of the dead, which his translator rendered as 'skeletons.'] They have white faces and white bodies, disheveled hair, and wear kilts of black and white striped cloth." This story describes how two Yaya men come to Oraibi to trade for tobacco, and portrays them as speaking a language that is not understood by the Hopis.

21. Presumably the description of a heavy, stocky person is to suggest the image of a bear, which later becomes the insignia of this group.

22. Masipa, or Old Shongopovi, was down below present-day Shongopovi on the east side of the mesa. Its ruins are still visible on both sides of an unpaved road running from the blacktop highway. At the date of writing, a few walls were standing and a large stone-lined spring could be seen.

23. Voth, *ibid.*, pp. 30–36, relates two variants of this myth as heard in the Second Mesa villages of Shipaulovi and Mishongnovi. For another variant, see Courlander, *ibid.*, pp. 82–95.

24. The main cliff ruins in the Tsegi Canyon complex are now called Keet Seel, Inscription House and Betatakin. All of them are regarded by Hopis as part of Kalewistema.

25. As indicated later (p. 78), the Horn Clan was accompanied to its destination by its affiliated Antelope, Deer and Grass Clans.

26. Jesse W. Fewkes, in his *Tusayan Migration Traditions*, p. 585, reproduces chronologies of clan arrivals as stated by several First Mesa sources. No two of these chronologies are exactly alike. In all the chronologies, however, the Water Clan is listed somewhat after the Bear, Snake and Horn, either before or after the Squash and Reed clans. In two chronologies the Bear Clan is first, in two others the Snake Clan. As noted elsewhere in Mr. Yava's narration, the Reed Clan claims to have been the original settler on First Mesa.

27. The strange being on the roof at night, grinding with the metate, appears in a number of stories and is generally taken to be a sorcerer, witch or some supernatural being. A similar event takes place in the story of the abandonment of Huckovi. (See "The Flight from Huckovi" in Courlander, *ibid.*, pp. 127ff.) The song (which also appears in the Huckovi story) is intended to have an ominous import, though the meaning of the words is not known.

28. In an account taken down by Voth, *ibid.*, p. 52, from a Shipaulovi informant, it is not the young man but an old one, a powaka or sorcerer, who is killed and buried. Before placing him in the ground they affix the horn to his head, and he later becomes transformed into the great horned water serpent.

29. Apparently the North Star.

30. Some versions of the Palatkwa story say that the children caught up with the clans only at Homolovi, the third stop en route to First Mesa.

31. For a pictorial representation of this kachina personage, see Jesse W. Fewkes, *Hopi Kachinas Drawn by Native Artists*, plate LX, p. 181.

32. Fewkes, *ibid.*, pp. 42–56, describes the Paleuleukanti festival in considerable detail. He notes (p. 42): "This festival . . . is an excellent one in which to study Hopi symbolism, for many masked personages appear in the dramatizations in the kivas and on the plazas outside. . . . The proceedings in the kivas are theatrical exhibitions that vary from year to year accordingly as one chief or another controls the different acts. . . . The audience consisted mainly of women and children, who occupied one end of the room. . . . Everyone was gladly welcomed to see the performance, and there were probably not a dozen persons on the mesa who did not attend."

33. The ruins of Puye are west of Santa Clara Pueblo in New Mexico, north of Los Alamos.

34. Fewkes, in *Hopi Kachinas*, p. 23, gives January as Pamüryawû and the dance as Pamürti. He describes the occasion as a dramatization of the return of the sun.

35. Kerosene lanterns were introduced at a later date for lighting kivas. Some kivas now use propane gas lamps, and in 1976 a New Oraibi kiva was wired for electricity.

36. The Editor was unable to ascertain which of the many Fewkes publications Yava had in mind.

37. Recorded and set down by Walter Dyk, 1938.

38. The Editor has supporting evidence for the Hopis' high opinion of Fewkes. Once when he was photographing a pictograph near Walpi, an elderly Hopi riding by on a mule called out as he passed, "Read Fewkes, you'll find it all there."

39. The publication referred to appears to be *A Pueblo Indian Journal, 1920–1921*, by Elsie Clews Parsons.

40. Voth, in *The Traditions of the Hopi*, pp. 244–46, records a version of this story given to him by a person from Shipaulovi. The Shipaulovi version, clearly in error, is merely a transposition of the Awatovi affair, even in many of its details. Fewkes, in his *Archeological Expedition to Arizona in 1895*, p. 635, also refers to the "destruction" of Sikyatki, though he says at one point: "There appears to be no good evidence that Sikyatki was destroyed by fire, nor would it seem that it was gradually abandoned." A Sun Clan member from Oraibi, Don Talayesva, narrated to the Editor an explanation of Sikyatki's demise featuring not a kachina race but a race between a swallow and a hawk.

41. Adolph Bandelier, *Final Report of Investigations among the Indians of the Southwestern United States, 1890–1892*, Vol. 2, pp. 371–72, indicates that a single Spanish missionary returned to Awatovi in 1700. However, this missionary probably had in his company a number of Indian assistants.

42. Note the recurring theme of the chief of a village causing it to be destroyed because of "corruption." This theme also appears in stories about the demise of Palatkwa and Pivanhonkapi. In a text printed by Voth, *ibid.*, p. 256, a narrator from Shipaulovi stated: "This is the way chiefs often punished their children (people) when they became 'bewitched.' That is one reason why there are so many ruins all over the country. Many people were killed in that way because their chiefs became angry and invited some chief or inhabitant from other villages to destroy their people." The frequency with which this theme surfaces in Hopi historical legends suggests that it is a free-floating motif used wherever suitable.

43. Hopi memories vary somewhat regarding which Second Mesa villages were involved. Sometimes Shongopovi is named, but most narrators indicate Mishongnovi. An account given in Voth, *ibid.*, pp. 251–52, says that the Oraibis recruited clan relatives from Mishongnovi, but that the chief of Shongopovi refused to allow his village to be drawn in.

44. See Appendix IV, p. 169, for song of the Two Horn priest in Awatovi.

45. See Appendix IV, p. 170, for initiation song in Laguna.

46. See Montgomery, Smith and Brew, *Franciscan Awatovi*, Papers of the Peabody Museum of American Archeology and Ethnology, Vol. XXXVI.

47. The Author originally had a brief description of the Kachina Society initiation in this section, but deleted it for reasons of propriety. Inasmuch as he himself was not a member of the Kachina kiva group, he felt that the information was not his to dispense.

48. A pictorial representation of Tunwup and Tumas is to be found in Fewkes, *Hopi Katchinas Drawn by Native Artists*, plate VII. Fewkes describes the ceremony as witnessed by him in this way (p. 77): "Details of the ceremonial Powamû child flogging at Walpi and Hano [Tewa Village] vary somewhat. In the Hano celebration an altar is made in the kiva at that time by the chiefs, Anote and Satele, both of whom place their official badges on a rectangle of meal drawn on the kiva floor. Into this rectangle the children are led by their foster parents and flogged in the presence of the inhabitants of the pueblo. The two floggers, Tunwup and Tumas, stand one on each side of the figure made of meal, holding their whips of yucca. As they dance they strike the boys or girls before them as hard as they can, after which they pass the whips to a priest standing by. After each flogging the yucca whips are waved in the air, which is called the purification. After the children have been flogged many adults, both men and women, present their bared bodies, legs, and arms to the blows of the yucca whips." Fewkes says further (p. 78): "It is probable that this supernatural being [Tunwup] was introduced from a ruin called Kicuba, once inhabited by the Kachina Clan."

49. For a description of the Grand Canyon sipapuni, see Mischa Titiev's article, "A Hopi Salt Expedition," p. 251. The same article, p. 250, notes that a cavelike formation nearby is described as the home of Masauwu, deity of death.

50. Two versions of this Maski story in Voth, *ibid.*, pp. 109ff. describe numerous *Inferno*-like punishments not mentioned in Mr. Yava's brief account.

51. This is the first mention of the protagonist's name. It is possible that Mr. Yava didn't think of the name earlier. However, in numerous Hopi narrations the protagonist is referred to merely as "the young man," "the woman," etc. Sometimes the name comes out as a seeming afterthought at the end.

52. The graphic depictions of punishments in Maski for sins committed while living, the pit of flames and the Last Judgment suggest Christian intrusions into Hopi belief, as does the carefree life of persons whose lives have been faultless. Hopi traditions are generally unmarked by Christian Church influence, and we can only ponder whether this view of Maski is an exception.

53. Unexplained, but of interest, is the Author's statement that the great personage to come would be a ka'ashitaka, "one who doesn't wet his head" (headwashing being an Oraibi tradition). Since the Hopis and Tewas have their headwashing rituals and

Christians their christenings, the identity of the Good Bahana remains a subject of considerable kiva debate.

54. Voth, *ibid.*, does not properly distinguish in his translation between Masauwu and a masauwu. He translates Maski as Skeleton House.

55. See Appendix III, Hopi Petition to Washington, p. 165.

56. See back note no. 24.

57. This account of the Oraibi Split conforms closely to that of an elderly Oraibi informant, Don Talayesva, who was present on the occasion of the open confrontation. As he described it to the Editor: "I can tell you exactly how it happened because I was involved in that business. I was about sixteen years old then. There was this group in Oraibi that was hostile to the whites. That was the problem. We all used to live peaceably together when I was a young boy, but about the time I was old enough to be in school we began to separate from our old way of life. And this group that was hostile to the government refused to send their children to school. They didn't want to get help from the government. They wanted to be left alone to go their own way. It got to be pretty bad in the village. Things got turned upside down. When we friendly people had our ceremonies, they [the Hostiles] had theirs by themselves. We were not living peaceably for quite a while, till 1906. That was when we decided to do something. It was on September the 8th, 1906, that it happened. We drove those hostile people from the village, out that way, and kept them gathered there. During the afternoon it was getting pretty bad. Yukioma, who was head of the Hostiles, wanted his people to stay in Oraibi. He wanted us [the Friendlies] to leave the village. So about three o'clock he made four lines on the ground and then he said, 'Well, it has to be this way now, that when you pass me over these lines it will be done. We're going to have a tug-of-war. If you push us over [the lines] we are the ones to leave.' So our chief called a lot of those strong men to do the work. He said, 'Well, we'll get together and push each other. We'll push them back that way. If we pass them over those four lines it will be done.' We had a hard struggle. Both of our chiefs were in the center, and they had a hard time to get their breath. And then we drove them over the four lines. Then 'it was done,' that's what Yukioma said. Before the setting of the sun he [and his group] departed. Our chief said, 'You people are supposed to go out to where you came from, Kawestima [Kalewistema], toward Kayenta, to live.' After the Hostiles left, someone carved three or four footprints in the rock showing where they went out toward the west. A fellow named Robert Silena and Charles Addington carved the words that Yukioma had said. When the Hostiles got to the place where they were going to stay, Hotevilla, they cut down some trees and made temporary hogans at first, then afterwards they made their stone houses." (See also Don Talayesva's account of the event in his autobiography *Sun Chief.*)

58. Eototo is said by some to be a Bear Clan deity, but he is also regarded as another personation of Masauwu, deity of the Fire Clan. Fewkes, in *Hopi Kachinas Drawn by Native Artists*, p. 182 fn., states his understanding that Eototo and Masauwu

both came from the village of Sikyatki, where they were considered to be equivalent germination deities.

59. The long shadow cast by Tawaquaptewa's declaration of an end of ceremonialism and chieftaincy in Oraibi was visible in a 1976 Hopi land dispute. A local branch of the Church of Latter-day Saints (Mormons) sought permission to use a piece of land near Oraibi for a new building. The request was contested by concerned Hopis, including Mina Lansa, mentioned in Mr. Yava's account. The Hopi Tribal Council asked for a report on the actual status of the land wanted by the church. The leader of the local LDS group sought testimony from elderly Hopis on this matter, and some of the testimony referred back to the facts and implications of Tawaquaptewa's actions, as these excerpts from the report (published in the Hopi newspaper *Qua'Töqti*, June 10, 1976) show:

"On May 18, Jason Tanakyouma and the Branch President [of the church] interviewed Homer Cooyama (Coyote Clan) of Kikenchmovi [New Oraibi]. Homer said he asked Chief Tawaquaptewa three times what he planned for his people (after the Oraibi Split in 1906) and that the Chief told him he had none. The Chief also told Homer that he would not pass his leadership position to anyone. Homer stated that because of the destruction of the religion at Oraibi, the Hopis have nothing to stand on, that there is no spiritual base. . . .

"On May 29, Emil Pooley visited Grace Myron of Shongopovi, former wife of Myron Poliquaptewa. She stated that she did not know if the land in question had been assigned [that is, by clan chiefs or the priesthood]. She also said that while Chief Tawaquaptewa had stated earlier that he was grooming Myron Poliquaptewa as his successor, shortly before he died the Chief requested that he be buried in the costume of his clan deity, Eototo, which he said would proclaim the end of religion (in Oraibi)."

There were those in Hotevilla, also, who believed that ceremonialism had been damaged beyond any repair. An article in the Hopi newspaper *Qua'Töqti*, September 12, 1974, recalled the struggle within the village over this issue and the question of non-cooperation with the Government as follows:

"A power struggle ensued after Yukioma's death in 1932. James Pongyayouma, maternal nephew [of Yukioma], and, therefore, legal heir according to tradition, was cast aside by forces led by Dan Kachongva, the son of Yukioma.

"According to Benjamin Wytewa, Sr., whose father was a Spider Clansman, and one of the lieutenants of Yukioma, the chieftain told Wytewa's father in his presence (Wytewa's) that the ceremonial and ritual cycle ended with the split at Oraibi, and that he did not want it revived in the new village (Hotevilla).

"However, at the insistence of former members of the various priesthood societies at Oraibi, he relented and gave his consent. But he predicted that it would not last, since it was not meant to be, Wytewa said.

"When Kachongva took control, he gathered around himself powerful men who by then had assumed leadership positions in the revived priesthood orders. They took the ultra-conservative position of wanting nothing to do with the bahana society, and at first resisted all attempts by the Government to educate their children.

"In order to forever discredit Pongyayouma and eliminate him as a threat to himself, Kachongva purportedly seduced Pongyayouma's wife, who died in disgrace a short time later. This forced Pongyayouma into exile."

60. Dr. H. C. Diehl heard another explanation of Teuvi's name, which he renders as Túve. Poli Bayestewa, Teuvi's grandson, said that his grandfather was an energetic man whose favorite expression was "Túve!"—"Let's go!"—from which he derived his nickname.

61. In his book *Sun Chief*, pp. 252–55, Don Talayesva describes a salt expedition to Zuni Lake.

62. The Hopi-Navajo land dispute, still unresolved at the time Mr. Yava was commenting on it, had its origins in an executive order issued by President Chester Arthur in 1882. That order set aside approximately two and a half million acres in northern Arizona "for the use and occupancy of the Moqui [Hopi] and other such Indians as the Secretary of the Interior may see fit to settle thereon." Although the area was commonly referred to as the "Arthur Reservation," it did not, in fact, establish final, legal boundaries for the Hopi territory. Scattered Navajo families were already living within the designated area in 1882, and by 1958 their numbers had increased to more than eight thousand. Although no Secretary of the Interior during those years officially settled Navajos or other Indians within the reserved area, no action was taken to prevent the increasing Navajo presence. The Hopis protested frequently about the Navajo encroachment on the lands they believed to have been permanently set aside for them. In the late 1930s the Navajo Service of the Bureau of Indian Affairs recommended division of the 1882 Reservation into grazing districts for what was said to be strictly land-management purposes. The most central of these was District 6, containing the main Hopi villages (except Moencopi) and 631,000 acres of land. In 1943 the BIA approved and implemented this plan. Meanwhile the Navajo population in the districts other than District 6 was increasing. In 1958 the Hopis went to court to stem the Navajo occupation of their lands. In 1962 the court ruled in the *Healing* v. *Jones* case that the Secretary of the Interior had tolerated use by the Navajos of the land outside of District 6, and by implication had settled them. Thus, the court ruled, the Navajos and Hopis had equal rights and interests in those areas. The decision legalized Navajo occupation. In December 1974 the U.S. Congress adopted a bill calling for six months of negotiations between the Hopis and Navajos with Federal mediation, with a court-ordered settlement to follow if the negotiations failed to reach an agreement. The settlement would provide for a final division of the "Joint Use" lands between Hopis and Navajos.

63. See Appendix I, p. 155, The 1890 Deal to Fill the Keam's Canyon School.

64. See Appendix II, p. 161, Hopi Chiefs' Meeting with the Commissioner.

65. See Appendix III, p. 165, Hopi Petition to Washington.

66. Mr. Yava did not cite specific examples of Hopi infringements, but Dewey Healing noted as follows:

"Over there by the Polacca Wash, Ned Nayatewa's son (Ned is kikmongwi of Walpi) wanted to put up a service station there. Some of his people advised him that the land belonged to the Hopi Mustard Clan. I suppose he got permission of some kind and then he went ahead and started to build his service station. But it was Tewa land, and we had a meeting about it up here on the [First] Mesa. The council put it to a vote to see whether we'd agree to let the station be completed there. We voted against it, because it was Tewa land. But we knew our vote wouldn't be final unless the Tribal Council supported us. Our Tewa leaders agreed with us and told the Tribal Council we didn't want to give up this Tewa land to a Hopi service station. There was a big discussion in the Tribal Council meeting. There were some Hopis there who argued very strongly against us, claiming the land wasn't ours but belonged to the Hopi Mustard Clan. The Tribal Council voted approval of the service station over our objections. After that we couldn't do anything. Later, when that man got his service station going, he spread out and took over still more Tewa land. We've had other cases like that as well."

67. Ruth Underhill, *Pueblo Crafts*, p. 99, says: "Before 1859, decorated pottery had almost ceased on the Hopi mesas. Then Nampeyo, a Tewa woman of Hano, adopted the designs of pottery dug up by archeologists at the ruined village of Sikyatki. Other First Mesa women, both Hopi and Tewa, have followed her."

68. One of the most hostile of anti-Council groups was composed of ultraconservatives in the village of Hotevilla. According to some Hopi testimony, the Hotevilla group called itself "the Hopi Independent Nation" and urged the Navajos not to negotiate with the Tribal Council on the land question. It contended that the Tribal Council was not a legitimate representative of traditional Hopi society. Some Hopis claim that this group was in contact with Germany and Japan during World War II (and later with the Soviet Union), and that it was responsible for an invasion of the villages by hippies in 1967.

Appendixes

Appendix I

The 1890 Deal to Fill the Keam's Canyon School

As Mr. Yava observes, it was agreed by the Bureau of Indian Affairs to send five Hopi leaders to Washington in exchange for their promise to let their children attend the Keam's Canyon Boarding School. The school had a capacity for forty or fifty Hopi students at the time, but only three students were enrolled. For some time Hopi leaders had been asking to be sent to Washington to talk to the Great Chief—the President—to voice their concerns about their land, the Navajos and other problems. It appears to have been Thomas Keam who initiated the "swap." In exchange for pledges by three village chiefs to fill the Keam's Canyon school, the Hopi leaders made the Washington trip at Government expense. Although greatly impressed with what they saw of the white man's world, they apparently made no impression on official Washington with their major problems. Considerable correspondence preceded the Washington visit, with Keam pressing the issue for the Hopis with the support of C. E. Vandever, the local Indian Affairs Agent. Keam always had in mind the uncertain land question, and presumably was hoping that the Hopi delegation might be able to convey its concerns to the Government. However, Washington officials seemed to think of a Hopi visit as a sightseeing junket. Their primary concern was to fill the new Keam's Canyon school. Here are some of the letters of the Keam's Canyon-Washington correspondence.

Keam's Canon A. O.
Jany 13, 1890

The Honorable O. I. Morgan,
Commissioner of Indian Affairs,
Washington, D.C.

Dear Sir:

During my stay in Washington last summer, I talked with you in reference to a promise made some of the principal chiefs of the Moqui Indians. This way; that they should visit Washington, and talk with their Great Chief on matters of importance to them.

155

At that time you desired me to write you this winter on the subject, as in the multiplicity of business it would no doubt pass from your mind.

When the matter was brought forward, and recommended by W. Oberly last winter; There were no incidental funds available for that purpose. W. Belt then informed me, he was not generally in favor of Indians visiting the East, but with the Moquis he considered it an exceptional case, and when funds were available he favored it.

On my return here I told the chiefs of the result of my talk, and they said they would wait anxiously for the time.

I rarely make a visit to the villages but they remind me of this promise, and say, that Indians from all the surrounding tribes have visited The Great Father in the East; they alone have not; although they have always been friendly, and do as The Great Chief desires.

One of the principal objects of this visit is, they tell me, to talk with you and settle the matter of yearly encroachments by Navajo herds, on the land and waters close to their villages. They also desire to see how the white man lives, and how he makes the different articles of clothing; impliments etc. they have seen here.

As none of this tribe has ever been East of Albuquerque, New Mexico; I believe it would result in great good. Being one of the most remote from civilization, and rarely leaving their homes, they have not the least idea, of this great country or its people. It would also have a beneficial effect on the school, which for some cause, the attendance is less now than at any time since its establishment. I have asked them why they do not send more children, when they express dislike for the Superintendent and his wife but fail to give me the reason. The Orabis have not sent a child yet, and say when asked "The Government does not protect us against the encroach-ments of the Navajos".

Agent Vandever visited here a short time ago and I talked with him on this matter, he expressed a desire to have the Moquis visit the East; also some of the leading Navajos, and settle the matter of Navajo encroachment on Moqui lands, and thereby prevent serious trouble, between the Moqui and surrounding Navajos.

Should you favor this visit, I would suggest the following head men of the Moquis; "Shimo", "Anowita", "Polacca", "Lalolami", and "Honani". These are the rulers and leading men from different villages, and represent the whole tribe.

Very respectfully
Your obt. Svt,
Thomas V. Keam

P.S. I have written this at the express wish of the chiefs.

T.V.K.

Personal. Keam's Canon A.O.
Feby 14, 1890.

The Honorable O. I. Morgan,
Commissioner of Indian Affairs,
Washington, D.C.

Dear Sir:

A few days ago the Superintendent of Moqui School, W. Baker, informed me he had received a letter from you, in reply to a wish expressed by the principal chiefs of that tribe, to visit Washington and talk with you on matters of important interest to them. He desired me to visit the villages with him, and impress the Indians with the importance of filling the school with their children.

On our arrival at the village the chiefs desired to hold the council in their principal "Kiva" or council chamber, as the subject was important and the talk should be straight. The contents of your letter was fully interpreted to them, when they expressed pleasure of hearing direct from you; but said they first desired to go to Washington, and see you before sending another child to school.

They told W. Baker of the kindly feelings that existed between the former employe's of the school, and the children as well as themselves— Now it was quite the reverse, they and the children disliked him very much, and they would not send another child to school as long as he remained. They desired to see their children happy, which made their hearts glad, but since his (Bakers) arrival there was nothing but discontent and dissatisfaction. Therefore they would like to see the "Great Father" and ask him to send a man whom they could like, and who would like them and their children, as they believed there were numbers of good white men in the East.

The following morning we succeeded in getting three boys to come, which is all the attendance at present, and one of the chiefs informed me today no more will come.

W. Bakers efforts are worthy of better success; but he is unfortunate in being placed among Indians, as his disposition will not enable him to make friends with them.

I have taken the liberty to write you personally on this matter, as you expressed a great desire to see this school a success, and it would ill become me after your kind expressions toward me, not to write you on a subject which I believe you attach great interest and importance to, and to which you have given bountiful aid.

Very truly yours,
Thomas V. Keam.

UNITED STATES INDIAN SERVICE,

Navajo Agency, N.M.
Feby 15, 1890

Hon. Commissioner of Indian Affairs
Washington, D.C.

Sir,

On the 12th inst. I telegraphed you that three Moquis Pueblo chiefs had sent me word that they will fill the school if given a trip to Washington, and asking what answer I should give them. I believe in allowing the chiefs to make the trip to the east, but do not believe it would be the proper thing to enter into such an agreement as that proposed by the chiefs. I believe they should be taught to send their children to school for the benefits to be derived from it, and I further believe that I can make them see it in that light, and by the proper effort fill the school. At the same time I believe it would be a great assistance to the work of education to send three of the leading men east on a trip. None of them have ever been farther from home than Holbrook, a village on the railroad about 90 miles from the reservation, consequently have not the remotest conception of how the world looks. By showing it to them and explaining that the white man is indebted to civilization and education for all he possesses they would probably heed the lesson. Certainly they would come home and talk of their trip to other members of the tribe as long as they live. The impressions left on their minds would be deep and lasting, and much good would certainly result. The same statement applies with equal force to the Navajos, and I would request that three of the leading men of each tribe be selected and sent together, as I firmly believe that incalculable good would result there from.

Very respectfully
Your obedient servant.
C.E. Vandever
U.S. Indian Agent

DEPARTMENT OF THE INTERIOR,
Office Of Indian Affairs

Washington, February 17, 1890

The Honorable
the Secretary of the Interior.

Sir:

I have the honor to transmit herewith a letter from Thomas V. Keam, who lives near the villages of the Moqui Indians in Arizona, in which he states that it is the desire of certain chiefs to visit this city, for the purpose of consulting in regard to their tribal matters and to see how the white man lives—a delegation of these Indians never having visited the East—in reply to which, the Superintendent of the Moqui Indian School was instructed, on the 28th ult, to tell the chiefs that on condition that they sent their children to school and kept the school well filled, their request would be considered. I am now in receipt of a telegram from Agent Vandever, under whose charge these Indians are, in which he states that three chiefs have send word that they will fill the school, if the government will permit them to come to this city.

As I think this is an exceptional case and that permission for a delegation of these Indians to come to this city would result in a benefit to the tribe in more ways than one, I respectfully recommend that authority be granted for the payment of the expenses of a delegation, to consist of the five chiefs named by Mr. Keam, viz; "Shimo", "Lalo-lami" and "Honani" [two names appear to have been omitted], with an Interpreter, and Agent Vandever in charge, in coming to this city, while here and in returning to their Agency; *provided* however, that before such authority is given the Agent, these chiefs shall guarantee to fill the Moqui Indian school with Indian children from the Moqui tribe, not only during the balance of the current fiscal year, but during the fiscal year 1891.

Payment of the expenses to be made from "incidentals in Arizona, 1890".

Very respectfully,
(Signed)   T. J. Morgan
Commissioner

DEPARTMENT OF THE INTERIOR
Office Of Indian Affairs,

Washington, March 8th 1890.

C. E. Vandever,
U.S. Indian Agent,
Navajo Agency, N.M.

Sir:

You are hereby advised that authority has been granted for the expenses of a delegation of five Moqui Chiefs—"Shimo", "Anowita", "Polacco", "Lalo-lami" and "Honani"—with an Interpreter, and yourself in charge, from the Moqui Agency, Arizona to Washington, D.C. and return, for the purpose of consulting in regard to their tribal matters and to see how the white man lives, in accordance with the wishes of said chiefs as set forth in a letter from Thomas V. Keam, who lives near the village of the Moquis in Arizona; *provided however*, that the said Chiefs shall first guarantee to fill the Moqui school with Indian children from the Moqui tribe, not only during the balance of the current fiscal year, but during the fiscal year 1891.

Referring to your letter of the 15th ult., requesting that three of the leading men of the Navajo tribe be also authorized to visit this city, you are advised that the funds applicable to this purpose are about exhausted, therefore your request cannot be complied with; however, you can bring this matter to the attendance of this Office after July 1st 1890, for consideration.

Very respectfully,
(Signed)   T. J. Morgan
Commissioner.
C.F.C.

Appendix II

Hopi Chiefs' Meeting with the Commissioner

The five Hopi village chiefs—Simo, Anawita, Polaccaca, Lololoma and Honani—met in Washington on June 27, 1890, with Commissioner Morgan. The following brief transcript appears to be the only record of that meeting, which seemingly consisted of brief statements by the chiefs and briefer comments by the Commissioner. Note that the Hopis were still called "Moquis"—a term approbrious to them—and it is doubtful that they referred to themselves as such as the transcript indicates they did. Note also that there is no reference to the burning question of land boundaries, and only slight mention of the Navajos. It is difficult to believe that this account covers all that was said after the Hopi leaders had travelled so far to put their grievances before the Commissioner (mistakenly addressed as the Great Father). Dr. H. C. Diehl, who provided this document to the Editor, commented: "When I have read the comments of the Indian leaders as reported by the Government, I wonder if such simpleton conversation really came from men who made the long trip to Washington (the first for Hopis in their history) or whether the Government faked these interviews." As is readily seen, the transcript badly mangles Hopi personal and place names.

CONFERENCE WITH MOQUI [i.e., HOPI] PUEBLOS
INDIAN OFFICE

June 27, 1890

Present Commissioner Morgan
Agent C.E. Vandever,
Thomas V. Keam, Interpreter,
Shimo, Tribal Chief
Polawa [Polaccaca], Chief Tewa,
An now ita, Chief Schichita navc,
Honani, Chief Cipaluvi
Lalolamy, Chief Orabi.

SHIMO. I have never seen the Great Father before. I am glad for what I have seen on the way here and look on your face now. On the way we saw great fields of corn and wheat and grass, every thing was green and beautiful, very different from our dry country, where we raise only a little for want of water. What we need is a water supply. We noticed that all the white people were busy at something. We let our horses loose in our few watering places and when we go after them we find them short. Some of the Navajos take them and they encroach on the water too. The Agent is far off; by the time he hears the horses are gone. Before we left home we lived, as it were, with closed eyes. What we had heard of Americans we could not believe. But now our eyes and our ears have been opened. We will tell the others when we get home what we have seen and those who live on the mesas may with help be willing to come down. We have lived on the mesas for fear of enemies, but there are no enemies now. All of us work hard. The women and children grind corn and work in the house and the men work in the fields from morning till night; our hands are blistered, but we accomplish little. But the white men got wonderful things done. They put up a house in a short time. We have to come from the top of the mesa for wood and water and it is a great deal of work. But our houses are there. If we could get assistance in building houses I would do all in my power to get the people to come down from the mesa. We need something for grinding corn too. I am old and grey and some of my hair is gone. Since the Americans came to the country we have better clothes and live differently. The Government has treated us kindly and we are thankful for that. If we could have some improvement about water, live down in the plain where the water is handy, we would be better off, and I will try and induce my people to do just as you advise. You have never heard of a Moqui going out and stealing from the whites, some of the Navajoes, though, are bad people. I see now how much more pleasantly the white people live. We want wagons and stoves and help to build houses so as to live more like the whites.

POLAWA [Polaccaca]. I am not a Moqui but a Tewa. Although my father has the old religion and all the old ideas, yet I have listened to the whites and have moved down from the mesa and have a good house and horses and cattle. We want horses and cattle, stoves and wagons. When I go back I think we will be willing to do as you ask. I am younger and stronger than most of these, and have taken the white man's way and I think after coming here and seeing things the others will do as I have done.

AN NOW ITA. We thank you for allowing us to come here. Our people wanted us to tell you how poor we are. Particularly we want sheep; we could sell the wool and buy what we need. The Navajoes have sheep and they do well. Also we want wagons and stoves. We have seen much on the way and coming here has done us good. We thank you. The Americans are great and strong and have big hearts. We are small and insignificant. When we left we had finished planting, we left our people to take care of our fields. They begged us to ask for assistance, and they will ask us how we succeeded, and what the Great Father will do for us. We shall have a long story to tell them of what we have seen.

HONANI. I also thank you for the chance to come here. My people told me to see everything, to find out how Americans live, whether there are many of them &c. I have seen wonderful things. What Indians want most is green grass. The Americans must have plenty of water. We have lived for years on the mesas, away from water. With assistance we will move into the valley near springs and our fields, and then if we had sheep we could sell wool and buy sugar and coffee and other good things and live like whites. We could look after our stock and get pay for what we do like white people. I am a young man and hope to do a good deal. Our horses are stolen by the Navajoes and the Agent can hardly help it. The Navajoes encroach on our water. The stealing of horses is a great trouble both to us and to the Agent. Often we cannot find out who stole the horses. We would like to have that stopped.

LALOLAMY. My people are blind. Their ears are closed. I am the only one. I am alone. They don't want to go in the white men's ways, although I am Chief. You are strong and have a good heart. You have much to do and many people to look after. I am thankful to see and I want your advice as to what to do with my people who are hard headed. We are very poor and very few, especially compared with the white people whom we have seen. All of it is very wonderful. We don't know much improving what little water we have and any assistance my people would be glad to get. I can tell my people now that I have seen you with my own eyes. I have seen for them. I want to know from you what is best to be done for them. Some of my people seem to have hearts of stone, blind eyes, deaf ears and don't believe what is told them. They are away from the world and know nothing except what is there where they live. This journey is a great thing for me. I never saw any thing in my life before. We raise corn, melons, peaches and some other vegetables and do fairly well, but here we have already seen melons and peaches. Ours are not ready yet. We work hard and our lives are centered in our work to raise what we can, and any assistance from you we will appreciate. Probably the hard headed and hearted people may sometimes believe what is told them. The Agent if he had not a good strong heart would not have been able to do what he has for the Navajoes and us.

Commissioner. I am glad you have enjoyed coming here, and I want you to go to Carlisle and to see all you can. As you see the white people are very much greater in numbers than you are. They are increasing very fast, and are very prosperous. They live in good houses and have good clothes and plenty to eat. Two things make them prosperous, one is that they educate all their children and keep them in school year after year, and they learn about books and how to do all kinds of things. The white people educate the women too, as you see here, and when they are educated they all work. These are the two things, we educate all our children and we all work. We are establishing schools for the Indian children, where they may be educated as white children are. If your children would go to those schools and stay as ours do, then your girls would learn to wash, iron, keep house, and your boys would learn farming, blacksmithing, carpentoring, &c., they could learn to do just as well as white children do. When you go to Carlisle you will see Indian girls and boys doing just as white boys and girls do.

I will talk with your Agent and see what can be done for you. He knows you and lives near you and you must take his advice. I shall be glad to do whatever I can for you, with whatever money Congress gives me to spend. All except this part of the cost was given the Indians.

To Agent Vandever:—How many families have moved down?

AGENT VANDEVER. Eight. This man [Polaccaca?—Ed.] has a good house, plastered, and he has a stove. All the eight except two have stoves.

COMMISSIONER. Provide those that are already down with stoves. I will authorize that so far as I have the power. If there is another company who want to go down from the mesa, help them to build.

AGENT VANDEVER. They need doors and windows. They should do the hauling themselves. I think about forty would go if some help were given them.

COMMISSIONER. Is there a carpenter at the school?

AGENT VANDEVER. Yes.

COMMISSIONER. I will spare the carpenter from the school for a while and will instruct him to show you how to build houses. So far as we give help it must be given to those who go down from the mesa.

AGENT VANDEVER. They have never got any thing for their sick and when they come to the school the Dr. does not give medicines or wait on them. He says the medicines are for the school. For implements next year, they need only hoes and axes.

COMMISSIONER. Next year I will try and have a blacksmith's shop established. I will ask the Secretary to authorize that. I will see what can be done towards furnishing medicines. The Agent is going down to stay with you for a month or two, and I will instruct the school carpenter to show you how to build houses and so far as I can I will help those who go down from the mesa. I cannot do very much, but I will do what I can.

Appendix III

Hopi Petition to Washington

In 1894, at the urging of Thomas Keam, the Hopi villages sent a petition to Washington urging that the Government cease its effort to reallocate clan lands and institute private individual holdings. The petition also requested a precise definition of the Hopi reservation. Keam apparently drafted the petition himself, in his own handwriting. The signers identified themselves by drawing their clan symbols, after which Keam wrote out their names. The document is a concise and eloquent description of Hopi landholding traditions and the difficulties of desert farming. As far as the Hopi elders know, there was no direct reply to the villages from anyone in Washington.

Moqui Villages
Arizona March 27 & 28, 1894

To the Washington Chiefs:

During the last two years strangers have looked over our land with spy-glasses and made marks upon it, and we know but little of what it means. As we believe that you have no wish to disturb our Possessions, we want to tell you something about this Hopi land.

None of us wer[e] asked that it should be measured into separate lots, and given to individuals for they would cause confusion.

The family, the dwelling house and the field are inseparable, because the woman is the heart of these, and they rest with her. Among us the family traces its kin from the mother, hence all its possessions are hers. The man builds the house but the woman is the owner, because she repairs and preserves it; the man cultivates the field, but he renders its harvest into the woman's keeping, because upon her it rests to prepare the food, and the surplus of stores for barter depends upon her thrift.

A man plants the fields of his wife, and the fields assigned to the children she bears, and informally he calls them his, although in fact they are not.

Even of the field which he inherits from his mother, its harvests he may dispose of at will, but the field itself he may not. He may permit his son to occupy it and gather its produce, but at the father's death the son may not own it, for then it passes to the father's sister's son or nearest mother's kin, and thus our fields and houses always remain with our mother's family.

According to the number of children a woman has, fields for them are assigned to her, from some of the lands of her family group, and her husband takes care of them. Hence our fields are numerous but small, and several belonging to the same family may be close together, or they may be miles apart, because arable localities are not continuous. There are other reasons for the irregularity in size and situation of our family lands, as interrupted sequence of inheritance caused by extinction of families, but chiefly owing to the following condition, and to which we especially invite your attention.

In the Spring and early Summer there usually comes from the Southwest a succession of gales, oftentimes strong enough to blow away the sandy soil from the face of some of our fields, and to expose the underlying clay, which is hard, and sour, and barren; as the sand is the only fertile land, when it moves, the planters must follow it, and other fields must be provided in place of those which have been devastated. Sometimes generations pass away and these barren spots remain, while in other instances, after a few years, the winds have again restored the desirable sand upon them. In such event its fertility is disclosed by the nature of the grass and shrubs that grow upon it. If these are promising, a number of us unite to clear off the land and make it again fit for planting, when it may be given back to its former owner, or if a long time has elapsed, to other heirs, or it may be given to some person of the same family group, more in need of a planting place.

These limited changes in land holding are effected by mutual discussion and concession among the elders, and among all the thinking men and women of the family groups interested. In effect, the same system of holding, and the same method of planting, obtain among the Tewa, and all the Hopi villages, and under them we provide ourselves with food in abundance.

The American is our elder brother, and in everything he can teach us, except in the method of growing corn in these waterless sand valleys, and in that we are sure we can teach him. We believe that you have no desire to change our system of small holdings, nor do we think that you wish to remove any of our ancient landmarks, and it seems to us that the conditions we have mentioned afford sufficient grounds for this requesting to be left undisturbed.

Further it has been told to us, as coming from Washington, that neither measuring nor individual papers are necessary for us to keep possession of our villages, our peach orchards and our springs. If this be so, we should like to ask what need there is to bring confusion into our accustomed system of holding corn fields.

We are aware that some ten years ago a certain area around our land, was proclaimed to be for our use, but the extent of this area is unknown to us, nor has any Agent, ever been able to point it out, for its boundaries have never been measured. We most earnestly desire to have one continuous boundary ring enclosing all the Tewa and all the Hopi lands, and that it shall be large enough to afford sustenance for our increasing flocks and herds. If such a scope can be confirmed to us by a paper from your hands, securing us forever against intrusion, all our people will be satisfied.

[The above Hopi petition was signed in clan symbols by 123 principals of kiva societies, clan chiefs and village chiefs of Walpi, Tewa Village, Sichomovi, Mishongnovi, Shongopovi, Shipaulovi and Oraibi.]

Appendix IV

Music Notation of Songs Referred to in the Text

1. "Creation Song of the Tewas"

2. "Song of the Two Horn Priest in Awatovi"

3. "Initiation Song in Laguna

Appendix V

Two Short NarrativeTexts by AlbertYava

Mockingbird, Giver of Birdcalls

When the world was young, the birds didn't have any way of communicating because they couldn't talk. Couldn't communicate with one another. The only one that was in a position to teach them was the mockingbird, called yalpa. He was the one who had given people their languages. He sent for all the fowls of the air and asked them to come together. He said to them, "We don't seem to have any language among us. So I'm in a position to teach you something. Now, you all listen to me. I'm going to give you your calls. If I want to call a rock hen, I'll say, 'Tchew tchew tchew,' and the rock hen will hear me. He'll wonder why I'm calling, and he'll come. If I want to have a red-tailed hawk come to the meeting, I'll make that shrill noise, 'Sieuuuu! Sieuuuu! Sieuuuu!' and the red-tailed hawk will know he's supposed to come. If I want to have an owl come to the meeting, I'll kind of cough, 'K'hu! K'hu! K'hu!' Owl will know I want him to come. I'm going to give every bird his call. When they hear these calls they'll know I am holding a meeting. Every bird should listen for his call." Mockingbird assigned all the calls. Whenever a bird heard what his call was supposed to be, he said, "That's all I want to know," and left.

The last bird was still there. He looked like the mockingbird. The mockingbird said, "Seems to me you look like me." It was the catbird. Looks just like the mockingbird. He said, "Yes, I believe I do." Mockingbird said, "Don't you want any call?" Catbird said, "No, I don't think I need to learn a call." "Why?" Catbird said, "Seems like you're not very popular with the other birds. Didn't you notice that as soon as they received their calls they flew right off? I think that the best thing for me is not to know any call. If I want to come to any meeting I can hear you calling the other birds, then I'll come. But I'll just sit quietly and not do any talking."

Mockingbird said, "Well, if you don't have any call, how are you going to make your announcement?" Catbird said, "Oh, I'll just flutter my wings."

Catbirds are the only ones that you hardly ever hear talking. All they say is, "Mieh! Mieh! Mieh!" That's all they say. The catbird decided that he didn't want a real call, because he was ashamed of his cousin, and he didn't want to be mistaken for him. He was afraid that if he had a call, other birds would think he was the mockingbird, who always talked too much.

Grey Hawk and the Field Mouse

This is a story told by Masaquaptewa about a field mouse that lived near the Corn Rock over at Second Mesa.

The people at Second Mesa were losing a lot of chickens. They prized chickens very much for their eggs, and the people got worried. They wondered where their chickens had been going. The chief of the village wanted to know what they could do about it. So he went to his war chief to see what the war chief thought about the matter. He took his pipe and tobacco along, and after they had passed the pipe to one another it was time to talk. They laid down the pipe and started to talk. The war chief asked, "What's the purpose of your visit, our father?" They always called the kikmongwi "our father."

"Well, son, I came here because people have been coming to me about their chickens. It seems as if somebody is taking them. People are worried. I want you to look into it and find out how the chickens are disappearing."

The war chief said, "All right, I'll detail some boys to go around and see what's happening to the chickens."

Along about noon, one of the boys spotted the old grey hawk on top of Corn Rock. The hawk was fluttering his wings. Soon as he saw a chicken down there in the yard he swooped down, picked it up and carried it to the top of Corn Rock. Ate a piece of the chicken up there. That evening one of the boys came to the war chief and said, "Now I know where the chickens are going, because I saw it with my own eyes. There's an old grey hawk on top of Corn Rock. He's the one that's been carrying away the chickens. But how can we get at Grey Hawk? You can shoot with bow and arrow, but you can't hit him. If you stand behind the rock your arrow won't reach him. And you can't climb that Corn Rock either. And you can't go up in the crevice." The war chief said, "Well, I'll think about it. Meanwhile we know where the chickens are going."

The field mouse happened to hear about all this, said, "I guess I'll make a visit to the chief myself." So he did. That night he went up to the chief's house, said, "Ha'u!" Chief said, "Come in!" In comes little old Field Mouse. Now, the chief is the protector, he's supposed to take care of the life and interests of whoever comes to him, even a small creature. He looked at the field mouse, said, "Come in, come in!" Field Mouse had his little old pipe and native tobacco. He lit up with a flint before the chief could get his own pipe ready, got ahead of him. (That's one thing you try to do, get ahead of the chief before he hands you his lighted pipe.) Chief took it. After he smoked he passed the pipe, saying, "My son." Field Mouse said, "My father." That's the way they're supposed to address one another. The chief said, "Now, what's on your mind?" The field mouse said, "You people seem to be having trouble with your chickens. I've been watching the hawk taking them away. But there's no way you can get rid of that hawk. I guess I'll have to do it for you." The chief said, "Well, son, my child, you're so small, how could you?" The field mouse said, "Oh, there's always a way to help." The chief said, "You can't shoot an arrow up there. You can't throw a spear. I don't see how you could help." The field mouse said, "I have a plan in my mind." "What is it?" "Well, I think I can entice the hawk to come down and try to pick me up. I live down there close to the Corn Rock. I'm going to tempt him to come down and catch me. I can go into my kiva. I'm going to get a sharp stick and put it in the ground. When he comes after me I'll get down next to the sharp stick, and the stick will pierce him."

The chief kind of laughed, said, "All right. I'll let you go ahead with your scheme." So after they agreed, they passed the pipe again. "Well," the field mouse said, "I'll let you know after four days, when I'm ready to have war with the grey hawk."

The field mouse went home, dressed himself like a warrior. On the appointed day he came out singing, mocking the grey hawk. Grey Hawk looked down, said to himself, "There's prize meat, I'm going to get him." So he started to flutter his wings, but field mouse was dancing around close to his hole, and he had a sharp stick sticking up from the ground right there. He kept mocking the grey hawk. Grey Hawk got angry, came down like a bullet to get the field mouse. The field mouse popped into his hole, but the grey hawk was coming down so fast he couldn't check his speed, and he hit the pointed stick head on. He impaled himself. The stick went right through his craw and killed him. Field Mouse took the dead hawk to the village chief. "Here you are," he said. "I got rid of your enemy." The chief said, "Did you really kill him?" Field Mouse said, "Yes. That stick went right through him. Killed him."

Well, the people were so glad that they put up a big feast in honor of the field mouse killing the grey hawk.

That was a story told by Masaquaptewa. Eddie Kennard got it from him and put down the text, then he brought it to me at Keam's Canyon and I corrected the Hopi words.

Publications Referred to by Author or Editor

Bandelier, Adolph. *Final Report of Investigations Among the Indians of Southwestern United States, 1890–1892* (two vols.).

Courlander, Harold. *The Fourth World of the Hopis.* New York: Crown Publishers, 1971.

Dyk, Walter (recorder/editor). *Son of Old Man Hat: A Navajo Autobiography.* New York: Harcourt Brace, 1938.

Fewkes, Jesse Walter. *Archeological Expedition to Arizona in 1895,* 17th Annual Report of the Bureau of American Ethnology (1895–1896). Washington, D.C., 1898.

——. *Hopi Katchinas Drawn by Native Artists,* 21st Annual Report of the Bureau of American Ethnology (1899–1900). Washington, D.C., 1903.

——. *Tusayan Migration Traditions,* 19th Annual Report of the Bureau of American Ethnology, part 2 (1901–1902). Washington, D.C., 1900.

Harrington, John P. *The Ethnogeography of the Tewa Indians,* 29th Annual Report of the Bureau of American Ethnology (1907–1908). Washington, D.C., 1916.

Montgomery, Ross G., Watson Smith, and Joseph Brew. *Franciscan Awatovi,* Peabody Museum Papers, vol. XXXVI. Cambridge, Mass., 1949.

Parsons, Elsie Clews. "A Pueblo Indian Journal, 1920–1921," *Memoirs of the American Anthropological Association,* no. 32, 1925.

Qua'toqti, Sept. 12, 1974; June 10, 1976, New Oraibi, Arizona.

Talayesva, Don C. *Sun Chief: The Autobiography of a Hopi Indian,* edited by Leo W. Simmons. New Haven: Yale University Press, 1942.

Titiev, Mischa. "A Hopi Salt Expedition," *American Anthropologist,* vol. 39, 1937.

Underhill, Ruth. *Pueblo Crafts.* Washington, D.C.: Bureau of Indian Affairs, 1944.

Voth, H. R. *The Traditions of the Hopi,* Field Columbian Museum Publication 96. Chicago, 1905.

Waters, Frank, and Oswald White Bear Fredericks. *Book of the Hopi.* New York: Viking Press, 1963.

Index

correspondence of on behalf of Hopis and Tewas, 155ff; role in drafting Hopi-Tewa petition to Washington, 165ff

Keuchaptevela, 35, 37, 53, 58ff, 69, 83ff passim; Catholic mission in, 89; move to top of mesa, 91

Keuchatewa, 116, 131

Kisiwu, Kisiwuva, 98

Kiva secrets, revelation of, 128-29

Kiwan Kachina mask in story, 63-65

Kootka, 61

Kwaiyegeh, 106

Kwakwan, Kwakwanteu. See One Horn Fraternity

Lagunas. See Kawaikas

Lalakon, 70, 74

Land problems, with Navajos, 120ff, 129; Chester Arthur solution for, 120-22; Hopi-Tewa mission to Washington to discuss, 122-23, 155ff; redistribution of Hopi clan holdings by U.S. Government, 123-24; petition to Washington regarding, 124, 165ff; grazing districts established, 127; difficulties between Hopis and Tewas, 131; importance of Tribal Council in dealing with, 134; position of Hotevilla conservatives on, 152 (n. 66)

Landholding tradition, 111, 115, 165ff

Language, village dialects of, 82

Lansa, Mina, assumes chieftaincy in Oraibi, 116

Le'etayo, 13

Literalness in Hopi and Tewa narratives, xi

Lololoma, 112, 123, 156, 160, 161, 163

Lowiwaya, 13

Mail, delivery of by riders and runners, 12-13

Masauwu, 37, 39, 49, 50ff, 58-59, 112; mask of, in story, 63-65, 69; shrine to, in Grand Canyon, 99; discussed, 106-7; described by Voth as "skeleton," 107; sparks in the night associated with, 107; traditional appearance of, 107-8; incident connected with, 108

Masipa, 36, 51-52, 145 (n. 22)

Masito, 52

Maski, description of, 99-100, 101-3; story about visit to, 100ff; possible Christian intrusion of concept, 148 (n. 52)

Maternal uncle, traditional authority of, 74

Meusiptanga, 88

Middle class developing on reservation, 137

Migrations, traditions of, 36ff, 43-45, 50ff, 57ff, 61-62, 68-69, 82, 86, 97

Mockingbird, theme of in myths, 5, 40, 78; story about, 171

Moencopi, 35; runners to from Oraibi, 13, 116; an offshoot of Oraibi, 116; a Corn Clan settlement, 116; friction between conservatives and progressives in, 117

Montgomery, Ross G., 148 (n. 46)

Mormons, at Joseph City, 13-14; at Tuba City, 117

Murals in kivas, 96-97

Muyingwa, 48

Nahtna, 74ff

Namoki, 80

Nampeyo, 132

Navajo Mountain. See Tokonave

Navajos, frictions with, 117ff

Nayatewa, Ned, 60

New Fire Ceremony, 75ff

Niman, 23, 24, 79, 97, 106, 113

Nitioma, 73ff passim

Nuvatikyao, 51, 79, 97-98; considered home of kachinas, 97

Oga'akeneh, 43-45

One Horn Fraternity, 2; initiation into, 2, 3, 8, 72ff; origin of at Palatkwa, 61, 69; teachings of, 70, 79; relationship to Lalakon, 70; exorcism ritual of, 110

Oraibi, breakup of, 11, 38, 53, 111ff, 149 (n. 57); founding of, 52; end of initiations in, 79; Catholic mission established in, 89; confrontation between Bear Clan and Fire Clan in, 112; push-of-war in, 113; destruction of ritual paraphernalia in, 115; raid against Walpi, story, 143 (n. 3)

Ortiz, Alfonso, xii

Oyaping, Nelson, 16

Pachaveu. See Invaya

Palatkwa, Palatkwapi, 8, 36, 41; destruction of, 37, 66-67; origin of Water Clan at, 61ff; story of, 62ff; other accounts of, 145 (n. 18)

Paleuleukang, 61ff; sacrifice to, 66-67; midwinter ceremonies for, 69

Paleuleukanti, 70, 146 (n. 32)

Parker, Arizona. See Colorado River Reservation

Parsons, Elsie Clews, 81, 144 (n. 8), 147 (n. 39)

Patowahkacheh, 55, 56

Pawbinele, Irving, 15-16, 24

Payupki and Payupkis, 1, 35, 38, 88, 129

Peki, 7, 19-20, 26, 105

Petrified wood, possibly sacred, 144 (n. 9)

Pictographs, 117, 143 (n. 3)

Pinini, 19

Pivanhonkapi, 38

Pokanghoya and Palengahoya, 8, 46-47, 48, 144 (n. 7)

Pokangs. See Pokanghoya and Palengahoya

Polacca, Polaccaca, Tom, 11, 12, 123, 130, 131, 156, 160, 161, 162

Poliquaptewa, Myron, named temporary Oraibi chief, 116

Popay, 90

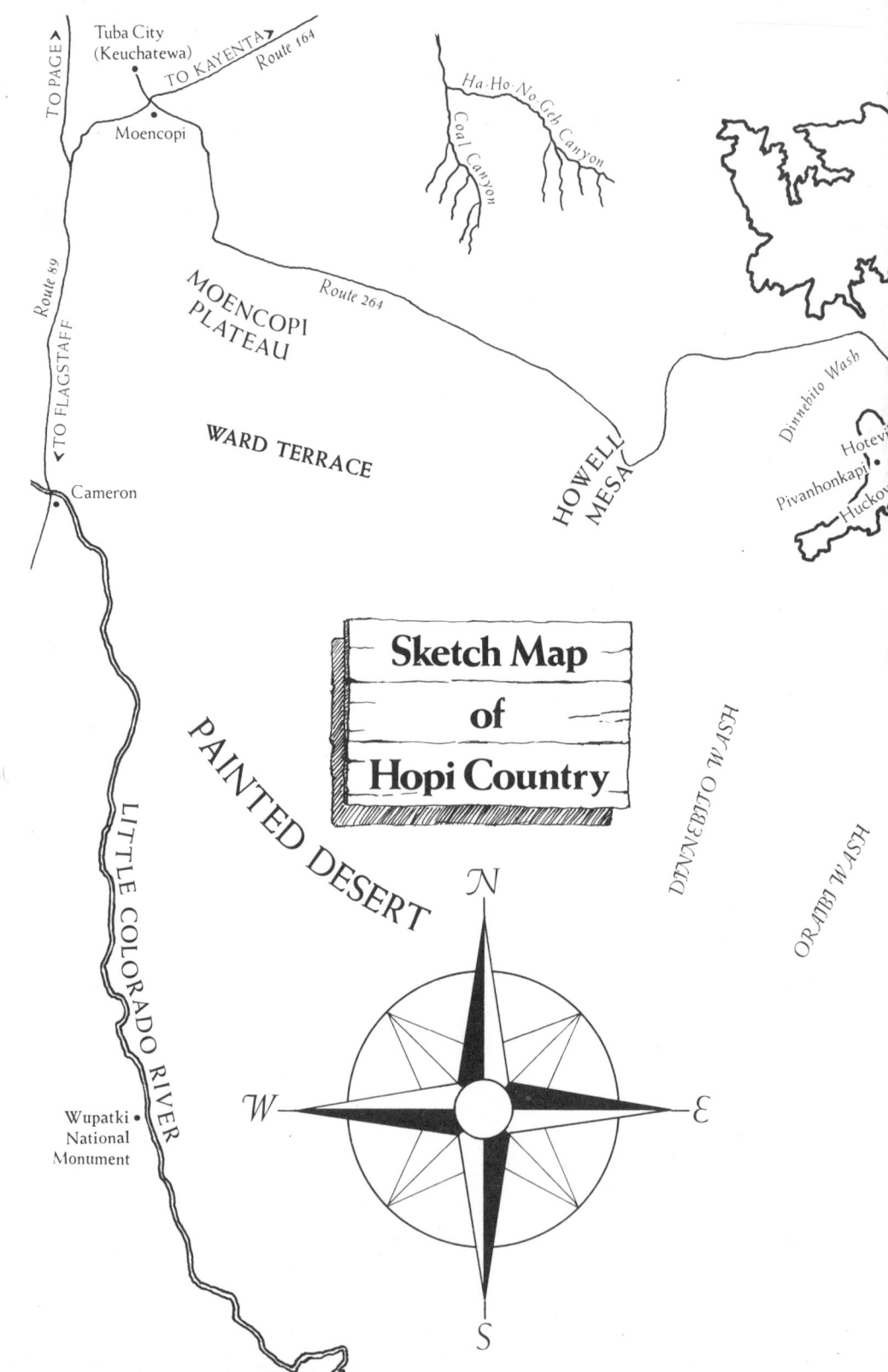

Sketch Map of Hopi Country